Clarifying the meanings of Stations of the Wayfarers

English and Arabic Edition

Dr. Qais Akram Mekki Hamouda

Second Edition – Revised Edition 1446 AH/2025 CE
ISBN: 979-8-9989305-1-5

Copyright © 2025 by Qais A. Mekki

Contents

Introducing the book, reason for writing, and its objectives

In the name of Allah, the Most Gracious, the Most Merciful.

All praise is due to Allah, the Lord of all worlds. O Allah, bestow Your blessings, peace, and grace upon our Master Muhammad, the Prophet sent as a mercy to all creation, and upon his family, companions, and those who follow him in righteousness until the Day of Judgment. Amen.

Allah the Exalted declares in His Noble Book:
"By the sun and its radiant brightness, and the moon as it reflects the sun's light! By the day as it reveals the world, and the night as it veils it! By the sky and its wondrous structure, and the earth and all its expanse! By the human soul and the perfection with which He fashioned it, instilling in it both its rebelliousness and its God-consciousness! Truly, he who purifies it has succeeded, and he who buries it in darkness has surely failed!" (Surah Ash-Shams 91:1–10).

This profound oath at the opening of Surah Ash-Shams—the longest oath in the Quran—emphasizes an undeniable truth: the purification of the soul (tazkiyah) is one of the purposes for which humanity was created, and it is an individual obligation (fard al-ayn) upon every Muslim, irreplaceable by any other act. The human soul is a battleground between transgression and piety. Its salvation depends on one's vigilance in purifying and nurturing it with goodness; its ruin lies in neglect and defilement through sin.

Among the profound teachings of the Prophet (peace be upon him) on the foundations of faith is the renowned Hadith of Jibril, narrated by Imams Muslim and Bukhari (below is Imam Muslim's wording). Umar ibn Al-Khattab (may Allah be pleased with him) reported:

Umar ibn al-Khattab reported: We were sitting with the Messenger of Allah, peace and blessings be upon him, one day, a man appeared with very white clothes and very black hair. There were no signs of travel on him and we did not recognize him. He sat in front of the Prophet, rested his knees by his knees, and placed his hands on his thighs. The man said, "O Muhammad, tell me about Islam." The Prophet said, "Islam is to testify there is no God but Allah and Muhammad is the Messenger of Allah, to establish prayer, to give charity, to fast the month of Ramadan, and to perform pilgrimage to the House if a way is possible." The man said, "You have spoken truthfully." We were surprised that he asked him and said he was truthful. He said, "Tell me about Iman (faith)." The Prophet said, "Faith is to believe in Allah, His angels, His Books, His Messengers, the Last Day, and to believe in providence, its good and its harm." The man said, "You have spoken truthfully. Tell me about Ihsan (excellence)." The Prophet said, "Ihsan (excellence) is to worship Allah as if you see Him, for if you do not see Him, He surely sees you." The man said, "Tell me about the final hour." The Prophet said, "The one asked does not know more than the one asking." The man said, "Tell me about its signs." The Prophet said, "The slave-girl will give birth to her mistress, and you will see barefoot, naked, and dependent shepherds compete in the construction of tall buildings." Then, the man returned, and I remained. The Prophet said to me, "O Umar, do you know who he was?" I said, "Allah and His Messenger know best." The Prophet said, "Verily, he was Gabriel who came to teach you your religion."

In this comprehensive hadith, we see the wise division of faith's foundations: Islam (outward acts of worship), Iman (inward beliefs), and Ihsan (excellence, heartfelt consciousness of Allah). These three pillars evolved historically into established Islamic sciences: Fiqh (jurisprudence) from Islam, Aqeedah (theology) from Iman, and Tazkiyah (spiritual purification) from Ihsan.

The people of the science of Ihsan (spiritual excellence) are the Sufis, who specialize in the purification of souls (tazkiyah) and nurturing hearts in the love and reverence of Allah. Here, we speak of true Sufism, as practiced by great imams such as Al-Hasan Al-Basri, Al-Harith Al-Muhasibi, Junayd Al-Baghdadi, Abdul Qadir Al-Jilani, and other giants of spiritual conduct, may Allah have mercy on them. These luminaries made the Sharia their judge, the Tariqah (spiritual path) their guide, and Tazkiyah (purification of the self) their fruit.

Tazkiyah is not merely a theoretical science confined to books; it is a journey walked alongside spiritually awakened guides (shuyukh), akin to learning medicine under practicing physicians. Just as medical students cannot become doctors by merely reading an anatomy textbook, spiritual seekers (murid) cannot purify their soul by solely studying Sufi literature. Rather, they must accompany those deeply rooted in divine knowledge (al-'arifun bi'Llah), who nurture souls through their luminous guidance and correct spiritual deviations with divinely inspired wisdom, and the seekers must maintain good companionship.

The Book "Stations of the Wayfarers (Manazil al-Sa'irin)" by Imam Al-Harawi:

Stations of the Wayfarers, authored by Shaykh Abdullah Al-Ansari Al-Harawi (d. 481 AH), stands among the most important works on the science of tazkiyah and spiritual journeying toward Allah. Imam Al-Harawi, a towering figure of 5th-century Sufism, seamlessly integrated exoteric and esoteric knowledge. He was a Hadith scholar, Hanbali jurist, and a divinely guided spiritual master (shaykh rabbani) renowned for grounding the methodology of tazkiyah in the Quran and Sunnah.

Stations of the Wayfarers is a meticulously structured spiritual guide outlining the seeker's journey to Allah through 100 "stations" (manazil), each divided into three levels: the beginner's stage, the intermediate stage, and the stage of the elite. These stations begin with repentance (tawbah) and self-vigilance (muraqabah) and culminate in divine unity (tawhid) and annihilation in the love of the Divine. The book details the seeker's ascension through each stage according to their spiritual readiness. Its systematic framework, clarity, and depth have earned it a unique status among works on spiritual conduct.

The book's influence transcends its era, remaining a beacon for seekers across centuries. It has become an essential reference for eminent scholars, with Sufi luminaries such as Shaykh Afeef-ud-Din Al-Tilimsani (d. 690 AH), Shaykh Kamal-ud-Din Al-Kashani (d. 735 AH), Shaykh Abdul Ra'uf Al-Munawi (d. 1031 AH), and contemporary scholar Dr. Yusri Jabr Al-Hasani composing extensive commentaries on it. These works affirm Stations of the Wayfarers as a foundational text in tazkiyah, capable of accommodating interpretations across diverse epochs.

Shaykh Al-Harawi authored this book nearly a thousand years ago. As with all languages, terminology evolves over time, and texts written a millennium ago may prove challenging for the general reader to comprehend. The purpose of this humble work before you is to make the meanings of Stations of the Wayfarers accessible by rendering it in concise, contemporary language. This adaptation is intended for those unfamiliar with classical texts and their specialized terminology, while preserving the core content as explained by reputable commentators, without elaboration, as prior scholars have already excelled in that regard. Our aim is to rephrase expressions into modern equivalents wherever possible, hoping this book becomes a key to unlock readers' hearts—may Allah protect and guide them—and inspire a thirst for deeper study, knowledge, and spiritual purification (tazkiyah) from its original sources.

To comprehensively understand the various terms and expressions used in our time, and to discern the most appropriate among them, I utilized the latest available computer technologies to research contemporary linguistic synonyms, coupled with meticulous personal verification to ensure alignment with the authoritative commentaries on the original text. I have also written it in three languages: Arabic, English, and Chinese, so that the benefit may be widespread, Allah willing.

However, simplifying the language of this profound text inevitably sacrifices some of the depth inherent in Shaykh Al-Harawi's (may Allah have mercy on him) original wording. The original text carries boundless subtleties; the Shaykh chose his words with precision to illuminate meanings from multiple angles. A single page of his work could fill volumes! Thus, I have included the original Arabic text alongside each chapter to remind readers of the source's profundity and emphasize the necessity of returning to it, to classical commentaries, and to the teachings of spiritually awakened scholars (shuyukh).

At the end of each chapter, I added brief reflections as advice to the reader - though not part of Shaykh Al-Harawi's original text - to aid in grasping the chapter's essence, labeled as: "Practical Summary & Advice".

If this work is well-received and time permits, I intend, Allah willing, to follow it with similar projects to revive the "sciences of the heart" ('ulum al-qulub) by rendering other foundational texts on tazkiyah accessible to our brothers, sisters, and children.

Finally, I kindly ask you not to hesitate in offering me your advice, correcting any mistakes you might find, suggesting improvements, or recommending alternative word choices in translation—especially my brothers and sisters who speak Chinese, as my proficiency in it is less than in Arabic and English. Please send your suggestions to the email: (advice.for.author@gmail.com). May Allah reward you abundantly.

I ask for your prayers for my parents and yours. Peace, mercy, and blessings of Allah be upon you.

Qais Akram Mekki Hamouda
Chicago, Ramadhan 1446 AH (2025 CE)

Book: Stations of the Wayfarers (Manazil al-Sa'irin)
Author: Abdullah Al-Ansari Al-Harawi

Shaykh Al-Harawi's Introduction (may Allah have mercy on him)

All praise is due to Allah, the One, the Unique, the Self-Sustaining, the Eternal, the Subtle, the Near. He showers the innermost hearts of the *ʿārifīn* (those who truly know Him) with noble words from the clouds of divine wisdom, unveils to them glimpses of His primordial light in the scrolls of nonexistence, guides them to the closest paths toward the primordial way, and returns them from the fragmentation of worldly distractions to the essence of eternity. He entrusts them with His treasures and deposits within them His secrets.

I bear witness that there is no deity but Allah, alone, without partner—the First, the Last, the Manifest, the Hidden. He stretched the shadow of multiplicity over creation for a long span, then made the sun of divine affirmation (*tamkīn*) a guide for His chosen ones. Finally, He gently withdrew the veil of separation from them, drawing them near to Him.

May Allah's blessings and peace be upon His intimate beloved, through whom He swore to uphold the truth: Muhammad, and his family, abundantly.

To proceed: A group of earnest seekers (*fuqarāʾ*) from Herat and beyond, desiring to understand the stations (*manāzil*) of those journeying toward the Truth—Exalted is His Name—persistently requested that I elucidate these stations in a way that illuminates their landmarks. After seeking Allah's guidance and assistance, I responded to their plea. They further asked me to organize these stations sequentially, indicating their interconnected branches, to avoid relying on others' words, and to condense the text for clarity and ease of memorization. I feared that elaborating on Abu Bakr Al-Kattani's statement, *"Between the servant and the Truth lie a thousand stations of light and darkness,"* would burden both them and myself.

Thus, I outlined the framework of these stations, which point to their completeness and ultimate aim. I pray that, with their sincere intention, they attain what Abu Ubaid Al-Basri described: *"Allah shows His servants, in their beginnings, what lies in their ends."* I structured the work into chapters and sections to avoid tedious elaboration and endless questioning, dividing it into 100 stations (*manāzil*) across ten parts.

As Junayd (may Allah be pleased with him) said: *"A servant may ascend from one state to a higher one, yet remnants of the prior state remain. From the higher state, he rectifies what was incomplete."* In my view, a servant cannot truly attain a station until he transcends it, then reflects upon it to perfect it. **Know that the travelers through these stations, are of an immense diversity and are not confined by rigid order nor halted by a finite endpoint.**

Numerous scholars—both classical and contemporary—have authored works on this subject. Yet, despite their merits, you may find most of them insufficient or incomplete. Some merely alluded to foundational principles without elaboration; others compiled anecdotes but failed to distill their essence or highlight their core wisdom. Some conflated the spiritual stations (*maqamat*) of the elect (*al-khassah*) with the basic obligations of the general populace (*al-'ammah*), while others mistook the ecstatic utterances (*shatḥ*) of the overwhelmed for established stations, conflating the expressions of the spiritually attained with universal truths. Most neglected to clarify the progressive stages (*darajat*) of this path.

Know that the scholars of this tradition agree: Just as a structure cannot stand without a foundation, the culmination of the spiritual journey (*nihayat*) is only valid if the beginnings (*bidayat*) are sound. Sound beginnings entail steadfastness in sincerity (*ikhlas*), adherence to the Sunnah, reverence for divine prohibitions through conscious fear (*khawf*), upholding sanctity, compassionately advising others, avoiding burdensome excess, and distancing oneself from those who corrupt one's time or tempt the heart.

In this matter, people are of three types:

1. **The Seeker (*al-Murid*)**: One who acts between fear and hope, striving toward divine love while embodying humility.
2. **The Sought (*al-Murad*)**: One raptured from the valley of dispersion (*tafriqah*) to the valley of divine unity (*jam'*).
3. **The Pretender**: All others are claimants, deluded by falsehood or self-deception.

All these spiritual stations (*maqamat*) are grouped into three ranks:

1. **The First Rank**: The seeker (*al-qasid*) embarks on the journey (*sirr*).
2. **The Second Rank**: The seeker enters a state of spiritual detachment (*ghurbah*).

3. **The Third Rank**: The seeker attains the witnessing (*mushahadah*) that draws them to the essence of divine unity (*ayn al-tawhid*) through the path of annihilation (*fana*).

Regarding the meaning of the first rank, Al-Husayn ibn Muhammad ibn Ali Al-Fara'idi narrated to us:
Ahmad ibn Muhammad ibn Hasanawiyah narrated to us, who heard from Al-Husayn ibn Idris Al-Ansari, who heard from Uthman ibn Abi Shaybah, who heard from Muhammad ibn Bishr (Al-Abdi), who heard from Umar ibn Rashid, from Yahya ibn Abi Kathir, from Abu Salamah, from Abu Hurairah (may Allah be pleased with him), who said:

The Messenger of Allah (peace be upon him) said: "Strive, for the devoted ones (*al-mufarridun*) have surpassed [others]." They asked, *"O Messenger of Allah, who are the devoted ones?"* He replied: "Those who are fervent in the remembrance of Allah Almighty. Through remembrance, their burdens are lifted, and they will come on the Day of Judgment lightened [of sins]."

This is a *hasan* (good) hadith. It was narrated uniquely by Umar ibn Rashid Al-Yamani from Yahya ibn Abi Kathir. Muhammad ibn Yusuf Al-Firyabi disagreed with Muhammad ibn Bishr Al-Abdi's chain, narrating it instead from Umar ibn Rashid, from Yahya, from Abu Salamah, from Abu Al-Darda (marfu'an, i.e., attributed to the Prophet). However, the correct attribution is to Abu Hurairah. It was also narrated by Bundar ibn Bishar from Safwan ibn Isa, from Bashir ibn Rafi' Al-Yamani (the Imam and Mufti of the people of Najran), from Abu Abdullah ibn 'Amr ibn Abi Hurairah, from Abu Hurairah (marfu'an). The strongest chain is that of Al-Ala ibn Abd Al-Rahman, from his father, from Abu Hurairah, from the Prophet (peace be upon him), recorded in *Sahih Muslim*. The people of Ash-Sham (appox. current day Syria) narrated this hadith from Abu Umamah (marfu'an). In all versions we see the wording: "The devoted ones (*al-mufarridun*) have surpassed [others]."

Regarding the meaning of "entering spiritual detachment (*ghurbah*)," Hamzah ibn Muhammad ibn Abdullah Al-Husayni narrated to us:
Abu Al-Qasim Abdul Wahid ibn Ahmad Al-Hashemi Al-Sufi narrated to us, saying: I heard Abu Abdullah Allan ibn Zayd Al-Dinawari Al-Sufi in Basra say: I heard Ja'far Al-Khuldi Al-Sufi say: I heard Junayd say: I heard Al-Sari from Ma'ruf Al-Karkhi from Ja'far ibn Muhammad from his father from his grandfather from Ali (may Allah be pleased with him) from the Messenger of Allah (peace be upon him), who said: "Seeking the Truth is a form of exile." This is a rare (*gharib*) hadith, which I have only recorded through the narration of Allan.

Concerning the meaning of "attaining divine witnessing (*mushahadah*)," Muhammad ibn Ali ibn Al-Husayn Al-Bashani (may Allah have mercy on him) narrated to us: *Muhammad ibn Ishaq Al-Qurashi narrated to us, who heard from Uthman ibn Sa'id Al-Darami, who heard from Sulaiman ibn Harb from Hammad ibn Zayd from Matar Al-Warraq from Abu Buraidah from Yahya ibn Ya'mur from Abdullah ibn Umar ibn Al-Khattab in the Hadith of Jibril's questioning of the Prophet (peace be upon him): Jibril asked, "What is Ihsan (excellence)?" The Prophet replied: "To worship Allah as though you see Him, for even if you do not see Him, He sees you." (Sahih Muslim).* This sound and rare hadith encapsulates the essence of this spiritual path.

I will elaborate on the degrees of each station (*maqam*) so you may distinguish the level of the general seeker (*al-'ammah*), the traveler (*al-salik*), and the realized one (*al-muhaqqiq*). Each has their own path, method, and orientation ordained for them. For each, a signpost is erected, a goal is set, and they are urged toward it. I pray Allah makes my purpose sincere, my path illuminated, and grants me manifest clarity. Truly, He is All-Hearing, Ever-Near.

Know that the ten divisions (*aqsam*) outlined in this book are:

The Division of Beginnings (*Bidayat*), The Division of Ethics (*Akhlaq*), The Division of Spiritual States (*Ahwal*), The Division of Gates (*Abwab*), The Division of Foundations (*Usul*), The Division of Divine Authorities (*Wilayat*), The Division of Culminations (*Nihayat*), The Division of Transactions (*Mu'amalat*), The Division of Valleys (*Awdiyah*)

The Division of Realities (*Haqa'iq*).

Part 1:Beginnings

The "Section of Beginnings" consists of ten chapters:

1. Spiritual Awakening (Al-Yaqzah)
2. Repentance (Al-Tawbah)
3. Self-Accountability (Al-Muhasabah)
4. Turning Back to Allah (Al-Inabah)
5. Contemplation (Al-Tafakkur)
6. Remembrance (Al-Tadhakkur)
7. Holding Fast to Allah (Al-I'tisam)
8. Fleeing to Allah (Al-Firar)
9. Spiritual Training (Al-Riyada)
10. Conscious Listening (Al-Sama')

Translation of the simplified Arabic text

Chapter 1: Spiritual Awakening

Allah the Exalted says: "Say, I only advise you of one thing: that you stand for Allah" (Quran 34:46).

"Standing for Allah" means awakening from the slumber of negligence and rising from laziness in worship.

This awakening is the first step where the heart is illuminated with awareness, allowing one to recognize Allah's blessings and obligations.

Spiritual awakening has three aspects:

1. Acknowledging Blessings:

- Reflect on Allah's blessings, even if they seem small.
- Admit your shortcomings in gratitude and recognize that all favors come solely from Allah.
- Compare your situation with those in hardship to appreciate what you have.

2. Reflecting on Sins:

- Seriously contemplate your sins; don't underestimate them.
- Fear their consequences and strive to repent.
- Ask Allah to purify your heart and help you avoid repeating them.

3. Guarding Time:

- Evaluate each passing day: Did your faith increase or decrease?
- Avoid wasting time in useless pursuits.
- Seek righteous company and learn from their advice.

How to Achieve This Awakening?

- Blessings are recognized through a mindful heart, gratitude, and humility.
- Sins are addressed by honoring Allah's rights, knowing your weaknesses, and believing in divine justice.
- Time is guarded by seeking knowledge, responding to goodness, and befriending the pious.

Key Takeaway:
The core of awakening is breaking free from bad habits that keep the heart dormant.

<u>Practical Summary & Advice:</u>
Spiritual awakening begins by pausing "autopilot" living and honestly evaluating your life:

- Daily, thank Allah for one blessing.
- Write down one sin you aim to abandon and seek His help.
- Every night, ask: "What did I add to my faith today?"
- Consistency in these steps will gradually redirect your heart toward Allah.

Translation of the simplified Arabic text

Chapter 2: Repentance

Allah the Exalted says: "And whoever does not repent, then they are the wrongdoers" (Quran 49:11).

Thus, Allah removes the label of "wrongdoer" from the repentant.

Conditions for Valid Repentance:

1. Acknowledging the Sin:
   - Realize that three things happen when you sin:
     - You left Allah's protection by committing it.
     - Your temporary joy in sinning.
     - Delaying repentance despite knowing Allah watches you.

2. Requirements of Repentance:

   - Regret: Feel sincere remorse.
   - Abandonment: Stop the sin immediately.
   - Seeking Forgiveness: Ask Allah earnestly.

3. Inner Truths of Repentance:

   - Recognize the gravity of your sin.
   - Doubt the acceptance of your repentance (avoid arrogance).
   - Forgive others' mistakes against you.

4. Secrets of True Repentance:

   - Distinguish between fearing Allah and fearing people.
   - Forget the sin after repenting (no revisiting it).
   - Repent continuously, even from shortcomings in your repentance.

Levels of Repentance:

- Ordinary Repentance: Leaving sins out of fear of punishment.
- Intermediate Repentance: Leaving sins due to shame (a mistake, as minor sins can accumulate).
- Special Repentance: Repenting from wasting time in disobedience.

How is Repentance Perfected?

- By repenting from everything that distances you from Allah, even the imperfections in your repentance!

Practical Summary & Advice:

Repentance is not mere words but sincere change:
1. Every night: Reflect: "Did I sin today? How can I fix it?"
2. After every sin: Pray: "O Allah, I repent. Help me never return to this."
3. Avoid people or places that tempt you to sin.

Repentance's door is always open – don't delay!

Translation of the simplified Arabic text

Chapter 3: Self-Accountability

Allah the Exalted says: "Fear Allah and let every soul look to what it has put forth for tomorrow" (Quran 59:18).

Self-accountability begins with sincere repentance.

To achieve this resolve, three foundations are needed:

1. Compare Blessings and Sins:
   - Reflect on Allah's countless blessings versus your mistakes.
   - This requires:
     - Awareness to recognize blessings.
     - Self-doubt (avoid overconfidence).
     - Distinguishing true blessings from life's tests.

2. Separate What's for Allah and What's for You:
   - Acknowledge that:
     - Sins expose your flaws.
     - Good deeds are Allah's grace, not your own merit.
     - Allah's judgment is just, not an excuse to justify errors.

3. Focus on Yourself, Not Others:
   - Pride may taint your good deeds.
   - Faults you criticize in others might exist in you.
   - Improve yourself; don't waste time judging others.

<u>Practical Summary & Advice:</u>

Self-accountability is growth, not self-punishment:

- Each morning: Write one blessing you're grateful for and one sin to avoid.
- Each night: Ask: "What did I do for my hereafter? Am I better than this morning?"
- Stop comparing yourself to others; focus on your spiritual journey.
- Progress comes through small consistent steps, not perfection!

Translation of the simplified Arabic text

Chapter 4: Turning Back to Allah

Allah the Exalted says: "Turn back to your Lord" (Quran 39:54).

Sincere return to Allah (Inabah) has three forms:

1. Repentant Return:
   - Returning to Allah to correct mistakes, like apologizing after sinning.
   - Requires three actions:
     - Freeing yourself from past sins' consequences.
     - Feeling remorse for your missteps.
     - Compensating for missed acts of worship.

2. Loyal Return:
   - Returning to Allah to fulfill your covenant with Him.
   - Requires three actions:
     - Abandoning the fleeting pleasure of sin.
     - Not belittling those unaware of Allah (fear for them, hope for yourself).
     - Critically examining your worship to refine it.

3. Responsive Return:
   - Returning to Allah in answer to your heart's call.
   - Requires three actions:
     - Relinquishing pride in your good deeds (all grace is from Allah).
     - Recognizing your constant need for His mercy.
     - Reflecting on Allah's subtle kindness in your life.

<u>Practical Summary & Advice:</u>

Inabah is a journey, not a single act:
- After each prayer: Pray: "O Allah, show me my flaws and help me fix them."
- Choose a friend who reminds you of Allah when you forget.
- Carry a notebook to jot moments you felt close to or distant from Allah.

Every return to Him – no matter how small – deepens your connection!

Translation of the simplified Arabic text

Chapter 5: Contemplation

Allah the Exalted says: "We revealed the Quran to you so you may clarify to people what was sent to them, so they may reflect" (Quran 16:44).

Contemplation (Tafakkur) is using spiritual insight to gain deep understanding.

It has three forms:

1. Contemplating Divine Oneness (Tawhid):

   - Reflecting on Allah's greatness and uniqueness, like diving into an endless ocean.

     - Escape drowning in its depth by:

       - Acknowledging the mind's limits in grasping Allah's perfection.
       - Stopping attempts to "figure out" Allah's essence.
       - Glorifying Him without likening Him to creation.

2. Contemplating Creation's Wonders:

   - Observing Allah's precise craftsmanship (sky, mountains, humans).

     - Requires three actions:

       - Noticing how blessings begin and unfold.
       - Interpreting divine signs in nature (e.g., rain as mercy).
       - Freeing the heart from distractions of desires.

3. Contemplating Actions and Intentions:

   - Analyzing daily deeds and motives.

     - Requires three actions:

       - Using Islamic knowledge to evaluate yourself.
       - Doubting your intentions (self-deception is easy!).
       - Understanding how your actions affect others.

<u>Practical Summary & Advice:</u>

Contemplation is a daily habit, not complex philosophy:

- 5 minutes each morning: Reflect on a Quranic verse or natural creation (e.g., a leaf) and ask: "What does this teach me about Allah?"
- Before decisions: Pause and ask: "Does this please Allah?"
- Journal weekly spiritual reflections.

Every sincere reflection brings you closer to wisdom!

Translation of the simplified Arabic text

Chapter 6: Remembrance

Allah the Exalted says: "None will remember except those who turn back [to Allah]" (Quran 40:13).
Remembrance (Tadhakkur) is higher than contemplation; contemplation is seeking wisdom, while remembrance is attaining it. It has three pillars:

1. Benefiting from Admonition:
   - Applying advice and warnings to your life.
   - Requires three conditions:
     - Feeling a deep need for advice.
     - Ignoring the advisor's flaws (focus on the message, not the person).
     - Remembering Allah's promise of reward and warning of punishment.

2. Extracting Lessons from Events:
   - Deriving wisdom from life's situations.
   - Requires three conditions:
     - A mindful mind linking causes to outcomes.
     - Understanding Allah's laws in creation (e.g., oppression leads to ruin).
     - Sincerity in seeking truth (no selfish motives).

3. Harvesting the Fruits of Reflection:
   - Transforming thoughts into beneficial actions.
   - Requires three conditions:
     - Shortening worldly hopes (act now, don't delay).
     - Pondering the Quran's meanings.
     - Avoiding excess in: frivolous socializing, empty wishes, worldly attachments, overeating, and oversleeping.

Practical Summary & Advice:
Remembrance is applying wisdom in practice:

- Daily: Read a short reminder (from Quran or wisdom) and ask: "How will I apply this today?"
- When hearing negative news: Seek lessons (e.g., "How can I avoid this mistake?").
- Reduce distractions (like TV or late-night leisure).

True remembrance makes you live consciously, not heedlessly!

Translation of the simplified Arabic text

Chapter 7: Holding Fast to Allah

Allah the Exalted says: "Hold firmly to the rope of Allah together" (Quran 3:103) and "Hold fast to Allah; He is your Protector" (Quran 22:78).

Holding fast (I'tisam) means clinging strongly to Allah, and it has three levels:

1. Ordinary Holding Fast (Beginners):
   - Adhering to Allah's commands by:
     - Believing in His promise (Paradise) and warning (Hell).
     - Respecting religious boundaries (prayer, fasting, etc.).
     - Treating people with fairness and certainty.
   - This is holding fast to the "rope of Allah" (Quran and Sunnah).

2. Special Holding Fast (Advanced):
   - Freeing oneself from worldly attachments by:
     - Controlling desires (e.g., reducing idle talk).
     - Being humble with others (no arrogance).
     - Cutting ties that distance you from Allah.
   - This is holding fast to the "trustworthy handhold" (sincerity to Allah).

3. Elite Holding Fast :
   - Achieving heart-connected devotion to Allah by:
     - Seeing His greatness in everything.
     - Submitting completely to Him in heart and actions.
     - Being constantly engaged in His remembrance.
   - This is holding fast to Allah Himself.

Practical Summary & Advice:

Holding fast is a journey of elevation:
- Start with basics: Pray regularly and read Quran daily.
- Gradually detach: Reduce one distracting habit (e.g., social media).
- Choose good company: Sit with those who remind you of Allah.

The tighter you hold to Him, the stronger your heart becomes!

Translation of the simplified Arabic text

Chapter 8: Fleeing to Allah

Allah the Exalted says: "So flee to Allah" (Quran 51:50).

Fleeing (Al-Firar) is escaping from the temporary to the Eternal.

It has three levels:

1. Ordinary Flight (Beginners):
   - Fleeing from:
     - Ignorance to knowledge (through study and action).
     - Laziness to diligence (with caution and resolve).
     - Inner turmoil to trust in Allah's mercy (through hope).

2. Special Flight (Advanced):
   - Fleeing from:
     - Theoretical talk to experiencing faith's sweetness (with the heart, not ears).
     - Ritualistic worship to the essence of piety (like sincerity).
     - Worldly attachments to spiritual detachment (from wealth or status).

3. Elite Flight :
   - Fleeing from:
     - Everything except Allah to Allah Himself (even spiritual concepts!).
     - Fleeing as an act to total surrender (like a child in a parent's arms).

<u>Practical Summary & Advice:</u>
Fleeing to Allah is liberation, not escapism:
- Start small: Dedicate 10 minutes daily to religious learning (e.g., studying a verse).
- Mind your intentions: Turn daily habits (like eating) into worship through gratitude.
- Avoid traps: Distance yourself from people or deeds that make you forget Allah.

True flight is living with Allah in every moment!

Translation of the simplified Arabic text

Chapter 9: Spiritual Training

Allah the Exalted says: "And those who give what they give while their hearts tremble" (Quran 23:60).

Spiritual training (Riyada) is nurturing the soul to embrace truth.

It has three levels:

1. Ordinary Training (Beginners):

- Refining Morals: Improve character through Islamic ethics (e.g., honesty, integrity).
- Purifying Actions: Sincerity in every deed (even small acts like removing harm from a path).
- Fulfilling Rights: Justice in dealings (returning deposits, avoiding fraud).

2. Special Training (Advanced):

- Eliminating Distractions: Avoid trivial pursuits (excessive joking, or gossip).
- Not Resting on Past Deeds: Never say, "I fasted all Ramadan; that's enough!"
- Continuous Learning: Apply knowledge rather than hoarding it.

3. Elite Training :

- Total Detachment: Abandon all distractions from Allah (even spiritual pride!).
- Divine Unity: See Allah's hand in every event (e.g., "This is from Allah's wisdom").
- Rejecting Compromises: Never trade obedience for sin (e.g., "I'll pray but backbite!").

Practical Summary & Advice:

Spiritual training is turning knowledge into action:

- Start with Ethics: Choose one trait (e.g., generosity) to practice for a week.
- Check Intentions: Before any act, ask: "Is this for Allah or people's praise?"
- Declutter Life: Reduce one time-wasting habit (e.g., mindless scrolling).

Consistent effort transforms you, step by step!

Translation of the simplified Arabic text

Chapter 10: Conscious Listening

Allah the Exalted says: "If Allah had known any good in them, He would have made them hear" (Quran 8:23).

True listening (Sama') is engaging the heart and mind. It has three levels:

1. Ordinary Listening (Beginners):

- Heeding Warnings: Fear Allah's punishment (e.g., stopping sin when reminded).
- Responding to Promises: Strive for His mercy (e.g., giving charity after hearing about Paradise).
- Recognizing Blessings: Acknowledge Allah's favors (health, safety).

2. Special Listening (Advanced):

- Decoding Symbols: Extract wisdom from events (e.g., rain as a sign of forgiveness).
- Understanding Purpose: See Allah's wisdom in everything (e.g., patience in illness elevates rank).
- Heartfelt Oneness: Detach from all but Allah (even spiritual distractions!).

3. Elite Listening :

- Purifying the Heart: Listening that removes veils (feeling Allah's presence in every heartbeat).
- Eternal Connection: Sensing you're part of His divine plan (like a drop in an eternal river).
- Returning to the Source: Seeing all endings tied to creation's beginning (death as a true start).

Practical Summary & Advice:

Conscious listening turns words into action and wisdom:

- Listen Actively: When reading Quran, imagine Allah speaking directly to you.
- Reflect: After every sermon, ask: "What does this teach me about Allah?"
- Journal: Write one moment daily where you felt deep meaning in what you heard.

True listening connects you to Allah in every detail!

2. Section of the Gates

The "Section of the Gates" comprises ten gates:

1. Sorrow (Al-Huzn)
2. Fear [of Allah] (Al-Khawf)
3. Compassionate Concern (Al-Ishfaq)
4. Humility [in Worship] (Al-Khushu')
5. Submissiveness (Al-Ikhbat)
6. Asceticism (Al-Zuhd)
7. Piety (Al-Wara')
8. Devotion (Al-Tabattul)
9. Hope [in Divine Mercy] (Al-Raja')
10. Longing [for Allah] (Al-Raghba)

Translation of the simplified Arabic text

Chapter 11: Grief

Allah the Exalted says: «They turned away while their eyes overflowed with tears out of grief» (Quran 9:92).

Grief is pain over what you've lost or failed to achieve. It has three levels:

1. Ordinary Grief (General People):
   - Grief due to:
     - Neglecting worship (e.g., missing prayers).
     - Falling into sins that distance you from Allah (e.g., lying).
     - Wasting time in useless pursuits.
2. Grief of the Determined (Serious Seekers):
   - Grief due to:
     - A heart distracted from Allah (even by permissible matters).
     - Inability to focus during worship (e.g., worldly thoughts in prayer).
     - Escaping grief through distractions (e.g., binge-watching instead of self-reflection).
3. Grief of the Elite (Advanced):
   - A rare grief felt only by those near Allah:
     - Pain from any temporary obstacle blocking their path to Him (even minor ones).
     - Anguish when sincere intentions are hindered (e.g., illness preventing group prayer).
     - Sensitivity to any deficiency in understanding Allah's wisdom (e.g., questioning trials).

<u>Practical Summary & Advice:</u>
Spiritual grief isn't weakness but a sign of a living heart:

- Don't fear grief: Journal: "I grieve because..." then ask Allah for help.
- Transform grief into action: If you regret wasted time, create a spiritual daily plan.
- Reflect: Read the Quranic verse above and ponder: "How does my grief draw me closer to Allah?"

Pure grief reminds you're still on the path – keep going!

Translation of the simplified Arabic text

Chapter 12: Fear

Allah the Exalted says: «[They] stand in awe of their Sustainer, who is above them» (Quran 16:50).

Fear is the loss of security due to awareness of Allah's punishment.

It has three types:

1. Ordinary Fear (General People):
   - Fear of Allah's punishment for sins (e.g., Hellfire).
   - Arises from:
     - Believing in Allah's warnings in the Quran.
     - Reflecting on past mistakes.
     - Contemplating the consequences of deeds on Judgment Day.

2. Fear of the Advanced (Serious Seekers):
   - Fear mixed with awe and spiritual sweetness, felt by those who:
     - Monitor every moment of their lives (even their breath!).
     - Fear self-deception by false comfort.
     - Taste faith's sweetness while fearing shortcomings.

3. Fear of the Elite :
   - Not conventional fear but profound reverence for Allah, manifesting as:
     - Feeling powerless before Allah's greatness during supplication.
     - Guarding the heart's sincerity even in joyful moments.
     - Inner collapse when witnessing Allah's beauty and power.

Practical Summary & Advice:

Healthy fear leads to piety:

- Channel your fear: Write down one sin you fear punishment for, and plan repentance.
- Check intentions: Before any act, ask: "Does this please Allah or deepen my fear of Him?"
- Daily reflection: Read "They stand in awe of their Sustainer, who is above them" and ponder: "How does my fear draw me closer to Allah?"

True fear isn't weakness—it redirects your heart toward obedience!

Translation of the simplified Arabic text

Chapter 13: Apprehensive Care

Allah the Exalted says: «[The righteous] will answer: "Behold, we were of old, filled with fear, amidst our kinsfolk"» (Quran 52:26).

Apprehensive care is fear blended with mercy, felt toward oneself and others.

It has three levels:

1. Ordinary Care (Beginners):
   - Fear for:
     - The Self rebelling against Allah (e.g., stubbornness in worship).
     - Good Deeds being wasted (e.g., charity without sincerity).
     - Others falling into error (while understanding their excuses).

2. Special Care (Advanced):
   - Fear for:
     - Time being split by worldly distractions.
     - The Heart being occupied away from Allah.
     - Certainty being weakened by doubts.

3. Elite Care :
   - Fear that prevents:
     - Pride in one's piety (e.g., feeling superior).
     - Quarrels with others (even if you're right).
     - Exceeding Limits in worship (e.g., fasting until exhaustion).

<u>Practical Summary & Advice:</u>

Apprehensive care balances fear and mercy:

- Daily ask: "Do I guard my faith as I guard my health?"
- Improve one relationship: Show compassion (e.g., to a struggling friend).
- Reflect on the verse: "We were of old, filled with fear, amidst our kinsfolk"—let this fear keep your heart alive!

Translation of the simplified Arabic text

Chapter 14: Humility

Allah the Exalted says: «Has the time not yet come for those who believe to humble their hearts to the remembrance of Allah and the truth He has sent down?» (Quran 57:16).

Humility (Khushu') is the heart's tranquility and submission before Allah's greatness. It has three levels:

1. Ordinary Humility (Beginners):

- Obedience to Commands: Following Allah's orders without resistance (e.g., praying attentively).
- Accepting Destiny: Embracing life's trials with patience (e.g., losing wealth or health).
- Humility Before Allah: Feeling the self's insignificance before the Creator.

2. Special Humility (Advanced):

- Self-Audit: Detecting flaws in oneself and deeds (e.g., questioning intentions behind charity).
- Acknowledging Others' Merit: Recognizing those superior in worship or ethics.
- Preparing for the Hereafter: Remembering death amid worldly comforts.

3. Elite Humility :

- Respect in Divine Presence: Even during spiritual experiences (e.g., avoiding pride in piety).
- Purifying Acts from Show-Off: Ignoring people's praise during worship.
- Seeing Allah's Grace: Knowing every good deed stems from Him, not oneself.

Practical Summary & Advice:

Humility is the key to connecting with Allah:

- Start small: Focus your heart in one rak'ah of prayer daily.
- Journal: Write one flaw you discovered in yourself today and seek Allah's help to fix it.
- Reflect on the verse: "Has the time not yet come...?" and ask: "Is my heart truly humble?"

True humility lets you see Allah in every detail!

Translation of the simplified Arabic text

Chapter 15: Spiritual Serenity

Allah the Exalted says: «And give glad tidings to those who humble themselves» (Quran 22:34).

Spiritual Serenity is the heart's tranquility and submission to Allah.

It has three levels:

1. Ordinary Serenity (Beginners):

- Conquering Desires: Using faith to transform worldly urges into worship (e.g., fasting to discipline the soul).
- Curing Negligence: Reminding oneself of Allah's watchfulness (e.g., dhikr during distractions).
- Harmony with Worship: Finding joy in obedience over fleeting pleasures.

2. Special Serenity (Advanced):

- Steadfast Will: Unshaken resolve during trials (e.g., praying despite illness).
- Heart's Peace: Calmness amid hardships (trusting Allah in crises).
- Overcoming Temptations: Resisting tests without faltering.

3. Elite Serenity :

- Indifference to Praise/Criticism: Acting solely for Allah, not people's opinions.
- Constant Self-Critique: Seeing your flaws before judging others.
- Absolute Humility: Never feeling superior, even to those who seem weak.

Practical Summary & Advice:
Spiritual serenity is the heart's refuge:

- Morning Routine: Pray "O Allah, make me among the humble" three times.
- Journal One Achievement: Done purely for Allah (not for praise).
- Reflect on the verse: "Give glad tidings to those who humble themselves"—ask: "Am I among them?"

True serenity is living as Allah wills, not as the world demands!

Translation of the simplified Arabic text

Chapter 16: Asceticism

Allah the Exalted says: «What is left [to you] by Allah is best for you» (Quran 11:86).

Asceticism (Zuhd) is complete detachment from worldly attachments.

It has three levels:

1. Ordinary Asceticism (Beginners):
   - Avoiding doubtful matters (even if permissible) due to fear of:
     - People's blame or criticism.
     - Damage to social reputation.
     - Resembling the immoral in behavior.

2. Special Asceticism (Advanced):
   - Contentment with minimal food and clothing to:
     - Free time for worship and reflection.
     - Strengthen resolve and self-control.
     - Emulate prophets and the righteous in simplicity.

3. Elite Asceticism :
   - Transcending asceticism itself by:
     - Deeming all you renounced worthless (the entire world is insignificant to Allah!).
     - Indifference to praise or blame.
     - Seeing everything as from Allah—no pride in your asceticism or deeds.

<u>Practical Summary & Advice:</u>

Asceticism isn't deprivation but liberation:

- Start small: Reduce one excess (e.g., clothes or food).
- Reflect on the verse: «What is left by Allah is best for you»—ask: "Do I prefer Allah's pleasure over my desires?"
- Read: «Know that the life of this world is but play and amusement…» (Quran 57:20) and ponder: "How can my asceticism bridge me closer to Allah?"

Translation of the simplified Arabic text

Chapter 17: Piety

Allah the Exalted says: «And purify your garments» (Quran 74:4).

Piety (Al-Wara') is extreme caution against displeasing Allah, even in permissible matters.

It has three levels:

1. Ordinary Piety (Beginners):

- Avoiding Major Sins: Like lying or stealing – to protect the soul.
- Increasing Good Deeds: Daily charity to compensate shortcomings.
- Guarding Faith: Avoiding places of fitnah (e.g., gatherings mocking religion).

2. Special Piety (Advanced):

- Caution in Permissible Acts: Avoiding overeating (even halal food) to protect health and time.
- Adhering to Islamic Etiquette: Lowering voices in markets to avoid showing off.
- Respecting Boundaries: Avoiding hurtful jokes labeled as "humor."

3. Elite Piety :

- Complete Purification: Avoiding distractions from Allah (e.g., limiting social media).
- Focus on Divine Unity: Not engaging in anything besides Him, even during leisure.
- Avoiding Gray Areas: Leaving lucrative jobs that distract from prayer.

Practical Summary & Advice:

Piety is guarding the heart from hidden sins:

- Daily Audit: Ask before sleep: "Did I do anything today that angered Allah?"
- Pick One Habit: Reduce idle talk or guard your gaze.
- Reflect on: «Purify your garments»—outer purity reflects inner purity!

Translation of the simplified Arabic text

Chapter 18: Complete Devotion

Allah the Exalted says: «And devote yourself to Him with utter devotion» (Quran 73:8).

Complete Devotion (Al-Tabattul) is total detachment from distractions to focus solely on Allah.

It has three levels:

1. Ordinary Devotion (Beginners):

- Cutting Worldly Ties: Renouncing pursuit of praise, wealth, or status.
- Accepting Divine Decree: Letting go of fear of the future or regret for the past.
- Ignoring People's Opinions: Prioritizing Allah's pleasure over people's approval.

2. Special Devotion (Advanced):

- Freeing the Heart from Desires: Resisting the urge to show off or compete.
- Tasting Divine Closeness: Finding joy in supplication over worldly pleasures.
- Seeing Allah's Signs: Reflecting on the creation of heavens and earth during worship.

3. Elite Devotion :

- Absolute Focus on Allah: Detaching the heart from all but Him, even during daily tasks.
- Perfecting Spiritual Integrity: Purifying intentions in every act, no matter how small.
- Preparing for the Hereafter: Living as if each day is the last in this world.

Practical Summary & Advice:
Complete Devotion (Al-Tabattul) liberates the heart from chains:

- Daily Practice: Dedicate 10 minutes to reflecting on a Quranic verse or sincere prayer.
- Choose One Act: Do it purely for Allah (e.g., helping someone secretly).
- Reflect on: «I created the jinn and mankind only to worship Me» (Quran 51:56).

Devotion to Allah isn't escapism—it's living with a free heart!

Translation of the simplified Arabic text

Chapter 19: Hope

Allah the Exalted says: «You have indeed in the Apostle of God a good example for everyone who looks forward [to God] and the Last Day» (Quran 33:21).

Hope is the heart's attachment to Allah's mercy, but it can weaken resolve if it turns into complacency.

It has three levels:

1. Ordinary Hope (Beginners):
   - Hope for Reward: Striving in prayer and fasting for Paradise.
   - Joy in Worship: Finding happiness during acts of devotion.
   - Abandoning Sins Gradually: Leaving sins out of hope for forgiveness.

2. Special Hope (Advanced):
   - Hope for Spiritual Ranks: Achieved by:
     - Renouncing worldly pleasures (e.g., reducing food and idle talk).
     - Adhering to knowledge and action (e.g., seeking beneficial knowledge).
     - Strictly observing Islamic boundaries (e.g., never delaying prayer).

3. Elite Hope :
   - Longing to Meet Allah: The highest hope, manifesting as:
     - Constant heartache to see Allah in the Hereafter.
     - Indifference to worldly glitter.
     - Bitterness in life without closeness to Allah.

Practical Summary & Advice:

True hope balances fear and aspiration:

- Start your day optimistically: Pray: "O Allah, I hope for Your mercy and repent for my shortcomings."
- Reflect on the verse: «In the Apostle of God you have a good example» - follow the Prophet's (peace be upon him) path for genuine hope.
- Journal moments of hope: Write weekly about an experience where you felt Allah's mercy.

Don't let hope make you lazy – let it fuel your actions!

Translation of the simplified Arabic text

Chapter 20: Spiritual Longing

Allah the Exalted says: «[They] call upon Us with yearning and awe» (Quran 21:90).

Spiritual longing is the heart's intense desire to draw closer to Allah. It surpasses mere hope, as it requires continuous action.

It has three levels:

1. Ordinary Longing (Knowledge-Based):
   - Rooted in knowledge of worship's virtues and sin's consequences.
   - Drives you to:
     - Excel in worship (e.g., prolonging prostration).
     - Avoid spiritual laziness (e.g., daily remembrance (dhikr) routine).
     - Reject weak excuses for neglecting duties.

2. Special Longing (State of Devotion):
   - Manifests as:
     - Total effort to achieve the goal (e.g., sacrificing time/wealth for Allah).
     - Unwavering resolve even in hardships.
     - Abandoning excess permissible acts that distract from Allah.

3. Elite Longing (Divine Witnessing):
   - Complete Devotion to Allah:
     - Pure spiritual companionship free from hypocrisy.
     - Unbreakable determination against challenges.
     - Union with Allah, leaving no desire for anything else.

<u>Practical Summary & Advice:</u>
True longing fuels the journey to Allah:

- Set a Spiritual Goal: Complete the Quran monthly or feed a needy person weekly.
- Daily Self-Check: "Did I truly draw closer to Allah today?"
- Reflect on: «When My servants ask you about Me, I am near» (Quran 2:186) - Allah is with you every step!

3- Section of Transactions:

The Section of Transactions consists of ten chapters:

1. Custodianship (Ar-Ri'ayah)
2. Vigilance (Al-Muraqabah)
3. Sanctity (Al-Hurma)
4. Sincerity (Al-Ikhlas)
5. Refinement (At-Tahdhib)
6. Steadfastness (Al-Istiqamah)
7. Reliance (At-Tawakkul)
8. Entrustment (At-Tafwid)
9. Confidence (Ath-Thiqa)
10. Submission (At-Taslim)

Translation of the simplified Arabic text

Chapter 21: Custodianship

Allah the Exalted says: «But they did not honor it as it should have been honored» (Quran 57:27).

Custodianship is protection fueled by care.

It has three levels:

1. Custodianship of Deeds (Worship):

- Perfecting Acts: Praying and giving charity sincerely, not for praise.
- No Boasting: Treating obedience as a duty, not a badge of honor.
- Humility: Viewing good deeds as Allah's gift, not personal effort.

2. Custodianship of States (Heart's Condition):

- Monitoring Intentions: Ensuring worship is free from show-off (e.g., fasting for Allah, not weight loss).
- Avoiding Arrogance: Never feeling spiritually superior.
- Rejecting Pretense: Not portraying oneself as "righteous" publicly.

3. Custodianship of Time (Time Management):

- Focus on the Moment: Avoid distractions during worship (e.g., work thoughts in prayer).
- Trust Divine Planning: Believe Allah will fix matters if intentions are pure.
- Inner Peace: Let go of past/future; embrace a present close to Allah.

Practical Summary & Advice:

True custodianship is serving Allah in every detail:

- Before any act: Ask: "Is this for Allah or another motive?"
- Daily 5-minute check: Review intentions (e.g., after Asr prayer).
- Reflect on: «Worship your Lord until certainty comes» (Quran 15:99) - sincerity is the key to acceptance!

Translation of the simplified Arabic text

Chapter 22: Vigilance

Allah the Exalted says: «[They] respect neither kinship nor treaty with a believer» (Quran 9:10).

Vigilance is constant awareness of Allah's presence. It has three levels:

1. Ordinary Vigilance (Beginners):

- Continuous Journey to Allah: Through:
    - Magnifying Allah in the heart (e.g., reflecting on His greatness during supplication).
    - Feeling shortcomings as motivation (e.g., giving more charity after missing a prayer).
    - Joy in obedience as a divine gift (e.g., weeping humbly in prayer).

2. Special Vigilance (Advanced):

- Awareness of Allah's Watchfulness: By:
    - Accepting divine decree without complaint (e.g., enduring illness patiently).
    - Avoiding futile arguments that distance from Allah.
    - Reckless behaviors that weaken faith.

3. Elite Vigilance :

- Ascending to the Highest Ranks:
    - Seeing Allah's wisdom in every event (e.g., contemplating creation).
    - Noticing eternal signs in temporal life (e.g., linking events to divine wisdom).
    - Transcending self-awareness (living with Allah without ego).

Practical Summary & Advice:

Vigilance is the essence of spiritual awakening:

- Start with micro-awareness: Pause every hour for 2 minutes to remember Allah's name "Ar-Raqeeb" (The Watchful).
- Combat distractions: Write "Allah sees me" on a sticky note as a daily reminder.
- Reflect on: «Does he not know that Allah sees?» (Quran 96:14)—Allah is with you in every breath!

Translation of the simplified Arabic text

Chapter 23: Sanctity

Allah the Exalted says: «Whoever honors the sacred ordinances of Allah, it is best for him with his Lord» (Quran 22:30).

Sanctity is profound respect for Allah's boundaries. It has three levels:

1. Ordinary Sanctity (Beginners):
   - Honoring Allah's Commands & Prohibitions:
     - Not out of fear (e.g., praying to avoid Hell).
     - Nor for reward (e.g., charity for Paradise).
     - Nor to impress others (e.g., fasting for praise).
   - The goal: Sincerity to Allah alone.

2. Special Sanctity (Advanced):
   - Engaging with Texts Simply:
     - Avoid forced interpretations of Quran/Hadith.
     - Reject exaggerated depictions (e.g., describing Paradise/Hell beyond scriptural evidence).
     - Never claim exclusive religious understanding without proof.

3. Elite Sanctity :
   - Guarding the Heart from Subtle Deviations:
     - Prevent self-confidence from becoming audacity toward Allah (e.g., delaying repentance).
     - Avoid turning joy in worship into complacency about accountability.
     - Protect spiritual focus from worldly distractions during remembrance.

Practical Summary & Advice:

True sanctity is honoring Allah in secret and public:
- Self-Audit: Before any act, ask: "Does this honor Allah's boundaries or cross them?"
- Read Texts Simply: Don't overcomplicate Quran/Hadith with philosophy.
- Journal: List three sacred priorities (e.g., prayer on time, kindness to parents).

Sanctity isn't fear—it's love and reverence for the Almighty!

Translation of the simplified Arabic text

Chapter 24: Sincerity

Allah the Exalted says: «Is it not to Allah that sincere devotion is due?» (Quran 39:3).

Sincerity is purifying deeds for Allah alone.

It has three levels:

1. Ordinary Sincerity (Beginners):

- Detaching Deeds from Self: Worship without seeking praise (e.g., praying humbly).
- No Expectation of Reward: Giving charity without waiting for gratitude.
- Dissatisfaction with Deeds: Viewing worship as Allah's gift, not personal success.

2. Special Sincerity (Advanced):

- Shame in Deeds: Feeling inadequate even when striving (e.g., fasting while doubting acceptance).
- Hiding Good Deeds: Helping others secretly.
- Acknowledging Allah's Grace: Recognizing success in worship is from Allah, not oneself.

3. Elite Sincerity :

- Freedom from Self-Monitoring: Worship becoming second nature (like breathing).
- Living as a Witness to Allah's Will: Letting deeds flow by His power, not ego.
- Rejecting Spiritual Pretense: Never claiming piety, even if you do good constantly.

Practical Summary & Advice:
Sincerity is the key to accepted deeds:
- Before any act: Ask: "If no one saw me, would I do this the same way?"
- Choose a secret deed: Help a neighbor anonymously.
- Reflect on: «They were commanded only to worship Allah, sincere in devotion» (Quran 98:5) - Allah sees hidden intentions!

Translation of the simplified Arabic text

Chapter 25: Refinement

Allah the Exalted says: «When it [the star] set, he said: "I do not love things that set"» (Quran 6:76).

Refinement is training the soul to abandon bad habits and deviations.

It has three levels:

1. Refinement of Worship:
   - Enhancing Worship Quality:
     - Avoid ignorance (e.g., praying without understanding supplications).
     - Reject mechanical routines (e.g., dhikr without focus).
     - Continuously improve devotion (e.g., deepening humility in prayer).

2. Refinement of the Heart's State:
   - Controlling Spiritual Emotions:
     - Prevent joy in obedience from becoming arrogance (e.g., boasting about fasting).
     - Avoid empty formalism (e.g., focusing on prayer's form over essence).
     - Shun self-interest during worship (e.g., praying only for worldly success).

3. Refinement of Intentions:
   - Purifying Inner Motives:
     - Eliminate forced obedience (e.g., charity due to social pressure).
     - Guard against spiritual laziness (e.g., skipping daily Quran reading for trivial reasons).
     - Avoid futile debates that weaken faith (e.g., arguing over unseen matters).

Practical Summary & Advice:

Refinement is transforming habits into worship:

- Daily Self-Evaluation: Ask: "Did I improve my worship today?"
- Replace One Habit: Swap social media scrolling with reading two Quranic verses before bed.
- Reflect on: «Successful is he who purifies it [the soul]» (Quran 91:9) – purification (tazkiyah) is the ultimate success!

Translation of the simplified Arabic text

Chapter 26: Steadfastness

Allah the Exalted says: «Remain steadfast [exclusively] to Him» (Quran 41:6).

Steadfastness is unwavering commitment to Allah's path.

Steadfastness breathes life into spiritual states; just as outward deeds grow for ordinary believers, inward states flourish through it. It is a bridge between valleys of distraction (deviation) and peaks of closeness to Allah (secure spiritual connection).

It has three levels:

1. Beginners' Steadfastness (Moderation in Worship):
   - Balance in Acts:
     - Avoid extremes (e.g., consecutive fasting beyond capacity).
     - Stay within sincerity's bounds (no desire for praise).
     - Follow the Prophet's (peace be upon him) teachings without innovation.

2. Advanced Steadfastness (Heart's Purity):
   - Rejecting Pretense:
     - Witness divine truths with a pure heart (e.g., worship as if seeing Allah).
     - Never claim special spiritual knowledge.
     - Maintain inner vigilance (monitor and dismiss negative thoughts).

3. Elite Steadfastness (Total Detachment):
   - Transcending Self-Awareness:
     - Forget being "steadfast" (live for Allah, not self-image).
     - Stop chasing perfection (perfection belongs to Allah).
     - Witness that Allah alone sustains you (absolute trust in Him).

<u>Practical Summary & Advice:</u>
Steadfastness is consistency, not perfection:
- Daily Prayer: "O Allah, keep my heart firm on Your religion."
- Small Habit: Pray two rak'ahs of Duha daily.
- Reflect on: «Those who say, 'Our Lord is Allah,' then remain steadfast» (Quran 41:30) - great reward awaits the steadfast!

Translation of the simplified Arabic text

Chapter 27: Reliance

Allah the Exalted says: “Put your trust in Allah if you are [truly] believers” (5:23).

Reliance (Tawakkul) is entrusting all matters to God—their true Owner—and fully depending on His plan and wisdom.

This station is difficult for ordinary people, as it requires complete surrender, while the sincere (the elite) find it easy, for they know God alone controls the universe, and no one else holds power over anything.

Reliance has three levels, all suitable for common people:

1. First Level: Reliance while actively pursuing worldly means (like work or treatment), but with the intention of occupying the soul and benefiting others - not claiming that effort alone brings success.

2. Second Level: Reliance while abandoning attachment to requests (i.e., not pleading anxiously) and ignoring causes; to train the soul in surrender and focus the heart on worship and faith's duties.

3. Third Level: Reliance with certainty that God is the true Owner of all things. Here, the servant doesn't even “think” about reliance, knowing God alone manages affairs, so the heart rests from the burden of control.

True servitude means realizing God is the sole Disposer of creation, and humans own nothing.

Summary & Practical Advice:

- Reliance isn't just a word but a trust nourished by certainty that God suffices His servant.
- Start training yourself to surrender in small situations: say “God is enough for me” when leaving home, or release anxiety over a lost opportunity. Remember: “When you have decided, place your trust in God” (3:159).
- Don't despair if you cling to means—the soul needs training.
- Reflect on Quranic verses like “Whoever relies on God, He is sufficient for them” (65:3), and surrender your heart to God step by step.

Translation of the simplified Arabic text

Chapter 28: Entrustment

Allah the Exalted says: "And I entrust my affair to God, for God is ever Seeing of [His] servants" (40:44).

Entrustment (Tafweed) is surrendering all matters to God without hesitation. It is higher than reliance (Tawakkul), as reliance follows visible causes, while entrustment is absolute surrender before and after them - it is the essence of spiritual integrity.

It has three levels:

1. First Level: Acknowledging you have no real power to guarantee outcomes. Thus, neither become arrogant in your efforts (e.g., thinking your deeds shield you from God's decree), nor despair in failure, nor rely solely on your intentions.

2. Second Level: Recognizing your utter helplessness. Here, you see no act can save you (e.g., assuming prayers alone suffice without heart's piety), no sin can destroy you (as forgiveness belongs to God), and no cause justifies greed for results.

3. Third Level: Witnessing with your heart that God alone manages the spiritual states of "separation" (Tafriqa) and "togetherness" (Jam'). Separation (Tafriqa) is feeling distant from God (e.g., confusion or distress), and Togetherness (Jam') is tasting nearness to Him (e.g., serenity). He alternates you between them to purify your faith.

Summary & Practical Advice:

- Entrustment is relinquishing control and seeing God as the true Actor in all things.
- Start your day by saying: "God is sufficient for me, and He is the best Disposer of affairs," and reflect on: "You cannot will unless God wills" (76:30).
- If you experience spiritual distress (Tafriqa), know it's a phase to cleanse your heart. If you taste peace (Jam'), know it's His gift.
- Recite Surah Al-Fatiha mindfully, repeat: "You alone we worship, You alone we ask for help," and trust God manages your states with unfathomable wisdom.

Translation of the simplified Arabic text

Chapter 29: Trust

Allah the Exalted says: "If you fear for him, cast him into the river" (28:7).

Trust is the soul of reliance (Tawakkul), the foundation of entrustment, and the essence of surrender to God. It is not mere calmness but certainty that God's decree is good, even if wisdom is hidden.

Trust has three levels:

1. First Level (Despair of Resistance): Despairing of your ability to change God's decree, thus ceasing to argue with fate and abandoning reckless actions opposing His wisdom.

2. Second Level (Security from Fear): Feeling complete security against losing what God has ordained. Here, you either attain the peace of contentment, the richness of certainty that God suffices you, or steadfast patience like a mountain.

3. Third Level (Witnessing God's Management): Seeing with the heart's eye that God is the Primary Manager of all things. Thus, you exit the confusion of human plans, stop exhausting yourself with reliance on means, and leave affairs to Him alone.

Summary & Practical Advice:

- True trust is living as if you see God's hand working in every detail.
- Start practicing it in simple situations: If anxious about livelihood or health, repeat: "God is sufficient for me; there is no god but Him. In Him I trust" (Quran 65:3).
- Reflect on: "And God is enough as a Trustee" (4:81).
- Avoid overcomplicating plans;
- read Surah Al-Qasas mindfully, remembering how Musa's mother cast him into the river with blind trust, and God preserved him.
- Trust requires daily training—let your heart anchor in faith.

Translation of the simplified Arabic text

Chapter 30: Submission

Allah the Exalted says: "But no, by your Lord, they will not [truly] believe until they make you [O Prophet] judge in all their disputes, then find no discomfort in their hearts over your judgment and submit completely" (4:65).

Submission is the pinnacle of responding to God. It shares with trust and entrustment the essence of reliance on God, but it is the highest station for ordinary seekers.

It has three stages:

1. First Level: Accepting what contradicts human logic (e.g., matters of the unseen), submitting to decrees unexplained by reason (e.g., life's fluctuations), and responding to spiritual calls even if daunting (e.g., sacrificing worldly attachments).

2. Second Level: Abandoning reliance on theoretical knowledge for heart-based experience (e.g., replacing debate with humility), and releasing attachment to religious formalities for spiritual truths (e.g., moving from ritual to essence).

3. Third Level: Dissolving your will into God's will. Here, you no longer even "see" yourself as submitting, for you witness that God Himself has submitted you to Him - you become a mirror reflecting His will.

Summary & Practical Advice:
Submission is discarding every "why?" and "how?".

- Train yourself to accept painful decrees calmly. Reflect on: "It is not for a believing man or woman to have choice in their matter when God and His Messenger have decided" (33:36).
- If you face unbearable trials, recall Prophet Yunus (Jonah) in the belly of the whale, crying out in darkness: "There is no god but You! Glory be to You! I have been of the wrongdoers!" (21:87). God answered and saved him.
- Practice submission daily: end prayers with, "My Lord, do not leave me to myself even for a blink," and trust God writes good for you wherever you turn.

4- The Section of Ethics

The Section of Ethics comprises ten chapters:

1. Patience (Al-Ṣabr)
2. Contentment (Al-Riḍā)
3. Gratitude (Al-Shukr)
4. Modesty (Al-Ḥayā')
5. Truthfulness (Al-Ṣidq)
6. Altruism (Al-Īthār)
7. Good Character (Al-Khuluq)
8. Humility (Al-Tawāḍuʿ)
9. Noble Chivalry (Al-Futuwwah)
10. Cheerfulness (Al-Inbisāṭ)

Translation of the simplified Arabic text

Chapter 31: Patience

Allah the Exalted says: "And endure patiently, for your patience is only by God" (16:127).

Patience is restraining the soul from complaint despite inner pain. It is among the hardest stations for ordinary people and seems as a desolate road on the path of divine love and monotheism.

It has three levels:

1. First Level (Patience Against Sin):
Avoiding sins out of fear of God's punishment or shame before Him. This patience protects faith and preserves the heart's purity.

2. Second Level (Patience in Obedience):
Persisting in acts of worship (like prayer and fasting) with sincerity and learning their details to perfect them.

3. Third Level (Patience in Trials):
Accepting tribulations through three keys:

- Remembering the immense reward for patience.
- Awaiting God's relief with certainty.
- Comparing trials to past blessings to ease suffering.

The Quran alludes to these levels (Quran 6:200):

- "Be patient" (in trials).
- "Restrain yourselves" (from sin).
- "Be steadfast" (in obedience).

Degrees of Patience:

- Patience for God (Ordinary): Patience driven by fear of punishment or hope for reward.
- Patience by God (Seekers): Patience through reliance on God's strength and mercy.
- Patience upon God (Wayfarers): Patience rooted in knowing trials are blessings to elevate the soul.

<u>Summary & Practical Advice:</u>
Patience isn't mere "waiting" but a school for nurturing faith. Train yourself by:

- First Level: Avoiding one daily sin (e.g., gossip) while reflecting on Hell's torment.
- Second Level: Performing Fajr prayer regularly and improving your ablution or focus.
- Third Level: When grief strikes, list God's past blessings and reflect on: "With hardship comes ease" (94:6).

Patience requires heart awareness: Repeat: "O Allah, help me remember You, thank You, and worship You well."

Translation of the simplified Arabic text

Chapter 32: Contentment

Allah the Exalted says: "Return to your Lord, well-pleased and pleasing [to Him]" (89:28).

Contentment is complete acceptance of God's decree without complaint or desire to alter it. It is a path closed to grievance and a core requirement for seekers of God.

Contentment has three levels:

1. First Level (Ordinary Contentment):

- Accepting God as the sole Lord and rejecting worship of others.
- Requires:
    - Loving God above all else.
    - Glorifying Him above all else.
    - Obeying Him before all else.
- This contentment purifies the heart from major shirk (associating partners with God).

2. Second Level (Contentment with God):

- Accepting all God's decrees, whether seemingly good or bad.
- Requires:
    - Equanimity toward blessings and trials.
    - Avoiding disputes with others over God's will.
    - Ceasing to seek changes to divine decree.
- This contentment marks the beginning of the path for the elite (the close ones).

3. Third Level (Contentment in God's Contentment):

- Dissolving your will into God's will, seeking only His pleasure, not your own.
- Here, even paradise or hell cease to matter - God's pleasure is your sole aim.

Summary & Practical Advice:

Contentment is not passive surrender but a heart's strength revealing beauty in every decree. Train yourself by:

- First Level: Daily recite: "I am content with God as my Lord and Islam as my religion," and reflect on: "Whoever submits their face to God while doing good has grasped the firmest handhold" (31:22).
- Second Level: When afflicted, say: "Praise God in every circumstance," and read Prophet Ayyub's story: "Adversity has touched me, and You are the Most Merciful" (21:83).
- Third Level: Dedicate time daily to recite "God is pleased with them, and they are pleased with Him" (5:119). Reflect on the mutual contentment between you and God. Ask: "Do my actions please God?" Let this question refine your intentions before deeds.

Translation of the simplified Arabic text

Chapter 33: Gratitude

Allah the Exalted says: "But few of My servants are grateful" (34:13).

Gratitude is recognizing blessings as gifts from God and acknowledging Him as the Giver. It has three pillars:

1. Acknowledging blessings: Knowing all you have is by God's grace.
2. Accepting blessings: Using them in obedience to God.
3. Praising through them: Thanking God with heart, tongue, and actions.

Gratitude has three levels:

1. First Level (Gratitude for Blessings):
   - Thanking God for visible favors (e.g., health, wealth).
   - Even non-Muslims share this and Allah accepts it and multiplies its reward.
2. Second Level (Gratitude in Trials):
   - Thanking God during hardships by surrendering the heart and avoiding complaint.
   - Here, the believer shows contentment with God's decree, concealing pain to uphold servitude.
   - Such grateful ones are the first invited to Paradise.
3. Third Level (Gratitude Beyond Circumstances):
   - Seeing God as the true Bestower in all situations, detached from the event itself.
   - Here, the heart dissolves in divine love, indifferent to ease or hardship—both reflect His wisdom.

Summary & Practical Advice:

True gratitude is seeing God's hand in everything. Start your day with "Praise be to God, by whose grace all good is perfected," and take practical steps:

- First Level: Write three new blessings you're grateful for daily.
- Second Level: When afflicted, say: "Praise God in every circumstance," and reflect on: "If you are grateful, I will certainly give you more" (14:7).
- Third Level: Shift your perspective; instead of asking, "Why me?" ask: "What wisdom does God intend here?"

Translation of the simplified Arabic text

Chapter 34: Modesty

Allah the Exalted says: "Does he not know that God sees [all]?" (96:14).

Modesty is a virtue that prevents you from vile acts out of awe that God is watching. It is the key path for those close to God.

Modesty has three levels:

1. First Level (Modesty of Awareness):
    - Arises from knowing God always watches you. It drives you to avoid sins, makes wrongdoing repulsive, and silences complaints.

2. Second Level (Modesty of Closeness):
    - Stems from feeling deeply connected to God. It makes you prefer solitude with Him over worldly interactions and fills your heart with divine tranquility.

3. Third Level (Modesty of Divine Presence):
    - Emerges from awe in God's majesty. Here, His presence is indescribable, inseparable, and boundless.

Summary & Practical Advice:

Modesty is a shield against sin. Train yourself by:

- First Level: Before acting, say: "God is watching me," and reflect on: "God is ever Watchful over you" (4:1).
- Second Level: Dedicate daily time to solitude with God (e.g., Duha prayer or supplication), sensing His presence.
- Third Level: Recite Surah "Al-Mulk" (67) before sleep, contemplating God's grandeur in creation, and pray: "O Allah, grant me modesty that guards me from disobeying You."

Translation of the simplified Arabic text

Chapter 35: Truthfulness

Allah the Exalted says: "When the matter is resolved, if they were true to God, it would be better for them" (47:21).

Truthfulness is aligning your actions and intentions with the essence of faith in God - it is the foundation of all good.

Truthfulness has three levels:

1. First Level (Sincerity of Intention):

   - Purifying your deeds solely for God, free from hypocrisy or worldly gain.
   - Its sign: Never breaking promises, avoiding bad influences, and persistently striving for good.

2. Second Level (Truthfulness in Detachment):

   - Living solely for the Truth, constantly acknowledging your flaws, and never compromising religious obligations.

3. Third Level (Truthfulness in Alignment):

   - Harmonizing your deeds and states with God's pleasure until His approval becomes your sole motive.
   - Here, even your best deeds may seem imperfect, as you realize perfection belongs to God alone.

Summary & Practical Advice:
True truthfulness is seeing God in every step. Train yourself by:

- First Level: Ask before any act: "Why am I doing this?" Reflect on: "Those who bring the truth and believe in it - they are the righteous" (39:33).
- Second Level: Daily write down one flaw you acknowledge and seek forgiveness.
- Third Level: Shift focus from "How to please people?" to "How to please God?".

Translation of the simplified Arabic text

Chapter 36: Altruism

Allah the Exalted says: "They give others preference over themselves, even if they are in need" (59:9).

Altruism is prioritizing others' good over your own, even when you need it.

It has three levels:
1. First Level (Altruism Toward People):
   - Prioritizing others' interests in permissible matters, provided it:
     - Doesn't violate Islamic law.
     - Doesn't waste your time or energy.
   - Achieved through three means:
     - Respecting others' rights.
     - Rejecting greed.
     - Seeking a noble character.
2. Second Level (Altruism for God's Pleasure):
   - Prioritizing God's pleasure over people's approval, even if it causes worldly hardship.
   - Achieved through three means:
     - Purity from selfishness.
     - Understanding Islam's essence (total submission to God).
     - Strong patience in trials.
3. Third Level (Altruism Beyond Ownership):
   - Realizing that ownership is an illusion—everything belongs to God. Even when you give, you're merely a vessel for His will.
   - Here, you don't "see" yourself as altruistic. Your ego dissolves; you seek no reward nor fear blame, knowing all acts belong to God.

Summary & Practical Advice:

True altruism is forgetting yourself for God and others. Train yourself by:

- First Level: Donate something you need (e.g., food or time) to someone needier. Reflect on: "Whatever good you send ahead for yourselves, you will find it with God" (2:110).
- Second Level: Choose God's pleasure over people's approval (e.g., rejecting bribes or defending the oppressed). Reflect on: "God loves the doers of good" (3:134).
- Third Level: Mindfully, ponder: "To God belongs the dominion of the heavens and the earth" (3:189). Ask: "Do I own anything to give?".

Translation of the simplified Arabic text

Chapter 37: Noble Character

Allah the Exalted says: "And indeed, you are of a great moral character" (68:4).

Noble character is the essence of Sufism, summarized in doing good and avoiding harm. It rests on three pillars: knowledge of ethics, generosity in giving, and patience in adversity.

Noble character has three levels:

1. First Level (Understanding Human Nature):
   - Recognizing people's limitations and destinies, avoiding unrealistic expectations.
   - Fruits of this level:
     - People feel safe from your harm.
     - They love you.
     - You become a means for their guidance.

2. Second Level (Refining Character with God):
   - Acknowledging your faults require repentance, and God's blessings demand gratitude.
   - Here, you attain constant contentment with God's decree, seeing no personal merit in obedience.

3. Third Level (Transcending Ordinary Morality):
   - Reaching a state where your character is purified; good deeds flow naturally without struggle.
   - Beyond this, you rise above pretense and conventional morals, as actions stem directly from divine connection.

Summary & Practical Advice:

Good character reflects true faith. Train yourself by:

- First Level: Treat someone who annoys you kindly, remembering the Prophet's ﷺ saying: "I was sent to perfect noble character."
- Second Level: Each night, write one fault you acknowledged and one blessing you thanked God for.
- Third Level: Pray two rak'ahs seeking better character, and reflect on Surah "Al-Ḥujurāt" (49), especially: "The noblest among you in God's sight is the most righteous" (49:13).

Translation of the simplified Arabic text

Chapter 38: Humility

Allah the Exalted says: "The servants of the Most Merciful walk upon the earth in humility" (25:63).

Humility is complete submission to God's will, avoiding arrogance or futile arguments.

It has three levels:
1. First Level (Humility Toward Religion):
   - Total acceptance of divine laws without opposing religious texts with personal opinions.
   - Requires:
      - Belief that salvation lies in following revelation, not debate.
      - Trust that righteousness is the path to safety.
      - Understanding that divine truths surpass human arguments.

2. Second Level (Humility with Creation):
   - Accepting others as they are:
      - Contentment with their God-ordained status.
      - Not retaliating against harm and accepting apologies.
   - Treating even adversaries kindly, as they are God's servants.

3. Third Level (Humility with the Truth):
   - Abandoning ego entirely:
      - Relinquishing personal opinions in serving God.
      - Not demanding rights in relationships.
      - Forgetting oneself in worship, seeing no "personal merit."

Summary & Practical Advice:
Humility is the believer's crown. Train yourself by:

- First Level: Recite "They walk upon the earth in humility" daily, imagining walking reverently as if carrying a sacred book.
- Second Level: If wronged, say: "O Allah, forgive them; they know not," and recall the Prophet's (peace be upon him) saying: "Whoever humbles himself for God, God elevates him."
- Third Level: End each day asking: "Did I do anything solely for God today?" Reflect on Surah "Luqmān" (31), especially: "Do not turn your cheek arrogantly from people, nor walk proudly on earth" (31:18).

Translation of the simplified Arabic text

Chapter 39: Spiritual Chivalry

Allah the Exalted says: "They were youths who believed in their Lord, and We increased them in guidance" (18:13).

Spiritual Chivalry is the essence of spiritual nobility, meaning freedom from selfishness and renouncing personal rights.

Spiritual Chivalry has three levels:

1. First Level (Basic Tolerance):
   - Avoiding disputes, overlooking others' faults, and forgetting past harm.

2. Second Level (Active Grace):
   - Approaching those who avoid you, honoring those who hurt you, and apologizing to those who wrong you—not by suppressing anger but purifying the heart.

3. Third Level (Complete Detachment):
   - Transcending abstract rational proofs (relying on human logic without divine guidance or a teacher's instruction), expecting no reward for deeds, and abandoning formalities in worship.

Warnings:

- Those who need a mediator to reconcile with an enemy or accept their apology (i.e., cannot reconcile with them directly), or those who find it difficult to apologize to others, have not grasped true Spiritual Chivalry.
- Those who seek divine truths through mere rational arguments (without spiritual guidance or revelation) cannot claim Spiritual Chivalry.

Summary & Practical Advice:
Spiritual Chivalry is living like the "Youths of the Cave" - steadfast in faith. Train yourself by:
- First Level: Write three recent situations where you felt anger, analyzing them through tolerance.
- Second Level: Offer a symbolic gift to someone who wronged you. Reflect on: "Good and evil are not equal. Repel [evil] with what is better" (41:34).
- Third Level: Pray two rak'ahs seeking sincerity in shunning showing off behaviors and ponder the story of the "People of the Cave" (Surah Al-Kahf).

Translation of the simplified Arabic text

Chapter 40: Spiritual Openness

Allah the Exalted says: "Will You destroy us for what the foolish among us have done? This is but Your trial - You lead astray whom You will and guide whom You will" (7:155).
Spiritual Openness (Al-Inbisāṭ) is the heart's purity and effortless interaction with creation and God.

It has three levels:
1. First Level (Openness with Creation):

- Dealing with people simply and generously, free from selfishness or fear of loss.
- Giving your time and resources without hesitation, accepting others' flaws, trusting God as the Provider.

2. Second Level (Openness with the Truth/God):

- Breaking free from fear of punishment or greed for reward, connecting to God as if speaking to a close friend.
- Here, nothing - material causes or human ties - blocks your connection to God.

3. Third Level (Openness in Withdrawal):

- Attaining inner peace where no effort is needed to "be open," as your heart is perpetually connected to God.
- Here, boundaries between "openness" and "withdrawal" vanish; you rest in divine serenity without external displays.

Summary & Practical Advice:
Spiritual Openness is living with a heart light as a butterfly. Train yourself by:

- First Level: Help a stranger without expecting thanks. Reflect on: "Whatever good you spend will be repaid to you" (2:272).
- Second Level: Pray two rak'ahs intending closeness to God, and recite: "O Allah, make me among those who are grateful when blessed and patient when tested."
- Third Level: Recite Surah "Ar-Ra'd" (13) mindfully, especially: "Those who believe and whose hearts find rest in the remembrance of God—surely, it is in the remembrance of God that hearts find rest" (13:28). Repeat daily: "God is sufficient for me, and He is the best Trustee" 100 times.

5- The Section of Foundations

The Section of Foundations comprises ten chapters:

1. Intention (Al-Qaṣd)
2. Determination (Al-ʿAzm)
3. Will (Al-Irādah)
4. Etiquette (Al-Adab)
5. Certainty (Al-Yaqīn)
6. Spiritual Intimacy (Al-Uns)
7. Remembrance (Al-Dhikr)
8. Poverty (Al-Faqr)
9. True Wealth (Al-Ghinā)
10. Station of the Desired (Maqām al-Murād)

Translation of the simplified Arabic text

Chapter 41: Intention

Allah the Exalted says: "If anyone leaves home, migrating for God and His Messenger, and death overtakes him, his reward is secured with God" (4:100).

Intention (Al-Qaṣd) is the unwavering resolve to obey God, with three levels:

1. First Level (Initial Intention):

- Forming a pure intention, training to eliminate hesitation, and distancing from worldly motives.
- Example: Intending to fast solely for God, avoiding vanity.

2. Second Level (Serious Resolve):

- A determination that ignores obstacles, removes hardships, and simplifies challenges.
- Example: Continuing worship despite distractions, rejecting weak excuses.

3. Third Level (Complete Intention):

- Total surrender to God's will, immediate response to His commands, and immersion in divine love until self dissolves.
- Here, the servant feels their actions are mere reflections of God's will.

Summary & Practical Advice:

True intention is a compass directing every step toward God. Train yourself by:

- First Level: Write one sincere intention each morning (e.g., helping someone or reading Quran). Reflect on: "And there are those who would dedicate their lives to Allah's pleasure" (2:207).
- Second Level: If tempted to delay a good deed, pray: "O Allah, help me remember You, thank You, and worship You well," then act immediately.
- Third Level: Spend 5 minutes daily in silence, asking: "Is what I'm doing now pleasing God?" Ponder Surah "Al-ʿAnkabūt" (29), especially: "Whoever strives, strives only for themselves" (29:6).

Translation of the simplified Arabic text

Chapter 42: Determination

Allah the Exalted says: "When you have decided, place your trust in God" (3:159).

Determination is the practical fulfillment of intention, whether willingly or reluctantly.

It has three levels:

1. First Level (Basic Determination):

- Rejecting spiritual stagnation and seeking divine knowledge.
- Preserving the light of faith in the heart.
- Resisting personal desires through willpower.

2. Second Level (Advanced Determination):

- Immersing fully in observing God's signs in creation.
- Illuminating the heart to see the path of truth clearly.
- Gathering inner strength to remain steadfast.

3. Third Level (Complete Determination):

- Understanding hidden motives behind determination (e.g., seeking reward or fearing punishment).
- Transcending the need for "determination" as human effort, relying entirely on God's guidance.
- Reaching a stage where actions flow naturally from complete surrender to God's will, without pretense.

Summary & Practical Advice:
True determination transforms your will into a bridge to God. Train yourself by:

- First Level: Dedicate 5 minutes each morning to recite "When you have decided, place your trust in God" and write one daily commitment (e.g., avoiding gossip or helping someone).
- Second Level: Pray two rak'ahs seeking steadfastness, reflecting on: "Those who strive for Us - We will guide them to Our paths" (29:69).
- Third Level: Before any act, ask: "Is this for God or my ego?" Ponder Surah "Ash-Sharḥ" (94) mindfully.

Translation of the simplified Arabic text

Chapter 43: Will

Allah the Exalted says: "Say: Everyone acts according to their own disposition" (17:84).

Will (Al-Irādah) is the driving force toward the Truth, with three stages:

1. First Level (Foundational Will):
   - Abandoning bad habits through beneficial knowledge.
   - Connecting with the righteous sincerely and cutting distracting ties.

2. Second Level (Advanced Will):
   - Transcending attachment to temporary spiritual states (e.g., joy or sorrow).
   - Finding comfort in God in all circumstances, balancing trials and blessings.

3. Third Level (Complete Will):
   - Total immersion in worship while maintaining uprightness.
   - Refining ethics continuously until actions mirror faith naturally.

Summary & Practical Advice:
True will transforms desires into fuel for drawing closer to God. Train yourself by:

- First Level: Write one habit to abandon (e.g., delaying prayer) and pair it with a positive act (e.g., daily Quran reading). Reflect on: "God does not change a people's state until they change themselves" (13:11).
- Second Level: If spiritually distressed, pray two rak'ahs and repeat: "O Turner of Hearts, make my heart steadfast in Your faith."
- Third Level: End each day asking: "Am I content with my ethics today?" Ponder Surah "Al-Qaṣaṣ" (28), especially: "My success lies only with God" (28:56).

Translation of the simplified Arabic text

Chapter 44: Etiquette

Allah the Exalted says: "Those who guard the limits set by God" (9:112).

Etiquette (Al-Adab) is maintaining balance between extremes (exaggeration and deficiency) by understanding the harm of transgression.

It has three levels:

1. First Level (Emotional Regulation):

   - Preventing fear from turning into despair.
   - Restraining excessive hope from becoming arrogance.
   - Controlling joy to avoid recklessness.

2. Second Level (Spiritual Elevation):

   - Transforming fear into reverence (restraint).
   - Elevating hope into trust in God's mercy (expansion).
   - Refining joy into contemplation of the Creator's greatness (witnessing).

3. Third Level (Natural Etiquette):

   - Understanding etiquette without pretense.
   - Reaching a stage where ethics become innate, as a gift from God.
   - Freedom from the burden of obligation, as etiquette becomes second nature.

Summary & Practical Advice:

True etiquette is when your actions mirror a pure heart. Train yourself by:

- First Level: Daily monitor your emotions. Ask: "Does my fear of God lead to hope or despair?" Reflect on: "Be mindful of God, and God will teach you" (2:282).
- Second Level: Pray two rak'ahs thanking God for balance. Ponder Surah "Al-Ḥashr" (59), especially: "Do not be like those who forgot God, so He made them forget themselves" (59:19).
- Third Level: Write three ethical traits you love about yourself and thank God for them nightly.

Translation of the simplified Arabic text

Chapter 45: Certainty

Allah the Exalted says: "And on earth, there are signs for those with certainty" (51:20).

Certainty (Al-Yaqīn) is unshakable trust in God that transforms faith into tangible reality.

It has three stages:

1. First Stage (Knowledge-based Certainty):
   - Believing in visible truths (e.g., God's existence through creation) and unseen truths (e.g., resurrection).
   - Example: Trusting God's control over your heartbeat, even if unseen.
2. Second Stage (Vision-based Certainty):
   - Moving from theoretical faith to heartfelt witnessing, like knowing fire's heat without touching it.
   - Here, doubt dissolves, and faith becomes light dispelling all shadows.
3. Third Stage (Ultimate Truth Certainty):
   - Experiencing faith as an existential reality, where divine presence overwhelms you until your will dissolves into His.
   - Here, you feel every atom in the universe glorifies God, and you join this divine chorus.

<u>Summary & Practical Advice:</u>

Certainty is seeing God's hand in everything. Begin your journey step-by-step:

- First Stage: Reflect daily on a cosmic sign (e.g., the sky or a plant) and recite: "Our Lord, You did not create this in vain" (3:191).
- Second Stage: Dedicate 10 minutes daily to ponder God's names and their manifestations in your life.
- Third Stage: Read Surah "Adh-Dhāriyāt" (51) mindfully, imagining all creation's praise, and pray: "O Allah, make me among the certain."

Translation of the simplified Arabic text

Chapter 46: Spiritual Intimacy

Allah the Almighty says: "And if My servants ask you about Me - behold, I am near..." (Quran 2:186).

Spiritual Intimacy (Al-Uns) is the essence of closeness to Allah, divided into three levels:

1. First Level: Spiritual Intimacy through Divine Signs:
The heart finds joy in remembering Allah, nourishes itself through His words, and contemplates His signs in creation. Like a child delighted by a toy, the believer delights in Allah's remembrance.

2. Second Level: Spiritual Intimacy through the Light of Insight:
Here, the heart perceives hidden truths through the light of faith. However, this stage is marked by spiritual turbulence and a sense of dissolving in divine love. The mind becomes overwhelmed, patience weakens, and worldly knowledge fades. It is linked to the supplication: "O Allah, grant me longing to meet You without suffering or misguidance."

3. Third Level: Spiritual Intimacy through Dissolution in Divine Presence:
The believer reaches a state where their self-awareness fades before Allah's majesty. It cannot be described, confined, or fully grasped - it is a divine gift of indescribable peace.

<u>Summary & Practical Advice:</u>
Intimacy with Allah is a journey: it starts with remembrance, ascends through faith, and culminates in absolute serenity.

- Consistently remember Allah (speak less except in good, keep your tongue moist with His remembrance).
- Reflect on Quranic verses, such as: "Those who believe and whose hearts find peace in the remembrance of Allah - surely it is in the remembrance of Allah that hearts find peace" (Quran 13:28).
- Be patient; closeness is achieved step by step. The more you love Allah, the deeper your intimacy with Him.

Translation of the simplified Arabic text

Chapter 47: Remembrance

Allah the Almighty says: "And remember your Lord whenever you forget..." (Quran 18:24).

Remembrance (Dhikr) is liberation from heedlessness and forgetfulness, divided into three levels:

1. First Level: Outward Remembrance
This involves verbal praise, supplication, or Quran recitation. Like a traveler calling out to their guide, the believer calls upon Allah verbally to stay connected.

2. Second Level: Hidden Remembrance
Here, remembrance becomes a secret of the heart. The believer abandons spiritual laziness, remaining constantly aware of Allah's presence - as if conversing with a beloved friend without pause.

3. Third Level: True Remembrance
The believer realizes that Allah is the One who remembers and encompasses them with care before they even remember Him. Their personal effort in remembrance fades, recognizing that every act of remembrance is ultimately a gift from Allah.

<u>Summary & Practical Advice:</u>
Dhikr is a weapon against forgetfulness and nourishment for the soul.

- Make Dhikr a daily habit (morning, evening, and during work).
- Reflect on the verse: "O you who believe! Remember Allah with much remembrance" (Quran 33:41).
- Move beyond verbal repetition; let Dhikr flow from your heart. The deeper your awareness of Allah, the sweeter remembrance becomes.

Translation of the simplified Arabic text

Chapter 48: Poverty

Allah the Almighty says: "O mankind! It is you who stand in need of Allah…" (Quran 35:15).

Poverty (Al-Faqr) is liberation from the illusion of self-sufficiency and reliance on Allah alone.

It has three levels:

1. First Level: Poverty of the Ascetics:
This involves detaching from worldly possessions, desires, and opinions - neither praising nor criticizing the world. Like a traveler shedding baggage to ease their journey, the ascetic abandons the world to focus on Allah.

2. Second Level: Returning to Divine Grace:
Here, the believer stops relying on their own deeds, recognizing that all grace comes from Allah. The veil of pride in spiritual status lifts, and the heart no longer clings to spiritual states or stations - like a traveler who forgets their effort to remember only their Wise Guide.

3. Third Level: True Poverty (Sufi Poverty):
The believer reaches complete dependence on Allah, stripped of self-will and enveloped in divine purification. Like a child trusting their mother entirely, they possess nothing but trust in the Most Merciful.

Summary & Practical Advice:
Poverty to Allah is the key to liberation from illusions and attaining certainty.

- Always remember: "Allah is the Rich, and you are the poor" (Quran 47:38).
- Do not be deceived by your efforts; every good is Allah's gift.
- Draw closer to Allah through gratitude, not claims. The poorer you are to Him, the richer you become in His mercy.

Translation of the simplified Arabic text

Chapter 49: True Wealth

Allah the Almighty says: "And He found you in need and made you self-sufficient" (Quran 93:8).

True wealth (Al-Ghina) is the profound fulfillment rooted in closeness to Allah, divided into three levels:

1. First Level: Wealth of the Heart
The heart becomes free from attachment to material means, accepts divine decree without resistance, and avoids disputes. Like a farmer who diligently tends his crops but entrusts their growth to Allah's mercy—unfazed by delayed rain or scarcity, knowing sustenance lies solely in Allah's hands.

2. Second Level: Wealth of the Soul
The soul aligns with obedience to Allah, abandoning what displeases Him and acting without hypocrisy. Like an honest merchant content with lawful gains, the soul finds richness in sincerity.

3. Third Level: Wealth through the Divine (Al-Haqq)
This highest stage has three phases:

- Phase One: Feeling that Allah remembers and cares for you constantly.
- Phase Two: Reflecting eternally that Allah is the First, with nothing before Him.
- Phase Three: Dissolving in the awareness of Allah's presence, finding sufficiency in Him alone.

Summary & Practical Advice:
True wealth lies not in possessions but in proximity to Allah.

- Remember: "There is no creature on earth but that its provision is [ordained] by Allah" (Quran 11:6).
- Work hard like the farmer, but trust outcomes to Allah.
- Reflect on the Quran, especially: "Verily, with hardship comes ease" (Quran 94:6).

The deeper your trust in Allah, the richer your soul becomes.

Translation of the simplified Arabic text

Chapter 50: The Station of the Desired

Allah the Almighty says: "And you did not expect that this divine writ would be bestowed upon you..." (Quran 28:86).

The Station of the Desired (Maqam Al-Murad) is a rank granted to select servants of Allah, elevated above ordinary seekers.

It has three levels:

1. First Level: Divine Protection
Allah safeguards His servant from deviation despite trials that push them toward heedlessness - such as reducing their desires, blocking worldly pleasures, or forcibly closing paths to sin. Like one rescued from drowning by divine intervention.

2. Second Level: Honor and Rectification
Allah removes the servant's flaws, shields them from sin, and grants them the ability to rectify mistakes. As He did for Solomon by replacing horses with the wind, or for Moses by forgiving him without severe reproach - signs of their elevated status.

3. Third Level: Divine Selection
Here, Allah chooses and purifies a servant exclusively for Himself. As He chose Moses when he sought fire and made him a prophet, or guides someone to a path only the chosen tread.

<u>Summary & Practical Advice:</u>
The Station of the Desired is a divine gift reminding us that Allah selects whom He wills by His mercy.

- Reflect on: "And if My servants ask you about Me - behold, I am near..." (Quran 2:186).
- Never despair of Allah's mercy; His selection transcends time or person.
- Seek sincerity in worship, and trust that Allah reforms the hearts of the pious.

6. Division of the Valleys

The Division of the Valleys consists of ten gates:

1. Spiritual Excellence (Ihsan)
2. Sacred Knowledge ('Ilm)
3. Divine Wisdom (Hikmah)
4. Inner Insight (Baṣīrah)
5. Spiritual Discernment (Firāsah)
6. Reverence (At-Taʿẓīm)
7. Spiritual Insight (Ilhām)
8. Divine Tranquility (Sakeenah)
9. Heart's Contentment (Ṭuma'nīnah)
10. Spiritual Ambition (Himmah)

Translation of the simplified Arabic text

Chapter 51: Spiritual Excellence

Allah the Almighty says: "Could the reward of goodness be anything but goodness?" (Quran 55:60).

Iḥsān (Spiritual Excellence) is the highest level of worship, defined by the Prophet (peace be upon him): "To worship Allah as if you see Him."

It has three degrees:

1. First Degree: Excellence in Intention
Purifying one's intention through knowledge (understanding truth), resolve (choosing good), and sincerity (freeing the heart from ego). Like a worker building a house meticulously for Allah's pleasure, not human praise.

2. Second Degree: Excellence in Actions
The believer carefully monitors their feelings and deeds: hides virtues to avoid hypocrisy, corrects mistakes sincerely, and maintains humility as if always before Allah. Like cleaning dust off a garment daily to keep it pure.

3. Third Degree: Excellence in Time
Living every moment in Allah's presence, never neglecting His remembrance, and striving ceaselessly to draw closer to Him. Like a traveler who never stops moving until reaching the summit.

<u>Summary & Practical Advice:</u>
Spiritual excellence (Iḥsān) is the path to spiritual perfection.

- Reflect on: "Do good, for Allah loves those who do good" (Quran 2:195).
- Start with your intention; purify it before every act.
- Self-reflect daily: Did you do anything today solely for Allah?

Translation of the simplified Arabic text

Chapter 52: Knowledge

Allah the Almighty says: "And We had endowed him with [special] knowledge from Ourselves" (Quran 18:65).

Knowledge is a light that dispels ignorance, rooted in evidence, and divided into three levels:

1. First Level: Evident Knowledge
Acquired through senses, experience, or reliable sources, like a student learning plant biology in a lab or studying history from verified texts.

2. Second Level: Hidden Knowledge
Grows in a pure heart through spiritual discipline and reveals itself to those with high aspirations in moments of solitude. Like a farmer patiently sowing seeds. Watching the plants grow, the farmer attains insight into unseen truths and differentiates between right and wrong.

3. Third Level: Divine (Ladunni) Knowledge
A direct gift from Allah, needing no mediation or proof. Like a flawless mirror reflecting sunlight, this knowledge illuminates purified hearts, unveiling divine mysteries.

Summary & Practical Advice:
Knowledge is a path to knowing Allah and self-purification.

- Reflect on: "Say: My Lord, increase me in knowledge" (Quran 20:114).
- Seek beneficial knowledge with sincerity, delving beyond the surface.
- Purify your heart through worship; divine knowledge is granted to pure souls.

Translation of the simplified Arabic text

Chapter 53: Divine Wisdom

Allah the Almighty says: "He grants wisdom to whom He wills, and whoever is granted wisdom has indeed been given abundant good" (Quran 2:269).

Divine Wisdom (Ḥikmah) is aligning things according to their rightful purpose.

It is divided into three levels:

1. First Level: Wisdom in Action
Giving each matter its due without excess or neglect, and acting at the right time. Like a farmer who sows seeds in spring and waits patiently for harvest at the appropriate time.

2. Second Level: Wisdom in Understanding
Recognizing Allah's wisdom in His warnings, His justice in His decrees, and His mercy even in His restrictions. Like a wise doctor who forbids a patient from harmful food out of compassion.

3. Third Level: Wisdom in Guidance
Attaining deep insight into truths, guiding others clearly, and directing them toward life's ultimate purpose: worshiping Allah. Like a teacher who adapts lessons so every student understands.

<u>Summary & Practical Advice:</u>
Wisdom is a treasure combining knowledge and action.

- Reflect on: "Invite to the way of your Lord with wisdom" (Quran 16:125).
- Pray for wisdom in every decision; being aware that delay in attaining something can be a blessing.
- Learn from experiences; the wise correct their course after every mistake.

Translation of the simplified Arabic text

Chapter 54: Spiritual Insight

Allah the Almighty says: "Say: This is my way - I invite to Allah with insight - I and those who follow me" (Quran 12:108).

Spiritual Insight is the light that dispels confusion.

It is divided into three levels:

1. First Level: Insight in Certainty
Trusting divine laws completely, as if seeing their outcomes, finding joy in obedience and aversion to sin. Like a ship captain following a compass precisely, knowing it ensures safe passage.

2. Second Level: Insight in Divine Justice
Understanding that Allah's guidance or trials hold wisdom and mercy, even if hidden. Like a surgeon performing a painful operation to save a patient—pain is temporary, healing is lasting.

3. Third Level: Insight in Divine Knowledge
Perceiving hidden truths through faith, discerning divine secrets with a pure heart, and distinguishing truth from falsehood with spiritual discernment. Like a lighthouse guiding ships through darkness.

<u>Summary & Practical Advice:</u>
Spiritual Insight is a gift illuminating the heart's path to Allah.

- Reflect on: "Have they not traveled through the land so their hearts may reason?" (Quran 22:46).
- Seek insight through prayer; trust that every trial holds wisdom.
- Purify your heart with remembrance; insight blossoms in pure souls.

Translation of the simplified Arabic text

Chapter 55: Spiritual Discernment

Allah the Almighty says: "In this, behold, there are messages indeed for those who can read the signs!" (Quran 15:75).

Spiritual Discernment (Firāsah) is perceiving hidden truths through divine light, without physical proof.

It has three levels:

1. First Level: Transient Discernment
A rare divine inspiration that suddenly guides the heart, like unknowingly speaking words that save a sincere seeker. This is not divination, as it comes from Allah, not human claims.

2. Second Level: Cultivated Discernment
Grows with strong faith and sincerity, revealed through divine insight. Like a farmer predicting rain through subtle natural signs.

3. Third Level: Secret Discernment
A pure divine gift needing no symbols, directly unveiled to a purified heart. Like a flawless mirror reflecting truth without distortion.

Summary & Practical Advice:
Spiritual Discernment is the soul's window to divine truths.

- Reflect on: "We propound these parables unto men so that they might think" (Quran 59:21).
- Purify your heart through worship; discernment is granted to pure souls.
- Distinguish discernment from astrology/fortune-telling; the former is divine, the latter forbidden.

Translation of the simplified Arabic text

Chapter 56: Reverence

Allah the Almighty says: "Why do you not stand in awe of Allah's majesty?" (Quran 71:13).

Reverence is humble submission to Allah's greatness.

It is divided into three levels:

1. First Level: Reverence in Obedience
Following Allah's commands without negligence, extremism, or excuses that weaken compliance. Like a student adhering to school rules diligently yet balanced.

2. Second Level: Reverence for Divine Decree
Accepting Allah's will without distorting it through arguments, rejecting it with limited knowledge, or seeking alternatives. Like a patient trusting a doctor's tough treatment plan for their own good.

3. Third Level: Reverence for Divine Authority
Making Allah the ultimate goal without intermediaries, never claiming a "right" to oppose His will. Like a child obeying parents wholeheartedly, seeing it as obedience to Allah.

<u>Summary & Practical Advice:</u>
Reverence reflects deep faith in Allah.

- Reflect on: "They did not appraise Allah with true appraisal" (Quran 6:91).
- Preserve prayer - the greatest act of reverence.
- Daily self-reflection: Did I misuse religious concessions? Did I accept Allah's decree with contentment?

Translation of the simplified Arabic text

Chapter 57: Spiritual Insight

Allah the Almighty says: "Said one who had knowledge from the Scripture: 'I will bring it to you before your glance returns to you'" (Quran 27:40).

Spiritual Insight (Ilhām) is a gift granted to pure hearts, surpassing spiritual discernment in clarity and permanence.

It has three levels:

1. First Level: Inspired Certainty
A sudden divine revelation - audible or internal - like a doctor divinely guided to diagnose a complex illness without tests.

2. Second Level: True Vision
Allah shows the servant truths that align with divine law, never crossing boundaries or erring. Like a leader divinely inspired to find escape routes in crises.

3. Third Level: Eternal Truths
A divine unveiling of cosmic secrets created by Allah since eternity. Like a scientist discovering a hidden natural law.

<u>Summary & Practical Advice:</u>
Spiritual Insight is a gift for sincere souls.

- Reflect on: "Be mindful of Allah, and Allah will teach you" (Quran 2:282).
- Purify your heart through prayer and charity; inspiration descends only on pure souls.
- Distinguish inspiration from illusions; ensure it aligns with divine law.

Translation of the simplified Arabic text

Chapter 58: Divine Tranquility

Allah the Almighty says: "It is He who sent down tranquility into the hearts of the believers" (Quran 48:4).

Divine Tranquility (Sakīnah) is a heavenly calm that strengthens hearts.

It is divided into three types:

1. First Type: Similar to The Tranquility of the Israelites
A gentle wind sent down in the Ark as a miracle for prophets, a honor for kings, and a sign of victory that terrifies enemies. Like a soldier feeling invisible courage in battle.

2. Second Type: Tranquility of the Divinely Inspired
Wisdom placed on the tongues of the righteous, revealing truths and dispelling doubts without ownership. Like a scholar grasping cosmic secrets without prior study.

3. Third Type: Tranquility of the Believers
A light and strength that brings peace, with three levels:

- First Level: Humble focus in worship, like a worshipper absorbed in prayer.
- Second Level: Calm dealing with others through justice and kindness, like a friend patient with others' flaws.
- Third Level: Contentment with divine decree, like a father losing his job yet trusting Allah's plan.

Summary & Practical Advice:
Tranquility is the key to a peaceful heart.

- Reflect on: "Those who believe and whose hearts find peace in the remembrance of Allah" (Quran 13:28).
- Engage in frequent remembrance (Dhikr); it brings calm and dispels worry.
- Interact humbly and trust Allah's plan, even in hardships.

Translation of the simplified Arabic text

Chapter 59: Inner Tranquility

Allah the Almighty says: "O reassured soul!" (Quran 89:27).

Inner Tranquility (Ṭuma'nīnah) is a permanent calm rooted in trust in Allah, distinct from temporary serenity.

It has three levels:

1. First Level: Tranquility of the Heart
The believer feels peace and confidence as remembrance of Allah fills their heart, turning fear into hope, hardship into acceptance, and trials into trust in divine reward. Like a child comforted by a parent's embrace.

2. Second Level: Tranquility of the Soul
The soul ascends by seeking understanding of creation's mysteries, longing to meet Allah, and unifying outward and inward faith. Like a researcher patiently studying the universe to uncover Allah's wisdom.

3. Third Level: Tranquility in Divine Proximity
The heart witnesses Allah's subtle grace and rests in the light of His eternal presence, like a ship sailing a calm ocean undisturbed by worldly storms.

Summary & Practical Advice:
Tranquility is the fruit of profound faith in Allah.

- Reflect on: "Those who believe and whose hearts find peace in the remembrance of Allah" (Quran 13:28).
- Cultivate Tranquility: Maintain remembrance (Dhikr) and recognize Allah's wisdom in all matters.
- Trust that trials are temporary; true comfort lies in closeness to Allah.

Translation of the simplified Arabic text

Chapter 60: Spiritual Resolve

Allah the Almighty says: "The sight did not swerve, nor did it transgress" (Quran 53:17).

Spiritual Resolve (Himmah) is the unwavering determination that directs the heart toward Allah.

It is divided into three levels:

1. First Level: Resolve to Purify
Cleanses the heart from attachment to the fleeting world, driving it to seek what lasts with Allah, and frees it from spiritual laziness. Like a traveler discarding excess baggage to move swiftly toward their goal.

2. Second Level: Resolve to Persevere
Grants unshakable determination in hardships, trust in Allah's promise, and readiness to sacrifice for truth. Like a soldier trudging a rugged path, confident of imminent victory.

3. Third Level: Resolve to Transcend
Elevates the heart above worldly status, focusing solely on closeness to Allah. Like a bird soaring in the sky, indifferent to what lies beneath.

<u>Summary & Practical Advice:</u>
Spiritual Resolve is the key to spiritual ascension.

- Reflect on: "By Allah's mercy, you were gentle with them. Had you been harsh, they would have fled from you" (Quran 3:159).
- Set your ultimate goal: Make Allah's pleasure your priority in every act.
- Never surrender to despair; high resolve turns obstacles into steps toward divine proximity.

7. Section of the Spiritual States

The "Section of the Spiritual States" comprises ten states:
1. Divine Love (Al-Maḥabbah)
2. Sacred Zeal (Al-Ghayrah)
3. Spiritual Longing (Ash-Shawq)
4. Spiritual Anxiety (Al-Qalaq)
5. Spiritual Thirst (Al-'Aṭash)
6. Spiritual Ecstasy (Al-Wajd)
7. Awe (Ad-Dahsh)
8. Spiritual Bewilderment (Al-Haymān)
9. Divine Flash (Al-Barq)
10. Spiritual Taste (Adh-Dhawq)

Translation of the simplified Arabic text

Chapter 61: Divine Love

Allah the Almighty says: "If any of you turn back from your faith, Allah will bring forth a people whom He loves and who love Him" (Quran 5:54).

Divine Love (Maḥabbah) is the highest form of closeness to Allah, guiding the heart to Him in all circumstances.

It has three levels:

1. First Level: Foundational Love
Purifies the heart from doubts, makes worship joyful, and eases hardships. Grows through gratitude for Allah's blessings, following the Prophet's (peace be upon him) teachings, and helping the needy. Like a traveler finding joy in their journey despite fatigue.

2. Second Level: Profound Love
Compels you to prioritize Allah's pleasure above all else. Your tongue constantly remembers Him, and your heart yearns to witness His signs. Nurtured by reflecting on Allah's attributes, studying His creation, and devout worship. Like a poet obsessed with their beloved.

3. Third Level: Transcendent Love
A love beyond words or symbols - akin to a blinding light that eclipses all else. This love is the soul's ultimate direction and the mark of true proximity to Allah.

<u>Summary & Practical Advice:</u>
Divine Love is the heart's path to Allah.

- Reflect on: "Those who believe are stronger in love for Allah" (Quran 2:165).
- Prioritize Allah's love: Remember Him constantly, serve His creation, and seek His pleasure in every deed.
- Persevere – do not despair if you haven't arrived yet to the Third Level - love grows through patience and sincerity.

Translation of the simplified Arabic text

Chapter 62: Sacred Zeal

Allah the Almighty says: "Bring them back to me!" – and he began stroking the legs and necks [of the horses] (Quran 38:33).

Sacred Zeal (Ghayrah) is a divine emotion emanating from love of Allah, that drives the heart to protect faith and rectify errors.

It has three levels:

1. First Level: Zeal for Lost Worship
Like someone reclaiming lost treasure, the believer feels anguish over time wasted in sin and hastens to repent. A merchant rebuilding their shop after a fire.

2. Second Level: Zeal for Wasted Time
Deep pain over moments that could have been spent in worship or goodness. This zeal reminds us that time is a non-renewable treasure. A student regretting neglected studies before exams.

3. Third Level: Zeal for Neglectful Hearts
A spiritual guide's anguish over those oblivious to Allah's remembrance, striving to purify their hearts. A surgeon performing delicate surgery to save a patient.

Summary & Practical Advice:
Sacred Zeal fuels self-reform and guiding others.

- Reflect on: "There is an excellent example for you in Abraham" (Quran 60:4).
- Guard your time - it's your spiritual capital.
- Never despair of reform; zeal begins with sincere steps.

Translation of the simplified Arabic text

Chapter 63: Spiritual Longing

Allah the Almighty says: "Whoever hopes to meet Allah - Allah's appointed time is sure to come" (Quran 29:5).

In the Sufi path, longing (Shawq) carries a paradox: Linguistically, longing is for the absent, yet their doctrine is based on "witnessing" Allah's eternal presence. Thus, the Quran uses "love" (not "longing") for Allah, as He is ever-present. Still, this spiritual longing is expressed in three levels:

1. First Level: Longing for Paradise
The believer seeks security from fear, joy after sorrow, and fulfillment through divine reward. Like a traveler yearning for homeland after a long absence.

2. Second Level: Longing for Allah
Grows from love of Allah's attributes, driving the heart to witness His grace, yet knowing He is ever-near. Like a student eager to learn from a mentor who is always present.

3. Third Level: Consuming Longing
A fiery desire that dissolves worldly pleasures, not due to Allah's absence, but intense nearness! Like a lover longing for their beloved despite their presence.

<u>Summary & Practical Advice:</u>
Spiritual longing reflects love for Allah, not His absence.

- Reflect on: "He is with you wherever you are" (Quran 57:4).
- Transform longing into action: Increase remembrance (Dhikr); Allah is closer than your jugular vein.
- Avoid material interpretations of longing; Allah is ever-present, and your longing signifies heart's connection to Him.

Translation of the simplified Arabic text

Chapter 64: Spiritual Anxiety

Allah the Almighty says: "I hastened to You, my Lord, that You might be pleased" (Quran 20:84).

Spiritual Anxiety (Qalaq) is a turmoil born of intense longing to meet Allah, weakening patience and agitating the heart.

It has three levels:

1. First Level: Anxiety of Separation
The believer feels distress that alienates them from people, wearies them of worldly life, and makes death seem like relief. Like a trapped animal desperate to escape.

2. Second Level: Anxiety of Helplessness
The mind becomes confused, advice falls on deaf ears, and energy drains in inner conflict. Like being caught in an unending storm.

3. Third Level: Consuming Anxiety
Relentless as an unquenchable fire, devouring the heart and leaving no room for peace or hope. Like a ship shattered by endless waves.

<u>Summary & Practical Advice:</u>
Spiritual anxiety reflects the heart's yearning for Allah but needs guidance.

- Reflect on: "Verily, with hardship comes ease. Indeed, with hardship comes ease" (Quran 94:5-6).
- Seek solace in patience and prayer: They are keys to calming anxiety.
- Stay connected: Share your struggles and learn from others' wisdom.

Translation of the simplified Arabic text

Chapter 65: Spiritual Thirst

Allah the Almighty says: "When the night grew dark upon him, he saw a star and said, 'This is my Lord!'" (Quran 6:76).

Spiritual Thirst ('Aṭash) is an intense longing for closeness to Allah—a dryness quenched only by His pleasure.

It has three levels:

1. First Level: The Beginner's Thirst
The believer seeks guidance, comforting words, or refuge. Like a student anxiously awaiting exam results.

2. Second Level: The Seeker's Thirst
The heart yearns for a day when Allah reveals secrets that fulfill it or a stage of rest on the journey. Like a desert traveler longing for an oasis.

3. Third Level: The Lover's Thirst
A longing unobscured by doubt, unseparated by illusions, satisfied only by a feeling of complete togetherness with Allah. Like a lover restless until meeting their beloved.

Summary & Practical Advice:
Spiritual thirst signifies a living heart.

- Reflect on: "Surely, it is in the remembrance of Allah that hearts find peace" (Quran 13:28).
- Quench your thirst with worship: Seek Allah through prayer and reflection.
- Persevere: Intense thirst precedes reaching the divine spring.

Translation of the simplified Arabic text

Chapter 66: Spiritual Ecstasy

Allah the Almighty says: "And We strengthened their hearts when they stood firm" (Quran 18:14).

Spiritual Ecstasy (Wajd) is a divine flame ignited by witnessing Allah's truths, purifying the heart.

It has three levels:

1. First Level: Fleeting Ecstasy
Temporary emotion triggered by a Quranic verse, a profound sight, or a deep thought. Like weeping at a moving Quran recitation, then returning to normal.

2. Second Level: Eternal Light
A spiritual glow enveloping the heart like primordial light, an inner call drawing one to Allah, or a force cleansing impurities. Like a tree shedding dead leaves to regrow.

3. Third Level: Transcendent Ecstasy
Complete detachment from the world, where the servant forgets themselves in divine presence. Like a bird freed from a cage, soaring unrestrained.

<u>Summary & Practical Advice:</u>
Ecstasy is a divine reminder of Allah's proximity.

- Reflect on: "Surely, it is in the remembrance of Allah that hearts find peace" (Quran 13:28).
- Seize these moments: Pray, supplicate, and recite the Quran during spiritual ecstasy.
- Embrace detachment: True purification brings you closer to Allah.

Translation of the simplified Arabic text

Chapter 67: Awe

Allah the Almighty says: "When they saw him, they were so astounded" (Quran 12:31).

Awe (Dahsh) is the bewilderment that strikes the heart when confronting Allah's greatness beyond human intellect, patience, or knowledge.

It has three levels:

1. First Level: The Seeker's Awe
The aspirant feels powerless when a spiritual experience surpasses their knowledge, drains their energy, or stuns their resolve. Like a student hearing a complex scientific theory for the first time.

2. Second Level: The Traveler's Awe
The soul is enveloped by a glimpse of divine light, forgetting time and space, dissolving in awe. Like one seeing the ocean for the first time, mesmerized by its waves.

3. Third Level: The Lover's Awe
A bewilderment that erases boundaries between servant and Lord - not through union, but through indescribable nearness. Like a child gifted a priceless treasure, speechless with joy.

<u>Summary & Practical Advice:</u>
Awe reveals the mind's inability to grasp Allah's perfection.

- Reflect on: "They did not appraise Allah with true appraisal" (Quran 6:91).
- Embrace amazement humbly: It's a gateway to knowing the Creator's majesty.
- Deepen your faith: Pray with devotion and reflect on the Quran.

Translation of the simplified Arabic text

Chapter 68: Spiritual Bewilderment

Allah the Almighty says: "And Moses fell down unconscious" (Quran 7:143).

Spiritual Bewilderment is a profound loss of composure in awe of Allah's majesty, deeper and more lasting than mere awe. It has three levels:

1. First Level: Initial Bewilderment
The servant is stunned upon first glimpsing Allah's mercy, realizing their own insignificance. Like standing before a vast ocean, feeling utterly small.

2. Second Level: Bewilderment of Discovery
The heart drowns in waves of divine secrets - marvels of creation and divine light - leaving it overwhelmed. Like a sailor astonished by raging waves while exploring the sea's depths.

3. Third Level: Bewilderment of Annihilation
Complete dissolution in witnessing Allah's eternal majesty, where self-awareness vanishes, and the mind is lost in divine revelation. Like a candle melting entirely into flame.

Summary & Practical Advice:
Bewilderment reveals human inability to grasp Allah's perfection.

- Reflect on: "Exalted is your Lord, the Lord of Honor, above what they describe" (Quran 37:180).
- Embrace humility: Let bewilderment purify your heart from arrogance.
- Channel this awe: Let it drive you to seek deeper knowledge and worship.

Translation of the simplified Arabic text

Chapter 69: Divine Flash

Allah the Almighty says: "When he saw a fire" (Quran 20:10).

The Divine Flash is a heavenly spark that illuminates the heart's path toward Allah, signaling the start of the spiritual journey. It differs from spiritual ecstasy (Wajd), which occurs after embarking on the path.

Devine Flash has three levels:

1. First Level: Flash of Hope
A spark that makes the believer see Allah's small blessings as immense, eases life's hardships, and instills acceptance of divine decree. Like finding a water droplet in the desert and seeing it as a treasure.

2. Second Level: Flash of Caution
A spark reminding the believer of negligence's consequences, reducing worldly attachment and urging inner purification. Like a traveler hastening steps upon hearing a danger warning.

3. Third Level: Flash of Grace
A spark creating unending joy, enveloping the heart in Allah's mercy, and filling it with pride in belonging to Him. Like rain reviving barren land.

Summary & Practical Advice:
The Divine Flash marks the journey's beginning.

- Reflect on: "Surely, it is in the remembrance of Allah that hearts find peace" (Quran 13:28).
- Welcome these flashes: They are Allah's invitation to draw closer.
- Persist in worship: The flash lights the path, but walking it requires your effort.

Translation of the simplified Arabic text

Chapter 70: Spiritual Taste

Allah the Almighty says: "This is a Reminder" (Quran 38:49).

Spiritual Taste (Dhawq) is the profound experience of faith's sweetness - more enduring than fleeting ecstasy (Wajd) and clearer than divine flashes (Barq).

It has three levels:

1. First Level: Taste of Conviction
The believer feels the certainty of faith, unshaken by desires, false hopes, or worldly attachments. Like distinguishing pure honey from artificial sweeteners.

2. Second Level: Taste of Will
The heart finds joy in divine intimacy, undistracted by worldly chaos or temptations. Like listening to a beautiful melody with full attention.

3. Third Level: Taste of Detachment
A direct spiritual feeling with Allah, where barriers vanish, and the servant perceives divine beauty. Like drinking from a pure spring that quenches thirst eternally.

<u>Summary & Practical Advice:</u>
Spiritual Taste is the fruit of sincerity.

- Reflect on: "Surely, it is in the remembrance of Allah that hearts find peace" (Quran 13:28).
- Document your spiritual experiences: They deepen your awareness of faith's taste.
- Seek Allah's pleasure, not mere taste: True spiritual taste follows sincerity.

8- Section of Divine Authorities (Wilayat)

The sction of Divine Authorities (*Wilayat*), consists of ten chapters:

1. Divine Glance (Al-Lahẓ)
2. Divine Moment (Al-Waqt)
3. Purity (Aṣ-Ṣafā')
4. Divine Joy (As-Surūr)
5. Inner Secret (As-Sirr)
6. The Breath (An-Nafas)
7. Spiritual Estrangement (Al-Ghurbah)
8. Immersion (Al-Gharaq)
9. Spiritual Absence (Al-Ghaybah)
10. Control (At-Tamakkun)

Translation of the simplified Arabic text

Chapter 71: The Divine Glance

Allah the Almighty says: "Look at the mountain; if it remains firm in its place, only then will you see Me" (Quran 7:143).

The Divine Glance is a fleeting spiritual insight revealing divine truths. It has three levels:

1. First Level: Glimpse of Divine Grace
Sudden awareness of Allah's blessings, humbling the servant into gratitude, yet mixed with fear of losing them. Like marveling at nature's beauty while fearing its impermanence.

2. Second Level: Glimpse of the Light of Insight
A flash revealing hidden truths through inspiration, purifying the heart and filling it with divine closeness. Like hearing a guide's voice in darkness leading to safety.

3. Third Level: Glimpse of Divine Unity
A spiritual vision dissolving worldly concerns, showing human efforts as insignificant before Allah's greatness. Like a scientist realizing their discoveries are but a speck in Allah's infinite knowledge.

Summary & Practical Advice:
Divine glimpses strengthen faith and proximity to Allah.

- Reflect on: "We will show them Our signs in the horizons and within themselves" (Quran 41:53).
- Document these moments: Writing deepens understanding and gratitude.
- Stay humble: Every spiritual glimpse is Allah's gift, not your achievement.

Translation of the simplified Arabic text

Chapter 72: Time

Allah the Almighty says: “Then you came [to Pharaoh] by My plan, O Moses” (Quran 20:40).

In the Sufi path, time has three dimensions, each with three levels:

1. First Dimension: Time of Longing and Awe
    - Level 1: Moments when the heart is drawn to Allah through pure hope or sincere fear, like awaiting a beloved's return.
    - Level 2: Time inflamed by divine love, where the servant yearns for closeness like a thirsty man for water.
    - Level 3: Time that blends joy in divine grace and fear of losing it.
2. Second Dimension: Time Between Knowledge and State
    - Level 1: Transition between religious knowledge and spiritual experience, like a student applying theory.
    - Level 2: Time witnessing the path's contradictions - certainty versus doubt.
    - Level 3: Time achieving balance between knowledge and action, making time a bridge to Allah.
3. Third Dimension: True Time (Timelessness)
    - Level 1: Moments where time dissolves, and the servant realizes Allah's control, like losing self-awareness in prayer.
    - Level 2: Time realizing the world's impermanence, leading to total reliance on Allah.
    - Level 3: Time illuminated by divine light, revealing creation anew, yet remaining within servitude.

<u>Summary & Practical Advice:</u>
Time is the vessel of deeds and life's value.

- Reflect on: “He is the One Who has made the night and the day successive for whoever desires to remember or desires gratitude” (Quran 25:62).
- Utilize every moment: In remembrance, obedience, and kindness.
- Trust Allah's plan: "True Time" is when the heart surrenders to Him.

Translation of the simplified Arabic text

Chapter 73: Purity

Allah the Almighty says: “And, verily, they are in Our sight among the chosen and the excellent!” (Quran 38:47).

Purity is freedom from spiritual blemishes and steadfastness in truth.

It has three levels:

1. Level 1: Purity of Knowledge

    - Clarifies understanding to recognize Allah's true path.
    - Reveals the ultimate purpose of sincere striving.
    - Aligns the seeker's intentions with goodness.

2. Level 2: Purity of State

    - The heart tastes the sweetness of a feeling akin to an intimate conversation with Allah.
    - The seeker witnesses Allah's mercy in all creation.
    - Worldly distractions fade in the light of divine presence.

3. Level 3: Purity of Connection

    - Human efforts dissolve in awe of Allah's greatness.
    - Theoretical knowledge becomes heart-certainty.
    - Burdens lift as the heart harmonizes with divine wisdom.

<u>Summary & Practical Advice:</u>
Purity is the heart's clear mirror.

- Reflect on: “Successful indeed is the one who purifies it” (Quran 91:9).
- Purify your heart: Through repentance and mindfulness of Allah.
- Seek certainty: The purer your heart, the closer you are to divine wisdom.

Translation of the simplified Arabic text

Chapter 74: Divine Joy

Allah the Almighty says: "Say: 'In the bounty of Allah and in His mercy - in that let them rejoice!'" (Quran 10:58).

Divine Joy (As-Surūr) is a pure bliss rooted in Allah's grace, distinct from worldly happiness. It is free from worldly spoilers, so Allah reserved its use in the Quran for happiness in the hereafter.

It has three levels:

1. Level 1: Joy of Spiritual Taste
   - Erases three sorrows:
     - Fear of losing connection with Allah.
     - Darkness of ignorance about His truths.
     - Loneliness of being distant from His love.

2. Level 2: Joy of Witnessing
   - Lifts the veil of limited human understanding.
   - Frees the heart from pretense and artificiality.
   - Elevates the soul above petty worldly choices.

3. Level 3: Joy of Divine Response
   - Erases loneliness through closeness to Allah.
   - Opens the door to heartful contemplation of divine beauty.
   - Revives the soul with the sweetness of nearness to Him.

<u>Summary & Practical Advice:</u>
True joy blooms near Allah.

- Reflect on: "Those who believe and whose hearts find rest in the remembrance of Allah" (Quran 13:28).
- Gratefulness: Every blessing from Him is a source of joy.
- Trust His plan: He suffices you against all worries.

Translation of the simplified Arabic text

Chapter 75: The Inner Secret

Allah the Almighty says: "Allah knows best what is in their hearts" (Quran 11:31).

Those endowed with the Inner Secret are Allah's chosen servants whose hearts guard profound devotion.

They are of three categories:

1. First Category: The Hidden Elite
   - Their aspirations transcend worldly limits.
   - Their intentions are pure as crystal.
   - They leave no visible trace, like divine treasures.

2. Second Category: The Discreetly Pious
   - They conceal greater truths beneath humble appearances.
   - Refined by humility and spiritual grace.
   - Their excellence is free from pretension.

3. Third Category: The Self-Forgetful
   - Divine love consumes them, making them unaware of their own virtue.
   - They possess sincerity they don't perceive and love they don't claim.
   - Their unique state reflects nearness to Allah without presumption.

Summary & Practical Advice:
The Inner Secret is the core of sincerity.

- Reflect on: "Does He who created not know? And He is the Subtle, the Acquainted" (Quran 67:14).
- Purify your inner self: Allah knows every hidden thought.
- Serve silently: Hidden deeds are most beloved to Him.

Translation of the simplified Arabic text

Chapter 76: The Breath

Allah the Almighty says: *"When he recovered, he cried: Glory be to You!"* (Quran 7:143).

In the spiritual journey, the breath (Al-Nafas) reflects the heart's connection with Allah.

It is divided into three levels:

1. First Breath: The Breath of Concealment
    - Arises when the heart feels distant from Allah.
    - Filled with suppressed grief and theoretical knowledge.
    - Its holder sighs like one in regret, speech reflecting inner struggle.

2. Second Breath: The Breath of Divine Manifestation
    - Emerges when light of knowledge illuminates the heart.
    - Transitions the seeker from joy to witnessing divine beauty.
    - Elevates beyond verbal description.

3. Third Breath: The Breath of Sanctity
    - Purified by Allah's light, linked to His eternal wisdom.
    - It is called the "Shell of Light" for its purity.
    - Represents peak closeness without dissolving the servant's identity.

Symbolic Meanings:
- Breath of Concealment: A lamp for those guarding their faith.
- Breath of Manifestation: A ladder to higher awareness.
- Breath of Sanctity: A crown for the spiritually realized.

<u>Summary & Practical Advice:</u>

The breath mirrors the soul's state.
- Reflect on: *"And remembers the name of his Lord and prays"* (Quran 87:15).
- Breathe mindfully: Let each breath remind you of Allah.
- Seek purity: Cleanse your heart to transform breath from grief to light.

Translation of the simplified Arabic text

Chapter 77: Spiritual Estrangement

Allah the Almighty says: "If only there had been among the generations before you people of wisdom who forbade corruption on earth - except a few whom We saved" (Quran 11:116).

Spiritual Estrangement is the seekers' isolation from their peers in society due to their adherence to piety, which distances them from worldly pursuits.

It is divided into three levels:

1 .Level 1: Physical Estrangement
- Leaving one's homeland for Allah's sake (e.g., migration).
- Such a person is honored as a martyr, spiritually connected to their homeland.
- They will be resurrected with the righteous, like Jesus (peace be upon him).

2 .Level 2: Moral Estrangement
- Being righteous in a corrupt society.
- A scholar among the ignorant, or a sincere believer among hypocrites.
- These are the "strangers" praised in prophetic traditions.

3 .Level 3: Spiritual Estrangement
- The estrangement of the God-conscious mystic (Al-'Arif).
- Their spiritual state transcends worldly labels and descriptions.
- Their high aspirations make them perpetual seekers of divine truth.

<u>Summary & Practical Advice:</u>
True estrangement is the price of divine proximity.

- Reflect on: "Indeed, those who say, 'Our Lord is Allah,' and then remain steadfast - the angels descend upon them…" (Quran 41:30).
- Choose divine approval: Even if it means standing alone.
- Persevere: The deeper your estrangement, the closer you are to Allah's mercy.

Translation of the simplified Arabic text

Chapter 78: Immersion

Allah the Almighty says: "And when they both submitted (to Allah), and he laid him prostrate upon his forehead" (Quran 37:103).

Immersion here signifies complete absorption in divine devotion.

It is divided into three stages:

1. Stage 1: Immersion of Knowledge into Action
    - The seeker aligns their deeds with their knowledge.
    - They grasp true sincerity, earning recognition among the righteous.

2. Stage 2: Immersion of Signs into Spiritual Unveiling
    - They speak through the heart's language, not habit.
    - Act based on spiritual insight, rising above worldly desires of the self.

3. Stage 3: Immersion of Witnessing into Unity
    - Enveloped by the light of certainty, perceiving all through divine wisdom.
    - Freed from worldly inclinations, their sole focus is Allah's pleasure.

<u>Summary & Practical Advice:</u>
True immersion is a total surrender to Allah.

- Reflect on: *"Whoever submits their whole self to Allah while doing good has grasped the firmest handhold"* (Quran 31:22).
- Unify your words and deeds: Let actions mirror your faith.
- Seek essence over form: Worship's core is the heart's surrender.

Translation of the simplified Arabic text

Chapter 79: Spiritual Absence

Allah the Almighty says: "And he turned away from them and said: 'Alas, my grief for Joseph!'" (Quran 12:84).

Spiritual Absence here refers to the heart's detachment from all but Allah.

It is in three stages:

1. Stage 1: The Seeker's Absence (Beginner)

   - Detaches from worldly attachments and obstacles to seek divine truths.
   - Struggles to break free from the self's desires and distractions.

2. Stage 2: The Traveler's Absence (Advanced)

   - Transcends superficial adherence to knowledge and rituals.
   - Moves forward with unwavering faith, abandoning spiritual laziness.

3. Stage 3: The Knower's Absence (Elite)

   - Becomes unaware of his own spiritual states, absorbed solely in Allah.
   - Resides in the "Fortress of Unity," free from self-centered concerns.

<u>Summary & Practical Advice:</u>
True absence is the heart's absorption in Allah.

- Reflect on: "Surely, in the remembrance of Allah do hearts find peace" (Quran 13:28).
- Purify your heart: Through constant remembrance and patience in obedience.
- Persist: Every effort brings you closer to spiritual liberation.

Translation of the simplified Arabic text

Chapter 80: Control

Allah the Almighty says: "And do not be disturbed by those who have no faith. " (Quran 30:60).

Control is the heart's unwavering stability in Allah's path, beyond mere tranquility.

It has three levels:

1. Level 1: Control of the Seeker (Beginner)
   - Combines:
     - Sincere intention guiding his journey.
     - Flashes of divine insight strengthening his faith.
     - A clear path providing ease in his efforts.

2. Level 2: Control of the Traveler (Advanced)
   - Combines:
     - Complete detachment from worldly distractions.
     - Moments of spiritual unveiling revealing divine truths.
     - Inner purity balancing him in all states.

3. Level 3: Control of the Knower (Elite)
   - Attains:
     - Heartfelt presence before Allah, beyond need for requests.
     - Divine light enveloping his being with certainty.
     - Ultimate stability where doubts cannot shake him.

<u>Summary & Practical Advice:</u>
Control is the fruit of patience and trust in Allah.

- Reflect on: "Seek help through patience and prayer" (Quran 2:45).
- Strengthen your resolve: Through consistent effort and daily remembrance.
- Ignore the doubters: Certainty is your strongest shield.

9. Division of Realities

The Division of Realities comprises ten chapters:

1. Divine Unveiling (Al-Mukashafah)
2. Witnessing (Al-Mushahadah)
3. Direct Vision (Al-Mu'ayanah)
4. Divine Life (Al-Hayah)
5. Divine Selection (Al-Qabd)
6. Spiritual Expansion (Al-Bast)
7. Spiritual Ecstasy (Al-Sakr)
8. Sobriety (Al-Sahw)
9. Divine Proximity (Al-Ittisal)
10. Separation (Al-Infisal)

Translation of the simplified Arabic text

Chapter 81: Divine Unveiling

Allah the Almighty says: "He revealed to His servant what He revealed" (Quran 53:10).

Divine Unveiling is the removal of veils between the servant and Allah to perceive divine truths.

It has three stages:

1. Stage 1: Unveiling Through Signs
   - The seeker infers from the phenomena of the universe the manifestations of the Creator, Glory be to Him, the Most High.
   - Intermittent glimpses confirm the path's validity, though gaps may occur.
   - The seeker reaches resilience against obstacles but may experience lapses.

2. Stage 2: Unveiling Through Steadfastness
   - Unveiling becomes continuous and unbroken.
   - The seeker attains unwavering focus, untouched by doubt or worldly desires.

3. Stage 3: Direct Witnessing
   - Immediate perception of truths without intermediaries.
   - Leaves no room for attachment to forms, culminating in pure heart-centered vision.

Summary & Practical Advice:
Divine Unveiling is a gift earned through sincerity.

- Reflect on: "It is not for any human that Allah should speak to him except by revelation or from behind a veil" (Quran 42:51).
- Purify your intention: Sincerity is the key to unveiling.
- Seek Allah's pleasure, not divine unveiling: He guides whom He wills.

Translation of the simplified Arabic text

Chapter 82: Witnessing

Allah the Almighty says: "In this, surely, is a reminder for whoever has a heart, or gives ear with a conscious mind" (Quran 50:37).

Witnessing is the complete lifting of veils to perceive the Truth directly, surpassing partial signs for absolute certainty.

It has three stages:

Stage 1: Witnessing Through Knowledge

- Transcending theoretical knowledge to perceive divine light.
- The seeker dissolves into divine radiance but still distinguishes between self and signs.

Stage 2: Direct Vision

- Immediate perception of the realities of the universe that negates the need for external proofs.
- The heart embodies purity, and words fail to describe the experience.

Stage 3: Unified Witnessing

- Complete heart-connectedness with the Truth, realizing divine oneness without confusion.
- The seeker swims in the ocean of divine presence, free from temporal and spatial limits.

<u>Summary & Practical Advice:</u>
Witnessing is the pinnacle of spiritual journeying.

- Reflect on: *"Shall I seek any judge other than Allah?"* (Quran 6:114).
- Purify your heart: Through sincerity and trust to receive divine insight.
- Seek depth: Do not be satisfied with appearances; Truth is seen with the heart before the eyes.

Translation of the simplified Arabic text

Chapter 83: Direct Vision

Allah the Almighty says: "Have you not seen how your Lord extends the shadow?" (Quran 25:45).

Direct Vision is perceiving truth through three means:

1. Sensory Vision (By Eyes)

    - Observing physical phenomena, like shadows, and physical items with the naked eye.

2. Heart's Vision

    - Certain knowledge beyond doubt, attained through deep faith.
    - Example: Recognizing Allah's greatness through His visible signs.

3. Soul's Vision

    - Spiritual illumination to perceive divine truths directly.
    - Pure souls resonate with divine beauty, drawing hearts closer to Him.

<u>Summary & Practical Advice:</u>
True vision is of the heart and soul.

- Reflect on: "He is with you wherever you are" (Quran 57:4).
- Purify your heart: Reflect on Allah's signs to attain inner sight.
- Look beyond the surface: Everything points to the Creator's majesty.

Translation of the simplified Arabic text

Chapter 84: Divine Life

Allah the Almighty says: "Or one who was dead, whom We gave life?" (Quran 6:122).

Divine Life here refers to three stages that revive the heart from ignorance and separation from Allah:

1. First Life: Life of Knowledge
   - Rescues you from the darkness of ignorance to the light of awareness.
   - Built on three pillars:
     - Fear of falling short in worship.
     - Hope in His mercy and forgiveness.
     - Love that binds you to Him.

2. Second Life: Life of Unity
   - Frees you from worldly distractions, uniting you with Allah's will.
   - Built on three pillars:
     - Dependence on Allah's support.
     - Humility in recognizing your weakness before His greatness.
     - Pride in choosing truth despite challenges.

3. Third Life: Life of Divine Closeness
   - Ego dissolves, and your existence aligns with divine truth.
   - Built on three pillars:
     - Awe that silences personal desires.
     - Presence filling your heart so you feel no separation.
     - Solitude where you connect with Allah without distractions.

<u>Summary & Practical Advice:</u>
True life is closeness to Allah.

- Reflect on: "Who was dead, whom We gave life and a light to walk among people" (Quran 6:122).
- Seek beneficial knowledge: It revives the heart from ignorance.
- Spend time in solitude: To ascend from superficiality to spiritual depth.

Translation of the simplified Arabic text

Chapter 85: Divine Selection

Allah the Almighty says: "And then We withdraw it [the shadow] unto Ourselves - a gradual withdrawal" (Quran 25:46).

Divine Selection refers to Allah choosing and preserving sincere servants in a special state of closeness.

They are of three types:

1. First Type: The Withdrawn Ones

- They completely isolate themselves from the world, unknown to others.
- Allah conceals their spiritual presence; they live in total obscurity, physically present but spiritually hidden.

2. Second Type: The Veiled Ones

- Allah hides their true status under ordinary appearances, making them indistinguishable.
- They may act ambiguously or simply in order to protect their spiritual purity.

3. Third Type: The Secretly Bonded

- Allah connects them to Him through an invisible bond, making them nearer to Him than anything.
- They are guarded even from themselves, unaware of their full reality.

<u>Summary & Practical Advice:</u>
Divine Selection is a sign of love and mercy.

- Reflect on: "He is with you wherever you are" (Quran 57:4).
- Avoid seeking fame: The best servants are those hidden from sight.
- Purify your intentions: Closeness to Allah is measured by sincerity, not visibility.

Translation of the simplified Arabic text

Chapter 86: Spiritual Expansion

Allah the Almighty says: "He multiplies you thereby" (Quran 42:11).

Spiritual Expansion is the heart's openness to goodness in three forms:

1. First Form: Expansion Through Mercy

- They live among people with compassionate hearts, illuminating them with faith's light while safeguarding their dignity.
- Their goal: Guiding others to truth with gentleness and wisdom.

2. Second Form: Expansion Through Steadfastness

- Their unshakable faith remains firm through trials and worldly distractions.
- Their hearts are serene, trusting Allah's divine decree.

3. Third Form: Expansion Through Guidance

- Like lamps on the path to Allah, they exemplify righteous conduct through knowledge and action.
- They are living models of devotion.

<u>Summary & Practical Advice:</u>
True expansion is effortless openness to goodness.

- Reflect on: "Keep yourself content with those who call on their Lord morning and evening" (Quran 18:28).
- Be merciful: A believer reflects Allah's mercy on earth.
- Strengthen your heart: Through remembrance and reflection on His signs.

Translation of the simplified Arabic text

Chapter 87: Spiritual Ecstasy

Allah the Almighty says: "…he asked, "My Lord! Reveal Yourself to me so I may see You." '" (Quran 7:143).

Spiritual Ecstasy is a state where the servant loses self-awareness due to overwhelming joy in divine proximity, unique to sincere lovers of Allah. It has three signs:

1. First Sign: Total Absorption in Allah
   - Forgets everything else, even matters deemed significant by others.

2. Second Sign: Immersion in Divine Longing
   - Dives into love for Allah without hesitation, as if swimming in endless light.

3. Third Sign: Indescribable Spiritual Joy
   - Overwhelmed by joy surpassing description, coupled with patience through trials.

Other states falsely called "ecstasy" – like greed or lust – are delusions unrelated to true spiritual ecstasy.

<u>Summary & Practical Advice:</u>
True ecstasy is the heart dissolving in love for Allah.

- Reflect on: "Those who believe are strongest in love for Allah" (Quran 2:165).
- Stay balanced: Do not let spiritual joy distract you from worldly duties.
- Seek sincerity: True ecstasy stems from pure love, not fleeting desires.

Translation of the simplified Arabic text

Chapter 88: Sobriety

Allah the Almighty says: "Until, when fear is lifted from their hearts, they say: 'What has your Lord said?' They say: 'The Truth'" (Quran 34:23).

Sobriety is an elevated state following ecstasy, marked by clarity and stability. It surpasses ecstasy as it embodies balance, not loss of awareness.

Its key traits:

1. Complete Clarity:

- The seeker perceives truths with an enlightened heart, free from confusion.
- No longer needs to seek or wait, having reached assured certainty.

2. Freedom from Constraints:

- Those whose lives align with Allah's are not at risk of committing sins, for their steadfastness on the path of truth safeguards them from making mistakes.
- They live in harmony with divine wisdom, trusting Allah's decree without anxiety.

3. Spiritual Purity:

- A flawless state, like a mirror reflecting divine light.
- Unshaken by worldly fluctuations, firm in faith.

<u>Summary & Practical Advice:</u>
Sobriety is the pinnacle of spiritual balance.

- Reflect on: "Say: He is my Lord; there is no god but Him. In Him I trust, and to Him I turn" (Quran 13:30).
- Seek clarity: Through reflection on Allah's signs and repentance.
- Stay steadfast: True certainty remains unshaken by circumstances.

Translation of the simplified Arabic text

Chapter 89: Divine Proximity

Allah the Almighty says: *"And then He drew near and came closer, until He was within two bows' length or even nearer"* (Quran 53:8-9).

Divine Proximity signifies intense closeness to Allah in three stages, without any notion of union or merging:

1. Stage 1: Bond of Reliance (Attachment to Allah)
   - Purifying Intent: Directing actions solely for Allah.
   - Refining Will: Freeing oneself from personal desires.
   - Achieving Stability: Steadfastness in spiritual obedience.

2. Stage 2: Bond of Witnessing (Heartfelt Vision)
   - Freedom from reliance on intellectual proofs.
   - Witnessing divine truths with unwavering certainty.
   - Clarity of heart, where mysteries dissolve.

3. Stage 3: Bond of Existence (Absolute Nearness)
   - Indescribable closeness, perceived as spiritual illumination.
   - Expressible only metaphorically, like light felt by the heart.

<u>Summary & Practical Advice:</u>
True proximity is the heart's nearness to Allah.

- Reflect on: *"When My servants ask you about Me, I am indeed near"* (Quran 2:186).
- Purify your intent: Closeness begins with sincerity.
- Never despair: Allah draws whom He wills by His mercy.

Translation of the simplified Arabic text

Chapter 90: Separation

Allah the Almighty says: "Allah warns you of Himself" (Quran 3:28).

Separation means severing attachment to all that distracts from Allah.

It has three forms:

1. First Separation: From the Material and Spiritual Worlds

- Ignoring their allure: Not obsessing over worldly pleasures or false spiritual gains.
- Independence from them: Relying solely on Allah for needs and aspirations.
- Indifference to them: Freeing the heart from fear or desire for creation.

2. Second Separation: From Awareness of Detachment Itself

- Reaching a state where you don't even think about being "detached," as your heart is fully absorbed in Allah.
- Like a fish in water that doesn't notice the water.

3. Third Separation: From the Concept of Connection

- Realizing closeness to Allah transcends labels of "connection" or "separation."
- Like sunlight: You see it but cannot own it, accepting its presence without grasping.

<u>Summary & Practical Advice:</u>
True separation is freeing the heart for Allah alone.

- Reflect on: "Say: Allah! Then leave them engrossed in their play" (Quran 6:91).
- Purify your heart: Through repentance and trust in Allah.
- Fear no loss: Whoever loses everything but Allah finds everything in Him.

10. Division of Ultimate Realities

The Division of Ultimate Realities comprises ten chapters:

1. Divine Knowledge (Ma'rifah)
2. Annihilation (Fana')
3. Divine Subsistence (Baqa')
4. Realization (Tahqeeq)
5. Devine Veiling (Talbees)
6. Divine Presence (Wujud)
7. Spiritual Detachment (Tajreed)
8. Singular Focus (Tafreed)
9. Togetherness (Jam')
10. Divine Oneness (Tawheed)

Translation of the simplified Arabic text

Chapter 91: Divine Knowledge

Allah the Almighty says: "When they listen to what has been sent down to the Messenger, you see their eyes overflowing with tears for recognizing the truth" (Quran 5:83).

Divine Knowledge is profound understanding of divine truths, divided into three levels:

Level 1: Knowledge of Attributes (For the General Public)
- Understanding Allah's attributes (mercy, justice) without likening them to creation.
- Based on:
    - Accepting attributes as revealed in the Quran.
    - Rejecting anthropomorphism (attribution of human characteristics or behavior to a god).
    - Acknowledging Allah's essence transcends human grasp.

Level 2: Knowledge of the Essence (For the Elite)
- Unifying Allah's attributes into a single perception of His essence.
- Achieved by:
    - Transcending intermediaries in understanding.
    - Releasing attachment to formalities.
    - Attaining heartfelt certainty in Allah's oneness.

Level 3: Absolute Knowledge (For the Elite of the Elite)
- Direct spiritual experience with Allah, beyond proof or words.
- Rooted in:
    - Heartfelt witnessing of divine proximity.
    - Moving beyond theory to lived experience.
    - Spiritual harmony with Allah without merging.

<u>Summary & Practical Advice:</u>
True knowledge dissolves the heart in love for Allah.

- Reflect on: "Of all of Allah's servants, only those who have knowledge are [truly] in awe of Him" (Quran 35:28).
- Seek beneficial knowledge: With humility, not for show.
- Go beyond the surface: Deeper knowledge strengthens certainty.

Translation of the simplified Arabic text

Chapter 92: Annihilation

Allah the Almighty says: "All that is on earth is perishing. But forever will remain the Face of your Lord" (Quran 55:26-27).

Annihilation is the dissolution of all except Allah in heart and existence, in three stages:

Stage 1: Annihilation of Knowledge and Perception

- Intellectual Annihilation: Realizing everything perishes except Allah.
- Denial of Dependency: Releasing reliance on creation.
- Annihilation in Truth: Experiencing divine oneness.

Stage 2: Annihilation of Witnessing

- Freedom from worldly or otherworldly desires.
- Letting go of even spiritual knowledge itself.
- Seeing only Allah in all things.

Stage 3: Annihilation of Annihilation

- The disappearance of the sense of "annihilation," as the heart mirrors divine light.

<u>Summary & Practical Advice:</u>
True annihilation is dissolving ego into love for Allah.

- Reflect on: "He is the First and the Last, the Manifest and the Hidden" (Quran 57:3).
- Purify your heart: Through repentance and detachment from all but Allah.
- Seek eternity: By working for the Hereafter, for only what is with Allah remains.

Translation of the simplified Arabic text

Chapter 93: Divine Subsistence

Allah the Almighty says: "And Allah is far superior and more lasting" (Quran 20:73).

Divine Subsistence refers to the eternal presence of Allah in the heart after all else vanishes.

It has three levels:

Level 1: Subsistence of the Known (Divine Reality)

- Awareness of Allah's existence remains as a tangible truth, even after abstract intellectual knowledge fades.

Level 2: Subsistence of the Witnessed (Spiritual Experience)

- Certainty that Allah—the Eternal Creator—remains after the ephemeral world perishes.
- The seeker feels as if they inhabit an immortal spiritual realm, untouched by physical decay.

Level 3: Subsistence of Eternal Truth

- Only Allah remains as an everlasting reality after all illusions perish.
- This stage transcends words: those who attain it need no explanation, and no explanation suffices for those who don't.

Summary & Practical Advice:
True subsistence is anchoring the heart to Allah alone.

- Reflect on: "Everything will perish except His Face" (Quran 28:88).
- Focus on the eternal: Invest time only in what brings you closer to Allah.
- Work for the Everlasting: This world is fleeting; what is with Allah is better and eternal.

Translation of the simplified Arabic text

Chapter 94: Realization

Allah the Almighty says: "Have you not believed? He said: Yes, but to reassure my heart" (Quran 2:260).

Spiritual Realization is attaining absolute certainty in Allah through three stages:

Stage 1: Realization from the Truth

- Purifying faith from doubt, ensuring knowledge is free from ignorance.
- Example: The certainty of Musa's mother when she cast her son into the river, trusting Allah's protection.

Stage 2: Realization by the Truth

- Harmonizing spiritual experiences with divine reality, free from contradiction.
- Example: Witnessing Allah's signs in creation without worldly distractions.

Stage 3: Realization in the Truth

- Dissolving all but Allah in the heart, rendering words or symbols unnecessary.
- Here, descriptions fade, as the heart mirrors divine presence without veils.

<u>Summary & Practical Advice:</u>
Realization is the pinnacle of certainty in Allah.

- Reflect on: "Those who believe and whose hearts find peace in the remembrance of Allah" (Quran 13:28).
- Seek inner peace: Through reflection on Allah's signs and dismissing doubts.
- Transcend the superficial: True certainty moves beyond the mind to the heart.

Translation of the simplified Arabic text

Chapter 95: Divine Veiling

Allah the Almighty says: "...We then would be leaving them more confused than they already are" (Quran 6:9).

Divine Veiling is Allah's wisdom in concealing truths according to His plan.

It has three forms:

First Veiling: Veiling Truth with Material Causes

- Allah presents events as tied to worldly causes (time, place, effort) to test people's faith.
- Example: Attributing success to human effort while ignoring divine decree.

Second Veiling: Veiling the Pious

- Allah conceals the spiritual states of the righteous to protect them from pride.
- Example: A worshiper who prays devoutly but hides their tears during supplication.

Third Veiling: Veiling of Prophets and Saints

- Prophets interact with people using tangible means, though they know Allah is the true source.
- Example: A prophet calling his people to fight while fully trusting Allah's victory.

Summary & Practical Advice:
Divine veiling is a wisdom beyond human grasp.

- Reflect on: "You cannot will unless Allah wills" (Quran 76:30).
- Seek understanding: Hidden truths serve divine purposes.
- Look beyond appearances: Allah's plan transcends surface judgments.

Translation of the simplified Arabic text

Chapter 96: Divine Presence

Allah the Almighty says:
- "Allah is ever Forgiving, Merciful" (Quran 4:110).
- "They would find Allah Forgiving, Merciful" (Quran 4:64).
- "And he finds Allah with him" (Quran 24:39).

Divine Presence is perceiving Allah's reality in the heart and creation. It has three levels:

First Level: Presence Through Knowledge

- Recognizing Allah's attributes (forgiveness, mercy) through His signs in creation.
- Example: A believer's certainty in Allah's mercy when repenting, bringing inner peace.

Second Level: Presence of the Divine Essence

- Faith in Allah's existence beyond human description or comparison.
- Example: Feeling Allah's nearness during supplication without physical imagery.

Third Level: Presence in Primordial Oneness

- Dissolving self-awareness in divine light while remaining conscious of Allah's greatness.
- Example: A worshiper absorbed in prayer, forgetting themselves yet aware of Allah's majesty.

<u>Summary & Practical Advice:</u>
True presence is the heart's connection to Allah.

- Reflect on: "He is with you wherever you are" (Quran 57:4).
- Acknowledge His blessings: Every atom reflects His existence.
- Purify your heart: Through sincerity to perceive truth with certainty.

Translation of the simplified Arabic text

Chapter 97: Spiritual Detachment

Allah the Almighty says: "Take off your sandals" (Quran 20:12).

Spiritual Detachment is freeing oneself from material distractions to focus on divine truth.

It has three stages:

Stage 1: Detachment of Certainty

- Moving beyond external proofs to unshakable inner conviction.
- Example: Believing in Allah without complex arguments, like a mother's instinctive sense of her child's presence.

Stage 2: Detachment of Knowledge

- Transcending intellectual understanding to direct spiritual experience.
- Example: Tasting the sweetness of faith in prayer, beyond philosophical debates.

Stage 3: Detachment of Self

- Forgetting even the awareness of detachment, wholly absorbed in Allah.
- Example: A scientist lost in research, but here, the focus is solely on Allah.

<u>Summary & Practical Advice:</u>
True detachment is purifying the heart for Allah alone.

- Reflect on: "I did not create jinn and humans except to worship Me" (Quran 51:56).
- Choose simplicity: In worship and thought, avoiding overcomplication.
- Strive daily: To cleanse your heart from worldly attachments.

Translation of the simplified Arabic text

Chapter 98: Singular Focus

Allah the Almighty says: "And they know that Allah is the Ultimate Truth" (Quran 24:25).

Singular Focus is directing the heart and deeds solely to Allah.

It has three stages:

1. Stage 1: Directing Intentions to Allah
    - Intense longing for Allah's pleasure above all else.
    - Profound love that eclipses all but Allah.
    - Heartfelt witnessing of Allah's oneness in everything.

2. Stage 2: Directing Actions by Truth
    - Pride in belonging to Allah's path without pretense.
    - Spiritual conduct reflecting pure devotion.
    - Vigilance in guarding the heart from worldly distractions.

3. Stage 3: Directing Call to Allah
    - Spreading goodness with simplicity and clarity.
    - Inviting others through actions, not just words.
    - Balancing truthfulness with compassion.

<u>Summary & Practical Advice:</u>
Singular focus is purity of heart and deed for Allah.

- Reflect on: "Say: He is Allah, the One" (Quran 112:1).
- Purify your intentions: Let every act be for Allah.
- Lead by example: Let your deeds speak before your words.

Translation of the simplified Arabic text

Chapter 99: Togetherness

God says: "And it was not you who threw when you threw, but it was God who threw" (8:17).

Togetherness (Al-Jam') is a state where whatever thoughts or actions that separates the servant and God vanishes. Symbols lose their necessity, and the heart transcends materialism (water and clay) after firm faith, purification from egoic stains, liberation from seeing causes as partners to God, and freedom from feelings of weakness.

It has three stages:

1. Unity of Knowledge: Worldly knowledge dissolves into divine light granted by God to sincere hearts.

2. Unity of Presence: The illusion of separation fades; one realizes their true existence is through God, not themselves.

3. Unity of Essence: All created signs disappear, leaving the seeker to see only God as the Source.

Togetherness is the pinnacle of the spiritual path and the shore of pure Oneness (Tawhid).

Summary & Practical Advice:
Togetherness is neither incarnation nor union. Togetherness means perceiving God's hand in all things, thereby freeing oneself from attachment to causes and becoming certain that hearts are in His hand alone

- Reflect on: "As for those who strive in Us - We surely guide them to Our paths" (29:69).
- Let your heart mirror divine light. Persist in remembrance (Surely in the remembrance of Allah do hearts find comfort. [13:28]).
- Begin with sincerity and patience; every step in self-purification draws you closer to Him.

Translation of the simplified Arabic text

Chapter 100: Divine Oneness

God says: "God bears witness that there is no deity save Him" (3:18).

Divine Oneness (Tawhid) is affirming God's absolute transcendence above all imperfection. Scholars and mystics affirm that Devine Oneness (Tawhid) is to purify faith in God alone. Other spiritual states may falter without this foundation.

Divine Oneness (Tawhid) has three levels:

1. Tawhid of the General People: Professing "There is no god but God" (as in Surah Al-Ikhlas: "He begets not, nor was He begotten. And none is like Him"). This level rejects obvious idolatry, defines Islamic identity, and suffices for most, provided the heart is sincere.

2. Tawhid of the Elite: Transcending reliance on worldly causes. Here, the seeker sees God as the True Actor behind all events, freeing the heart from dependence on tools or logic alone.

3. Tawhid of the Elite of the Elite: A indescribable state where human concepts dissolve. God's eternal essence is realized beyond symbols, words, or time. Even trying to describe it will be undermining it!

<u>Summary & Practical Advice:</u>
Tawhid is faith's core—from simple confession to awe before God's infinity.

- Reflect on: "He is the First and the Last, the Manifest and the Hidden" (57:3).
- Strengthen certainty that God alone controls all affairs. Ask yourself: Do I fear creation more than the Creator?
- Let Tawhid guide your life, and seek His help, for "Whoever believes in God, He will guide his heart" (64:11).

End of the Book. All gratitude is to Allah

www.ingramcontent.com/pod-product-compliance
Lightning Source LLC
Chambersburg PA
CBHW081527120626
46550CB00009B/2647

* 9 7 9 8 9 9 8 9 3 0 5 1 5 *

تقريب معاني كتاب منازل السائرين

Clarifying the meanings of Stations of the Wayfarer

الطبعةالانكيزية و العربية

English and Arabic Edition

الدكتور قيس أكرم مكي حمّودة

Dr. Qais Akram Mekki Hamouda

الطبعة الثانية – طبعة منقحة ١٤٤٦هـ /٢٠٢٥م

Second Edition – Revised Edition 1446 AH/2025 CE

ISBN: 979-8-9989305-1-5

حقوق الطباعة والنشر محفوظة للمؤلف

Copyright © 2025 by Qais A. Mekki

فهرس المحتويات

بسم الله الرحمن الرحيم

التعريف بالكتاب، والداعي لكتابته، والهدف منه

الحمد لله رب العالمين. اللهم صل و سلم و بارك على سيدنا محمّد النبي المبعوث رحمة للعالمين، وعلى آله وصحبه، ومن تبعه بإحسان الى يوم الدين، آمين.

أمّا بعد، فيقول الله تعالى في كتابه الكريم:

﴿ وَالشَّمْسِ وَضُحَاهَا ۝١ وَالْقَمَرِ إِذَا تَلَاهَا ۝٢ وَالنَّهَارِ إِذَا جَلَّاهَا ۝٣ وَاللَّيْلِ إِذَا يَغْشَاهَا ۝٤
وَالسَّمَاءِ وَمَا بَنَاهَا ۝٥ وَالْأَرْضِ وَمَا طَحَاهَا ۝٦ وَنَفْسٍ وَمَا سَوَّاهَا ۝٧ فَأَلْهَمَهَا فُجُورَهَا
وَتَقْوَاهَا ۝٨ قَدْ أَفْلَحَ مَن زَكَّاهَا ۝٩ وَقَدْ خَابَ مَن دَسَّاهَا ۝١٠ ﴾ (الشمس: ١-١٠).

هذا القَسَمُ العظيم في مطلع سورة الشمس، الذي يَعتلي بكثرَة المُقسَم به، إذ هو أطول قسمٍ في القرآن الكريم، ليُؤكِّد حقيقةً جَلِيَّةً: أنَّ تزكيةَ النفس هي من الغايات التي خُلِقَ الإنسانُ مِن أجلها، وأنَّها فريضةٌ عينيةٌ على كلِّ مُسلمٍ، لا يُجزِئُ عنها غيرُها. فالنفسُ الإنسانيةُ ميدانٌ للصراع بين الفجور والتقوى، وبقَدْرِ ما يَحرصُ العبدُ على تَطهيرها وتنميتها بالخير، تَفلحُ وتَنجو، وبقَدْرِ إهمالها وتدنيسها بالمعاصي، تَخيبُ وتَخسر.

ومن الأحاديث العظيمة التي بين النبي صلى الله عليه وسلم فيها أصول الدين، حديث جبريل المشهور، عندما جاء إلى النبي صلى الله عليه وسلم على هيئة رجل يسأله ويستفتيه عن بعض المسائل الهامة، والحديث رواه الإمامان مسلم و البخاري (وهذا لفظ مسلم) عن عمر بن الخطاب رضي الله عنه قال : بينما نحن عند رسول الله صلى الله عليه وسلم ذات يوم، إذ طلع علينا رجل شديد بياض الثياب، شديد سواد الشعر، لا يُرى عليه أثر السفر، ولا يعرفه منا أحد، حتى جلس إلى النبي صلى الله عليه وسلم، فأسند ركبتيه إلى ركبتيه، ووضع كفيه على فخذيه، وقال: يا محمد، أخبرني عن الإسلام؟ فقال رسول الله صلى الله عليه وسلم : (الإسلام أن تشهد أن لا إله إلا الله وأن محمدا رسول الله، وتقيم الصلاة، وتؤتي الزكاة، وتصوم رمضان، وتحج البيت إن استطعت إليه سبيلا) . قال : صدقتَ، قال : فعجبنا له يسأله ويصدقه. قال : فأخبرني عن الإيمان؟

قال : (أن تؤمن بالله وملائكته وكتبه ورسله واليوم الآخر، وتؤمن بالقدر خيره وشره) . قال : صدقت . قال فأخبرني عن الإحسان؟ قال : (أن تعبد الله كأنك تراه، فإن لم تكن تراه فإنه يراك) . قال : فأخبرني عن الساعة؟ قال : (ما المسئول عنها بأعلم من السائل) . قال : فأخبرني عن أمارتها؟ قال : (أن تلد الأمة ربَّتها، وأن ترى الحفاة العراة العالة رعاءَ الشاء يتطاولون في البنيان) . قال : ثم انطلق، فلبثتُ مليًا، ثم قال لي : (يا عمر، أتدري من السائل؟) . قلت : الله ورسوله أعلم . قال : (فإنه جبريل أتاكم يعلمكم دينكم).

في هذا الحديث الجامع، نرى التقسيمَ الحكيمَ لأصول الدين: الإسلامُ (العبادات الظاهرة)، والإيمانُ (العقائد الباطنة)، والإحسانُ (المراقبة القلبية). وهذه الأصول الثلاثة تَطوَّرَت عبرَ التاريخِ إلى علومٍ إسلاميةٍ راسخة: فـ"الإسلامُ" نشأ منه عِلْمُ الفقه، و"الإيمانُ" عِلْمُ العقيدةِ والكلام، و"الإحسانُ" عِلْمُ التزكيةِ والسلوك.

وأهلُ علم الإحسانِ هم الصوفيةُ، الذين تَخصَّصوا في علم تزكيةِ النفوسِ وتربيةِ القلوبِ على مَحبةِ اللهِ وخشيته. و نحن هنا نتحدَّثُ عن التصوُّفِ الحقّ الذي سارَ عليه أئمةٌ كالحسن البصري، والحارث المحاسبي، والجُنيد البغدادي، وعبدالقادر الجيلاني، وغيرهم من عمالقةِ السلوك، رحمهم الله جميعاً، الذين جعلوا الشريعةَ حاكماً والطريقةَ مرشداً، والتزكية ثمرةً.

والتزكيةُ ليستْ عِلماً يُكتَبُ في الكتبِ فحسب، بل هي مَشْيٌ على الدربِ مع الشيوخِ العارفين والصحبة الصالحة، كتعلُّم الطبِّ عند الأطباء؛ فكما لا يَكفي الطالبُ أن يقرأَ كتابًا في التشريحِ ليُصبحَ طبيبًا، كذلك لا يَكفي المُريدُ أن يقرأَ كُتبَ التصوُّفِ ليُزكِّيَ نفسَه. بل لا بدَّ مِن صُحبةِ العارفين بالله، الذين يُربُّونَ الأرواحَ بتوجيهاتهم النورانية، ويُصحِّحونَ الانحرافاتِ القلبيةَ بِحِكَمِهم الإلهية.

كتاب "منازل السائرين" للإمام الهروي:

يُعتبر كتاب "منازل السائرين" للشيخ عبدالله الأنصاري الهروي (المتوفى سنة ٤٨١ هـ) مِن أهمّ ما كُتِبَ في علم التزكية والسلوك إلى الله. فقد ألَّفه الإمام الهروي، أحد أبرز أعلام التصوف في القرن الخامس الهجري، والذي جمع بين علوم الظاهر والباطن، فكان

محدِّثًا وفقيهًا حنبليّاً، وشيخًا ربانيًّا يُشار إليه بالبنان في ترسيخ منهج التزكية القائم على الكتاب والسنة.

وكتاب "منازل السائرين" هو دليلٌ روحيٌّ مُحكَمٌ يَرسُمُ للمُريد طريقَ السير إلى الله عبر مئة "منزل" (مقام، مرحلة)، مقسَّمةً كلُّ منها إلى ثلاث درجات: درجة المبتدئين، ودرجة المتوسِّطين، ودرجة المحقّقين. تبتدئُ هذه المنازلُ بالتوبة والمراقبة، وتنتهي بالتوحيد والفناء في محبة الحق سبحانه، مع تفصيلٍ دقيقٍ لِكيفيةِ ترقِّي المُريد في كلِّ مرحلةٍ وفقَ استعداده الروحي. وقد حظي هذا الكتاب بمكانةٍ فريدةٍ بين كتب السلوك لِما يَمتازُ به مِن تنظيرٍ منهجيٍ يُجسّدُ مراحلَ السيرِ إلى الله بِوضوحٍ وعمقٍ.

ولم يقتصر أثره على عصره فحسب، بل ظلَّ مَنارًا يُهتَدى به عبر القرون، حتى أصبح مرجعًا أساسيًّا لِكبار المشايخ. وقد ألَّفَ حولَه عُلماءُ الصوفية شروحًا عديدةً، كشروح الشيخ عفيف الدين التلمساني (ت. ٦٩٠ هـ)، والشيخ كمال الدين الكاشاني (ت. ٧٣٥ هـ)، والشيخ عبدالرؤوف المناوي (ت. ١٠٣١ هـ)، و الشيخ المعاصر الدكتور يسري جبر الحسني، وغيرهم مِن الأعلام، مما يُؤكِّدُ مكانتَه كأحد النصوص التأسيسية في علم التزكية، وقدرتَه على استيعابِ تفاسيرِ العصورِ المُختلفة.

كتب الشيخ الهروي هذا الكتاب قبل حوالي ألف سنة، و كما في باقي اللغات، يتغير استعمال المصطلحات مع تغير الزمن، و قد يصعب على عامّة الناس فهم النصوص المكتوبة قبل ألف سنة. و قد جاءت فكرة هذا العمل المتواضع بين يديكم لتقريب معاني كتاب "منازل السائرين" بكتابته بلغة سلسة معاصرة مقتضبة سهلة المنال في هذا الزمان لمن ليس له اطلاع سابق لكتب القوم واصطلاحاتهم، مع الحفاظ على مضامينها كما أوضحها شُرّاح الكتاب المعتمدون، بدون شرح أو اسهاب، فقد كفى ووفّى من سبقنا بذلك، ولكن رأيت استبدال العبارات بعبارات مماثلة لها قدر الإمكان بلغة معاصرة، أملاً أن يكون هذا الكتاب مفتاحاً لقلوب القارئين - حفظهم الله ورعاهم - ان تتعطش لمزيد من البحث والمعرفة والتزكية من منابعها الأصليّة. وللإلمام بمختلف الاصطلاحات و التعابيرالمستعملة في وقتنا هذا، والتفاضل بينها لانتقاء الأنسب، استعنت بأحدث التقنيّات الحاسوبيّة المتوفّرة للبحث عن المرادفات اللغويّة في زماننا هذا، مع الفحص الشخصي الدقيق للتاكّد من توافق المعنى مع الشروح المعتمدة للنص الأصلي. كما كتبته في ثلاث لغات: العربية، والانكليزية، والصينية، لتعم الفائدة إن شاء الله تعالى.

ولكن من الضروري أن ندرك بأن تبسيط لغة هذا الكتاب العميق يحمل في طياته بالضرورة شيئاً من فقدان العمق الذي اختصت به تعبيرات الشيخ الهروي رحمه الله، إذ أن النص الأصلي يحمل في طياته إيحاءاتٍ لا تُحصى، فقد اختار الشيخ الهروي رحمه الله ألفاظه بدقةٍ تُضيء المعنى من زوايا متعددة، حتى إن شرح صفحةٍ واحدةٍ منه قد يستغرق مجلدات! لذا فقد ألزمت نفسي بإدراج النص الأصلي مع كل بابٍ تذكيراً بعمق الأصل وضرورة العودة إليه و إلى كتب الشُرّاح المعتمدة و الى سماع دروس الشيوخ العارفين.

في نهاية كل باب، أضفت بعض السطور، نصيحةً للقارئ العزيز والقارئة العزيزة، حول معنى الباب، وهي ليست من نص كتاب الشيخ الجليل الهروي، و لكنّي آمل أن تساعد في تذوّق معنى الباب.

و إذا لقي هذا العمل قبولاً، وأن كان في العمر بقيّة، فإني أنوي إن شاء الله تعالى، على طريق إحياء علوم التزكية، ان أتبع هذا الكتاب بأعمال أخرى لتقريب معاني امهات كتب التزكية لإخواننا و أخواتنا و ابنائنا و بناتنا.

و في الختام أرجو أن لا تبخلوا علي بنصائحكم، لتصحيح أي خطأ ترونه، أولتقديم اقتراح منكم، أو استعمال كلمة أخرى تفضّلونها في الترجمة، خاصّة أخوتي وأخواتي المتكلمين باللغة بالصينيّة فإتقاني لها أقل من العربيّة والانكليزيّة، ترسلونه الى البريد الاليكتروني (advice.for.author@gmail.com)، وجزاكم الله خيراً.

نسألكم الدعاء لوالدينا ووالديكم، والسلام عليكم ورحمة الله وبركاته.

قيس أكرم مكّي حمّودة
شيكاغو، في رمضان ١٤٤٦هـ (٢٠٢٥م)

كتاب : منازل السائرين

المؤلف : عبد الله الأنصاري الهروي

مقدّمة الشيخ الهروي رحمه الله

بسم الله الرحمن الرحيم

الحمد لله الواحد الأحد، القيوم الصمد اللطيف القريب الذي أمطر سرائر العارفين كرائم الكلم من غمائم الحكم وألاح لهم لوائح القدم في صفائح العدم، ودلهم على أقرب السبل إلى المنهاج الأول وردهم من تفرق العلل إلى عين الأزل وبث فيهم ذخائره وأودعهم سرائره.

وأشهد أن لا إله إلا الله وحده لا شريك له، الأول الآخر الظاهر الباطن الذي مد ظل التلوين على الخليقة مدا طويلا ثم جعل شمس التمكين لصفوته عليه دليلا، ثم قبض ظل التفرقة عنهم إليه قبضا يسيرا.وصلاته وسلامه على صفيه الذي أقسم به في إقامة حقه محمد وآله كثيرا.

وبعد، فإن جماعة من الراغبين في الوقوف على منازل السائرين إلى الحق عز اسمه من الفقراء، من أهل هراة والغرباء، طال علي مسألتهم إياي زمانا أن أبين لهم في معرفتها بيانا يكون على معالمها عنوانا. فأجبتهم بذلك بعد استخارتي الله واستعانتي به وسألوني أن أرتبها لهم ترتيبا يشير إلى تواليها ويدل على الفروع التي تليها وأن أخليه من كلام غيري وأختصره ليكون ألطف في اللفظ وأخف للحفظ وإني خفت أني إن أخذت في شرح قول أبي بكر الكتاني "إن بين العبد والحق ألف مقام من نور وظلمة" طولتُ عليّ وعليهم.

فذكرت أبنية تلك المقامات التي تشير إلى تمامها وتدل على مرامها.وأرجو لهم بعد صدق قصدهم ما قال أبو عبيد البسري "إن لله عبادا يريهم في بداياتهم ما في نهاياتهم". ثم إني رتبته لهم فصولا وأبوابا يغني ذلك الترتيب عن التطويل المؤدي إلى الملال ويكون

مندوحة عن التسآل فجعلته مائة مقام مقسومة على عشرة أقسام. وقد قال الجنيد "قد ينقل العبد من حال إلى حال أرفع منها وقد بقي عليه من التي نقل عنها بقية فيشرف عليها من الحالة الثانية فيصلحها".وعندي أن العبد لا يصح له مقام حتى يرتفع عنه ثم يشرف عليه فيصححه. **واعلم أن السائرين في هذه المقامات على اختلاف مفظع لا يجمعهم ترتيب قاطع ولا يقفهم منتهى جامع.**

وقد صنف جماعة من المتقدمين والمتأخرين في هذا الباب تصانيف عساك لا تراها أو أكثرها، على حسنها، مغنية كافية: منهم من أشار إلى الأصول ولم يف بالتفصيل، ومنهم من جمع الحكايات ولم يلخصها تلخيصا، ولم يخصص النكتة تخصيصا، ومنهم من لم يميز بين مقامات الخاصة وضرورات العامة، ومنهم من عد شطح المغلوب مقاما وجعل بوح الواجد ورمز المتمكن شيئا عاما، وأكثرهم لم ينطق عن الدرجات.

واعلم أن العامة من علماء هذه الطائفة والمشيرين إلى هذه الطريقة اتفقوا على أن النهايات لا تصح إلا بتصحيح البدايات كما أن الأبنية لا تقوم إلا على الأساس. وتصحيح البدايات هو إقامة الأمر على مشاهدة الإخلاص ومتابعة السنة وتعظيم النهي على مشاهدة الخوف ورعاية الحرمة والشفقة على العالم ببذل النصيحة وكف المؤنة ومجانبة كل صاحب يفسد الوقت وكل سبب يفتن القلب.

على أن الناس في هذا الشأن ثلاثة نفر: رجل يعمل بين الخوف والرجاء، شاخصا إلى الحب مع صحبة الحياء، فهذا هو الذي يسمى المريد، ورجل مختطف من وادي التفرق إلى وادي الجمع، وهو الذي يقال له المراد، ومن سواهما مدع مفتون مخدوع.

وجميع هذه المقامات تجمعها رتب ثلاث:
الرتبة الأولى: أخذ القاصد في السير.
الرتبة الثانية: دخوله في الغربة.
الرتبة الثالثة: حصوله على المشاهدة الجاذبة إلى عين التوحيد في طريق الفناء.

وقد اخبرنا في معنى الرتبة الأولى الحسين بن محمد بن علي الفرائضي قال: أخبرنا أحمد بن محمد بن حسنوية قال: أخبرنا الحسين بن إدريس الأنصاري قال: حدثنا عثمان بن أبي شيبة قال: حدثنا محمد بن بشر هو العبدي قال: حدثنا عمر بن راشد عن يحيى بن ابي كثير عن أبي سلمة عن أبي هريرة رضي الله عنه قال: قال رسول الله صلى الله عليه و

سلم: "سيروا سبق المفرّدون" ، قالوا: "يا رسول الله، وما المفردون"؟ قال: "المهتزون الذين يهتزون في ذكر الله عز و جل، يضع الذكر عنهم أثقالهم فيأتون يوم القيامة خفافا".وهذا حديث حسن، لم يروه عن يحيى بن أبي كثير إلا عمر بن راشد اليماني، وخالف محمد بن يوسف الفريابي فيه محمد بن بشير العبدي فرواه عن عمر بن راشد عن يحيى عن أبي سلمة عن أبي الدرداء مرفوعا. والحديث إنما هو لأبي هريرة، رواه بندار بن بشار عن صفوان بن عيسى عن بشير بن رافع اليماني إمام أهل نجران ومفتيهم عن ابي عبد الله بن عم أبي هريرة عن أبي هريرة مرفوعا. وأحسنها طريقا وأجودها سندا حديث العلاء بن عبد الرحمن عن أبيه عن أبي هريرة عن النبي ص صلى الله عليه وسلم وهو مخرج في صحيح مسلم. وروى هذا الحديث أهل الشام عن أبي أمامة مرفوعا. قال في كلها: "سبق المُفرِّدون".

وأخبرنا في معنى الدخول في الغربة حمزة بن محمد بن عبد الله الحسيني قال: حدثنا أبو القاسم عبدالواحد بن احمد الهاشمي الصوفي قال: سمعت أبا عبد الله علان بن زيد الدينوري الصوفي بالبصرة قال: سمعت جعفر الخلدي الصوفي يقول: سمعت الجنيد قال: سمعت السري عن معروف الكرخي عن جعفر بن محمد عن أبيه عن جده عن علي رضي الله عنه عن رسول الله ص صلى الله عليه و سلم قال "طلب الحق غربة". وهذا حديث غريب ما كتبته إلا من رواية علان.

وأخبرنا في معنى الحصول على المشاهدة محمد بن علي بن الحسين الباشاني رحمه الله قال: حدثنا محمد بن اسحاق القرشي قال: حدثنا عثمان بن سعيد الدارامي قال: حدثنا سليمان بن حرب عن حماد بن زيد عن مطر الوراق عن أبي بريدة عن يحيى بن يعمر عن عبدالله بن عمر بن الخطاب في حديث سؤال جبرائيل رسول الله ص صلى الله عليه و سلم قال: "ما الإحسان"؟ قال: "أن تعبد الله كأنك تراه فإن لم تكن تراه فإنه يراك". وهذا حديث صحيح غريب أخرجه مسلم في الصحاح. وهذا الحديث إشارة جامعة لمذهب هذه الطائفة.

وإني مفصل لك درجات كل مقام منها لتعرف درجة العامة منه ثم درجة السالك ثم درجة المحقق. ولكل منهم شرعة ومنهاج ووجهة هو مولاها قد نصب له علم هو له مبعوث واتيح له غاية هو إليها محثوث وإني أسأل الله أن يجعلني في قصدي مصحوبا لا محجوبا وأن يجعل لي سلطانا مبينا، إنه سميع قريب.

واعلم أن الأقسام العشرة التي ذكرتها في صدر هذا الكتاب هي: قسم البدايات، ثم قسم الأخلاق، ثم قسم الأحوال، ثم قسم الأبواب، ثم قسم الأصول، ثم قسم الولايات، ثم قسم النهايات، ثم قسم المعاملات، ثم قسم الأودية، ثم قسم الحقائق.

١- قسم البدايات

فأما قسم البدايات فهو عشرة أبواب وهي: اليقظة والتوبة والمحاسبة والإنابة والتفكر والتذكر والاعتصام والفرار والرياضة والسماع

نص الشيخ الهروي

١- باب اليقظة

قال الله عز و جل: ﴿ قُلۡ إِنَّمَآ أَعِظُكُم بِوَٰحِدَةٍۖ أَن تَقُومُواْ لِلَّهِ ﴾(سبأ: 46).

القومة لله هي اليقظة من سنة الغفلة، والنهوض من ورطة الفترة. وهي أول ما يستنير قلب العبد بالحياة لرؤية نور التنبيه.

واليقظة هي ثلاثة أشياء:

الأول، لحظ القلب إلى النعمة - على الإياس من عدها، والوقوف على حدها، والتفرع إلى معرفة المنة بها، والعلم بالتقصير في حقها.

والثاني، مطالعة الجناية - والوقوف على الخطر فيها، والتشمر لتداركها، والتخلص من ربقها، وطلب النجاة بتمحيصها.

والثالث، الانتباه لمعرفة الزيادة والنقصان في الأيام - والتنصل عن تضييعها، والنظر إلى الضن بها، ليتدارك فائتها، ويعمر باقيها.

فأما معرفة النعمة، فإنها تصفو بثلاثة أشياء:بنور العقل، وشيم برق المنة، والاعتبار بأهل البلاء.

وأما مطالعة الجناية، فإنها تصح بثلاثة أشياء: بتعظيم الحق، ومعرفة النفس، وتصديق الوعيد.

وأما معرفة الزيادة والنقصان في الأيام، فإنها تستقيم بثلاثة أشياء: بسماع العلم، وإجابة دواعي الحرمة، وصحبة الصالحين.

وملاك ذلك كله خلع العادات.

النصّ مكتوباً بلغة مبسّطة

١- باب اليقظة (الاستيقاظ الروحي)

قال الله تعالى: ﴿ قُلۡ إِنَّمَآ أَعِظُكُم بِوَٰحِدَةٍۖ أَن تَقُومُواْ لِلَّهِ ﴾ (سبأ: ٤٦).

المقصود بـ"القومة لله" هو الاستيقاظ من غفلة القلب، والنهوض من حالة التراخي والتكاسل عن الطاعة.

هذه اليقظة هي أول خطوة يُشرق فيها القلب بنور الوعي، فيبدأ بملاحظة نعم الله وحقوقه عليه.

اليقظة ثلاثة أنواع :

١. تذكُّر النعم :

- أن تنظر إلى نعم الله عليك، حتى لو كانت قليلة في نظرك.
- أن تعترف بأنك مقصِّر في شكرها، وأن الفضل في وجودها يعود إلى الله وحده.
- أن تتأمل في أحوال من ابتُلوا بالفقر أو المرض، فتُدرك قيمة ما عندك.

٢. مراجعة الأخطاء :

- أن تتأمل في ذنوبك وأخطائك بجدية، ولا تستخف بها.
- أن تخاف عواقبها، وتسعى للتوبة منها.
- أن تطلب من الله أن يُطهِّر قلبك منها، ويعينك على عدم العودة إليها.

٣ .مراقبة الوقت:

- أن تحسب كل يوم يمر: هل زاد إيمانك أم نقص؟
- أن تحافظ على وقتك، ولا تضيعه في ما لا يفيد.
- أن تستفيد من صحبة الصالحين، وتتعلم من نصائحهم.

كيف تصل إلى هذه اليقظة؟

- تذكُّر النعم يحتاج إلى: عقل واعٍ، وقلب شاكر، ومقارنة نفسك بمن هم أقل منك.
- مراجعة الأخطاء تحتاج إلى: احترام حقوق الله، ومعرفة ضعف نفسك، والإيمان بوعيد الله للعصاة.
- مراقبة الوقت تحتاج إلى: سماع المواعظ، والاستجابة لنداء الخير، ومصاحبة الصادقين.

الخلاصة:

مفتاح كل هذا هو التخلص من العادات السيئة التي تُثقل القلب، وتجعلك تعيش في غفلة.

موجز ونصيحة عملية:

اليقظة الروحية تبدأ بالتوقف عن "العيش الآلي" ومراجعة حياتك بصدق:

- خصص دقائق يوميًّا لتذكر نعمة واحدة وتشكر الله عليها.
- اكتب ذنبًا واحدًا تُريد التخلص منه، واطلب العون من الله لتركه.
- اسأل نفسك كل ليلة: "ماذا أضفت اليوم لإيماني؟".
- الاستمرار على هذه الخطوات البسيطة سيُعيد توجيه قلبك نحو الله، خطوة بخطوة.

نص الشيخ الهروي

٢- باب التوبة

قال الله عز و جل: ﴿ وَمَن لَّمْ يَتُبْ فَأُولَٰئِكَ هُمُ الظَّالِمُونَ ﴾(الحجرات: ١١)، فأسقط اسم الظلم عن التائب.
والتوبة لا تصح إلا بعد معرفة الذنب. وهي أن تنظر في الذنب إلى ثلاثة أشياء: إلى انخلاعك من العصمة حين إتيانه، وفرحك عند الظفر به، وقعودك على الإصرار عن تداركه مع يقينك بنظر الحق إليك.

وشرائط التوبة ثلاثة أشياء: الندم، والاعتذار، والإقلاع.
وحقائق التوبة ثلاثة أشياء: تعظيم الجناية، واتهام التوبة، وطلب إعذار الخليقة.
وسرائر حقيقة التوبة ثلاثة أشياء: تمييز التقية من العزة، ونسيان الجناية، والتوبة من التوبة أبدا، لأن التائب داخل في الجميع من قوله تعالى: ﴿وتوبوا إلى الله جميعا﴾(النور: ٣١) فأمر التائب بالتوبة.

ولطائف سرائر التوبة ثلاثة أشياء:
أولهما أن تنظر بين الجناية والقضية، فتتعرف مراد الله فيها إذ خلاك وإتيانها، فإن الله عز و جل إنما يخلى العبد والذنب لأحد معنيين: أحدهما أن تعرف عزته في قضائه وبره في ستره وحلمه في إمهال راكبه وكرمه في قبول العذر منه وفضله في مغفرته، والثاني ليقيم على العبد حجة عدله فيعاقبه على ذنبه بحجته.
واللطيفة الثانية: أن تعلم أن طلب البصير الصادق سيئته لم يبق له حسنة بحال لأنه يسير بين مشاهدة المنة وتطلب عيب النفس والعمل.
واللطيفة الثالثة: أن مشاهدة العبد الحكم لم تدع له استحسان حسنة ولا استقباح سيئة، لصعوده من جميع المعاني إلى معنى الحكم.

فتوبة العامة لاستكثار الطاعة. فإنه يدعو إلى ثلاثة أشياء إلى جحود نعمة الستر والإمهال، ورؤية الحق على الله، والاستغناء الذي هو عين الجبروت والتوثب على الله.

وتوبة الأوساط من استقلال المعصية. وهو عين الجرأة والمبارزة، ومحض التزين بالحمية، والاسترسال للقطيعة.

وتوبة الخاصة من تضييع الوقت. فإنه يدعو إلى درك النقيصة، ويطفئ نور المراقبة، ويكدر عين الصحبة.

ولا يتم مقام التوبة إلا بالانتهاء إلى التوبة مما دون الحق، ثم رؤية علة تلك التوبة، ثم التوبة من رؤية تلك العلة.

النصّ مكتوباً بلغة مبسّطة

٢- باب التوبة

قال الله تعالى: ﴿وَمَن لَّمْ يَتُبْ فَأُولَٰئِكَ هُمُ الظَّالِمُونَ﴾ (الحجرات: ١١).

فالله يرفع وصف "الظالم" عن التائب.

مقومات التوبة الصحيحة :

١ .معرفة الذنب:

- أن تدرك أن ثلاثة أمور صارت عند فعل المعصية:
  - خروجك من حماية الله حين أقدمتَ عليها.
  - فرحك المؤقت بفعلها.
  - أنك قد أخّرت التوبة رغم علمك أن الله يراك.

٢ .شروط التوبة:

- الندم: أن تحزن على ما فعلت.
- الإقلاع: أن تتوقف عن الذنب فورًا.
- الاعتذار: أن تطلب المغفرة من الله بصدق.

٣ .حقائق التوبة:

- أن تعترف بخطورة ذنبك.
- أن تشكّ في قبول توبتك (لا تثق بنفسك).
- أن تسامح الآخرين إذا أخطؤوا في حقك.

٤ .أسرار التوبة الداخلية:

- أن تُميّز بين التوبة الخالصة والخوف من الناس.
- أن تنسى ذنبك بعد التوبة ولا تعود إليه.
- أن تتوب دائمًا، حتى من تقصيرك في التوبة نفسها.

درجات التوبة:

- توبة العامة: ترك الذنب خوفًا من العقاب.
- توبة المتوسطين: أن يتوب من استصغار الذنب الصغير ثقة بكثرة الطاعات (وهذا خطر، فالصغيرة قد تكبر).
- توبة الخاصة: التوبة من تضييع الوقت في غير طاعة الله.

كيف تكتمل التوبة؟

- بالتوبة من كل ما يُبعدك عن الله، حتى من نقص توبتك نفسها!

موجز ونصيحة عملية:

التوبة ليست كلمات تُقال، بل قلبٌ نادم وعملٌ صالح:

- كل ليلة: افحص يومك واسأل: "هل أخطأت؟ وكيف أصلحه؟".
- بعد كل ذنب: قل بصدق: "اللهم إني تبتُ إليك، أعِنّي على عدم العودة".
- تجنب الأماكن أو الأشخاص الذين يدفعونك للخطأ.
- التوبة باب مفتوح دائمًا – لا تؤجلها!

نص الشيخ الهروي

٣- باب المحاسبة

قال الله عز و جل: ﴿ ٱتَّقُواْ ٱللَّهَ وَلۡتَنظُرۡ نَفۡسٌ مَّا قَدَّمَتۡ لِغَدٍۖ ﴾(الحشر:١٨).

وإنما يسلك طريق المحاسبة بعد العزيمة على عقد التوبة.

والعزيمة لها ثلاثة أركان:

أحدها: أن تقيس بين نعمته وجنايتك، وهذا يشق على من ليس له ثلاثة أشياء: نور الحكمة، وسوء الظن بالنفس، وتمييز النعمة من الفتنة.

والثاني: تمييز ما للحق عما لك أو منك، فتعلم أن الجناية عليك حجة، والطاعة عليك منة، والحكم عليك حجة ما هو لك معذرة.

والثالث: أن تعرف أن كل طاعة رضيتها منك فهي عليك، وكل معصية عيرت بها أخاك فهي إليك، ولا تضع ميزان وقتك من يديك.

النصّ مكتوباً بلغة مبسّطة

٣- باب المحاسبة (مراجعة النفس)

قال الله تعالى: ﴿ ٱتَّقُواْ ٱللَّهَ وَلۡتَنظُرۡ نَفۡسٌ مَّا قَدَّمَتۡ لِغَدٍۖ ﴾ (الحشر: ١٨).

المحاسبة هي مراجعة النفس بعد العزم على التوبة.

ولتحقيق هذا العزم ثلاثة أسس:

١ .مقارنة النعمة بالذنب:

- قارن بين نعم الله الكثيرة عليك وبين أخطائك.
- هذا يحتاج إلى:
  - فطنة لرؤية النعم.
  - شكٍّ في صلاح نفسك (لا تعتدّ بها كثيرًا).
  - تمييز النعمة الحقيقية من الاختبارات الصعبة.

٢ .فَرْقُ ما لله وما لك:
- اعترف أن:

- الذنب دليلٌ على تقصيرك.
- الطاعة نعمةٌ من الله، وليست مجهودك الشخصي.
- حكم الله عليك عدلٌ، وليس عذرًا لتبرير أخطائك.

٣ .عدم الانشغال بغيرك:

- كل طاعة تفرح بها في نفسك قد تكون مصدر كِبْرٍ.
- كل ذنب تلوم عليه أخاك قد يكون موجودًا فيك.
- ركز على تحسين نفسك، ولا تضيع وقتك في مراقبة الآخرين.

موجز ونصيحة عملية:

المحاسبة ليست تأنيبًا قاسيًا، بل فرصة للتطور:

- كل صباح: اكتب نعمة واحدة تشكر الله عليها، وذنبًا واحدًا ستتجنبه اليوم.
- قبل النوم: اسأل نفسك: "ماذا قدمت لغدي؟ هل أنا أفضل من الصباح؟".
- توقف عن مقارنة نفسك بالآخرين؛ ركز على مسارك الروحي الخاص.
- التقدم يأتي بخطوات صغيرة متتالية، لا بانتظار الكمال!

نص الشيخ الهروي

٤- باب الإنابة

قال الله عز و جل: ﴿وَأَنِيبُوٓاْ إِلَىٰ رَبِّكُمۡ﴾(الزمر:54).

الإنابة ثلاثة أشياء:
الرجوع إلى الحق إصلاحاً، كما رجع إليه اعتذاراً.
والرجوع إليه وفاءً، كما رجع إليه عهداً.
والرجوع إليه حالاً، كما رجع إليه إجابة.

وإنما يستقيم الرجوع إليه إصلاحاً بثلاثة أشياء: بالخروج من التبعات، والتوجع للعثرات، واستدراك الفائتات.
وإنما يستقيم الرجوع إليه وفاءً بثلاثة أشياء: بالخلاص من لذة الذنب، وبترك الاستهانة بأهل الغفلة تخوفا عليهم مع الرجاء لنفسك، وبالاستقصاء في رؤية علل الخدمة .
وإنما يستقيم الرجوع إليه حالاً بثلاثة أشياء: بالإياس من عملك، ومعاينة اضطرارك، وشيم برق لطفه بك.

النصّ مكتوباً بلغة مبسّطة

٤- باب الإنابة

قال الله تعالى: ﴿وَأَنِيبُوٓاْ إِلَىٰ رَبِّكُمۡ﴾ (الزمر: ٥٤).

الإنابة هي الرجوع إلى الله بصدق.
وهي ثلاثة أنواع:

١ .رجوع الإصلاح:
- العودة إلى الله لتصحيح الأخطاء، مثل الاعتذار بعد الذنب.

- يشترط له ثلاثة أمور:

  - التخلص من عواقب الذنوب السابقة.
  - الشعور بالألم للزلات التي ارتكبتها.
  - تعويض ما فاتك من طاعات.

٢ .رجوع الوفاء:

- العودة إلى الله وفاءً بعهدك معه.
- يشترط له ثلاثة أمور:

  - التخلي عن متعة الذنب حتى لو كانت صغيرة.
  - عدم الاستهانة بمن غفل عن الله (لا تحتقرهم، بل اخشَ عليهم وارجو لنفسك).
  - البحث عن نقاط الضعف في عبادتك لتحسينها.

٣ .رجوع الاستجابة:

- العودة إلى الله استجابةً لنداء قلبك.
- يشترط له ثلاثة أمور:
  - اليأس من الاعتماد على أعمالك الصالحة (فالفضل لله).
  - إدراك أنك مضطرٌ إلى رحمة الله دائمًا.
  - تذكُّر لطف الله الخفيّ عليك في كل لحظة.

<u>موجز ونصيحة عملية:</u>

الإنابة ليست خطوة واحدة، بل رحلة مستمرة:

- بعد كل صلاة: قل: "اللهم أرني عيوب نفسي، وأعنّي على إصلاحها".
- اختر صديقًا يُذكرك بالله إذا نسيت.
- احمل مفكرةً صغيرة لكتابة اللحظات التي شعرت فيها بقرب الله أو ابتعدت عنها.

كل رجوع إلى الله – ولو صغيرًا – يزيدك قربًا منه!

نص الشيخ الهروي

٥- باب التفكر

قال الله عز و جل:﴿ وَأَنزَلْنَآ إِلَيْكَ ٱلذِّكْرَ لِتُبَيِّنَ لِلنَّاسِ مَا نُزِّلَ إِلَيْهِمْ وَلَعَلَّهُمْ يَتَفَكَّرُونَ ﴾(النحل:٤٤).

إعلم أن التفكر تلمس البصيرة لاستدراك البغية.

وهو ثلاثة أنواع: فكرة في عين التوحيد، وفكرة في لطائف الصنعة، وفكرة في معاني الأعمال والأحوال.

فأما الفكرة في عين التوحيد، فهي اقتحام بحر الجحود، لا ينجى منه إلا الاعتصام بضياء الكشف، والتمسك بالعلم الظاهر.

وأما الفكرة في لطائف الصنائع، فهي ماء يسقي زرع الحكمة.

وأما الفكرة في معاني الأعمال والأحوال، فهي تسهل سلوك طريق الحقيقة.

وإنما يتخلص من الفكرة في عين التوحيد بثلاثة أشياء: بمعرفة عجز العقل، وبالإياس من الوقوف على الغاية، وبالاعتصام بحبل التعظيم.

وإنما تدرك لطائف الصنائع بثلاثة أشياء: بحسن النظر في مبادئ المنن، والإجابة لدواعي الإشارات، وبالخلاص من رق الشهوات.

وإنما يوقف بالفكرة على مراتب الأعمال والأحوال بثلاثة أشياء: باستصحاب العلم، واتهام المرسومات، ومعرفة مواقع الغير.

النصّ مكتوباً بلغة مبسّطة

٥- باب التفكُّر (التأمل الروحي)

قال الله تعالى:﴿وَأَنزَلْنَآ إِلَيْكَ ٱلذِّكْرَ لِتُبَيِّنَ لِلنَّاسِ مَا نُزِّلَ إِلَيْهِمْ وَلَعَلَّهُمْ يَتَفَكَّرُونَ﴾ (النحل:٤٤).

التفكُّر هو استخدام البصيرة لتحقيق الفهم العميق، وهو ثلاثة أنواع:

١ .التفكُّر في حقيقة التوحيد :

- التأمل في عظمة الله ووحدانيته، كالغوص في بحر عميق.
  - يُنجيك من الغرق فيه ثلاثة أمور:
    - اعترافك بأن العقل محدودٌ في إدراك كمال الله.
    - توقُّفك عن محاولة الوصول إلى "كيفية" ذات الله.
    - التمسك بتعظيم الله دون تشبيه.

٢ .التفكُّر في إبداع الخلق:

- النظر في دقة صنع الله (كالسماء، الجبال، الإنسان).
  - يحتاج إلى ثلاثة أمور:
    - ملاحظة بدايات النعم وكيف تتجلى.
    - تفسير الإشارات الإلهية في الكون (مثل المطر دليل رحمة).
    - التحرر من شهوات تشغل قلبك عن التأمل.

٣ .التفكُّر في أعمالك وأحوالك :

- تحليل نواياك وأفعالك اليومية.
  - يحتاج إلى ثلاثة أمور:
    - التزامك بالعلم الشرعي في تقييم نفسك.
    - شكّك في صدق نواياك (قد تخدع نفسك!).
    - فهم تأثير أفعالك على الآخرين.

<u>موجز ونصيحة عملية:</u>

التفكُّر ليس فلسفة معقدة، بل هو عادة يومية:

- خمس دقائق صباحًا: تأمَّل في آية قرآنية أو مخلوقٍ طبيعي (كورقة شجر) واسأل: "ماذا تعلمني عن الله؟"
- قبل أي قرار: توقف ثانيةً وفكر: "هل هذا يُرضي الله؟ "
- اكتب ملاحظاتك الروحية في دفترٍ صغير كل أسبوع.

كل تأمل صادق يقربك من الحكمة!

نص الشيخ الهروي

٦- باب التذكر

قال الله عز و جل: ﴿ وَمَا يَتَذَكَّرُ إِلَّا مَن يُنِيبُ ﴾(غافر:١٣).

التذكر فوق التفكر، فإن التفكر طلب، والتذكر وجود.
وأبنية التذكر ثلاثة أشياء:
الانتفاع بالعظة، واستبصار العبرة، والظفر بثمر الفكرة.
وإنما ينتفع بالعظة بعد حصول ثلاثة أشياء: بشدة الافتقار إليها، والعمي عن عيب الواعظ، وبذكر الوعد والوعيد.
وإنما تستبصر العبرة بثلاثة أشياء: بحياة العقل، ومعرفة الأيام، والسلامة من الأغراض.
وإنما تجنى ثمرة الفكرة بثلاثة أشياء: بقصر الأمل، والتأمل في القرآن، وقلة الخلطة والتمني والتعلق والشبع والمنام.

النصّ مكتوباً بلغة مبسّطة

٦- باب التذكُّر (الاستفادة من العِبَر)

قال الله تعالى: ﴿ وَمَا يَتَذَكَّرُ إِلَّا مَن يُنِيبُ﴾ (غافر: ١٣).

التذكُّر أعلى من التفكُّر؛ فالتفكُّر بحثٌ عن الحكمة، أما التذكُّر فهو وصولٌ إليها.

وله ثلاثة أركان:

١ .الانتفاع بالموعظة:
- أن تستفيد من النصائح والتحذيرات.
- يشترط له ثلاثة أمور:
  - شعورك بالحاجة الماسّة لهذه الموعظة.
  - ترك التركيز على عيوب الناصح (لا تنتقد شخصه، بل استمع لرسالته).
  - تذكُّر وعد الله بالثواب ووعيده بالعقاب.

٢ .رؤية العِبَر في الأحداث:
- أن تستخرج الدروس من مواقف الحياة.
- يشترط له ثلاثة أمور:

- عقلٌ واعٍ يربط الأسباب بالنتائج.
- معرفة سنن الله في الكون (مثل: الظلم يؤدي للهلاك).
- نيةٌ خالصة لطلب الحق (لا تبحث عن مصلحة شخصية).

٣ .حصاد ثمرة التأمل:
- أن تترجم أفكارك إلى أفعالٍ نافعة.
- يشترط له ثلاثة أمور:

- تقصير الأمل (لا تؤجل التغيير).
- تدبُّر القرآن وفهم معانيه.
- تجنُّب الإفراط في: الاختلاط باللهو، التمنّي الفارغ، التعلق بالدنيا، الشبع الزائد، النوم الكثير.

<u>موجز ونصيحة عملية:</u>

التذكُّر هو التطبيق العملي للحكمة:

- كل يوم: اقرأ موعظةً قصيرة (من القرآن أو حكمة) واسأل: "كيف أطبق هذا اليوم؟".
- عند سماع خبرٍ سلبي: ابحث عن العبرة (مثل: كيف أتجنب هذا الخطأ؟).
- خفِّف من الأشياء التي تُشتت قلبك (كالتلفاز أو السهر غير المفيد).

التذكُّر الحقيقي يجعلك تعيش بوعي، لا بغفلة!

نص الشيخ الهروي

٧- باب الاعتصام

قال الله عز و جل: ﴿واعتصموا بحبل الله جميعاً﴾(آل عمران:١٠٣)،
﴿وَٱعْتَصِمُواْ بِٱللَّهِ هُوَ مَوْلَىٰكُمْ﴾(الحج:٧٨).

الاعتصام بحبل الله هو المحافظة على طاعته مراقبا لأمره، والاعتصام بالله هو الترقي عن كل موهوم والتخلص من كل تردد. والاعتصام على ثلاث درجات:

اعتصام العامة: بالخبر، استسلاما وإذعاناً بتصديق الوعد والوعيد، وتعظيم الأمر والنهي، وتأسيس المعاملة على اليقين والإنصاف. وهو الاعتصام بحبل الله.

واعتصام الخاصة: بالانقطاع، وهو صون الإرادة قبضاً، وإسبال الخلق على الخلق بسطاً، ورفض العلائق عزماً. وهو التمسك ﴿بالعروة الوثقى﴾(البقرة:٢٥٦).

واعتصام خاصة الخاصة: بالاتصال، وهو شهود الحق تفريداً، بعد الاستخذاء له تعظيماً، والاشتغال به قرباً. وهو الاعتصام بالله.

النصّ مكتوباً بلغة مبسّطة

٧- باب الاعتصام

قال الله تعالى: ﴿وَاعْتَصِمُوا بِحَبْلِ اللَّهِ جَمِيعًا﴾ (آل عمران: ١٠٣)،
وقال: ﴿وَٱعْتَصِمُواْ بِٱللَّهِ هُوَ مَوْلَىٰكُمْ﴾ (الحج: ٧٨).

الاعتصام هو التمسك بالله بقوة. وهو ثلاثة مستويات:

١ .اعتصام العامة (المبتدئين):
التمسك بأوامر الله ونواهيه عبر:

- الإيمان بوعد الله (الجنة) ووعيده (النار).
- احترام الحدود الشرعية (الصلاة، الصوم، إلخ).
- التعامل مع الناس بالعدل واليقين.

- هذا هو التمسك بحبل الله (القرآن والسنة).

٢ .اعتصام الخاصة (المتقدمين):
- التحرر من التعلقات الدنيوية عبر:

- ضبط الرغبات (كالإقلال من الكلام الزائد).
- التواضع مع الخلق (عدم التكبر).
- قطع العلاقات التي تُبعد عن الله.

- هذا هو التمسك بـ "العروة الوثقى" (الإخلاص لله).

٣ .اعتصام خاصة الخاصة (الخواص):
- الوصول إلى مرحلة الاتصال القلبي بالله عبر:

- رؤية عظمة الله في كل شيء.
- الخضوع الكامل له بالقلب والجوارح.
- الانشغال بذكره دائمًا.

- هذا هو الاعتصام بالله نفسه.

<u>موجز ونصيحة عملية:</u>
الاعتصام بالله درجاتٌ متصاعدة:

- ابدأ بالأساسيات: حافظ على الصلاة واقرأ القرآن يوميًّا.
- تخلَّص تدريجيًّا: قلل من عاداتك واحدةً تُشتتك (كالتصفّح في الانترنت).
- اختر صُحبةً: اجلس مع من يذكرك بالله إذا نسيت.

كلما تمسكت بالله، زادت قوتك الداخلية وقربك منه!

نص الشيخ الهروي

٨- باب الفرار

قال الله عز وجل: ﴿ففروا إلى الله﴾(الذاريات:٥٠).
الفرار هو الهرب مما لم يكن إلى ما لم يزل.
وهو على ثلاث درجات:
فرار العامة: من الجهل إلى العلم عقداً وسعياً، ومن الكسل إلى التشمير حذراً وعزماً، ومن الضيق إلى السعة ثقةً ورجاءً.
وفرار الخاصة: من الخبر إلى الشهود، ومن الرسوم إلى الأصول، ومن الحظوظ إلى التجريد.
وفرار خاصة أالخاصة: مما دون الحق إلى الحق، ثم من شهود الفرار إلى الحق، ثم الفرار من الفرار إلى الحق.

النصّ مكتوباً بلغة مبسّطة

٨- باب الفرار (الهروب إلى الله)

قال الله تعالى: ﴿فَفِرُّوا إِلَى اللَّهِ﴾ (الذاريات: ٥٠).

الفرار هو الهروب من كل شيء زائل إلى الله الدائم.

وهو ثلاثة مستويات:

١ .فرار العامة (المبتدئين):
- الهروب من:

  - الجهل إلى العلم (بالدراسة والعمل).
  - الكسل إلى الاجتهاد (بالحذر والعزيمة).
  - الضيق النفسي إلى الثقة برحمة الله (بالأمل والرجاء).

٢ .فرار الخاصة (المتقدمين):
- الهروب من:

- الكلام النظري إلى اختبار حلاوة الإيمان (بالقلب لا بالأذن).
- العبادات الشكلية إلى جوهر التقوى (كالإخلاص).
- التمسك بالدنيا إلى التجرد الروحي (عدم التعلق بالمال أو المنصب).

٣ .فرار خاصة الخاصة (الخواص):
- الهروب من:

- كل ما سوى الله إلى الله نفسه (حتى من الأفكار الروحية!).
- الفرار كفعلٍ إرادي إلى الاستسلام الكامل (كطفل بين يدي والديه).

<u>موجز ونصيحة عملية:</u>
الفرار إلى الله ليس هروبًا من الحياة، بل تحرُّرٌ نحو الأفضل:

- ابدأ بالأساس: خصص 10 دقائق يوميًّا لتعلم دينك (كتفسير آية).
- انتبه للنوايا: حوِّل عاداتك اليومية (كالأكل) إلى عبادة بالشكر.
- تخلَّص من الفخاخ: ابتعد عن العلاقات أو الأعمال التي تُنسيك الله.

الهروب الحقيقي هو أن تعيش مع الله في كل لحظة!

نص الشيخ الهروي

٩- باب الرياضة

قال الله عز وجل: ﴿وَٱلَّذِينَ يُؤْتُونَ مَآ ءَاتَواْ وَّقُلُوبُهُمْ وَجِلَةٌ﴾(المؤمنون:٦٠).
الرياضة تمرين النفس على قبول الصدق.
وهي على ثلاث درجات:
رياضة العامة: تهذيب الأخلاق بالعلم، وتصفية الأعمال بالإخلاص، وتوفير الحقوق في المعاملة.
ورياضة الخاصة: حسم التفرق، وقطع الالتفات إلى المقام الذي جاوزه، وإبقاء العلم يجري مجاريه.
ورياضة خاصة الخاصة: تجريد الشهود، والصعود إلى الجمع، ورفض المعارضات والمعاوضات.

النصّ مكتوباً بلغة مبسّطة

٩- باب الرياضة (التدريب الروحي):

قال الله تعالى: ﴿وَٱلَّذِينَ يُؤْتُونَ مَآ ءَاتَواْ وَّقُلُوبُهُمْ وَجِلَةٌ﴾ (المؤمنون: ٦٠).

الرياضة هي تدريب النفس على قبول الحق والعمل به.

وهي ثلاثة مستويات:

١ .رياضة العامة (المبتدئين):

- تهذيب الأخلاق: تطوير شخصيتك عبر تعلُّم الأخلاق الإسلامية (كالصدق والأمانة).
- تصفية الأعمال: إخلاص النية في كل عمل (حتى لو كان بسيطًا كإماطة الأذى عن الطريق).
- توفير الحقوق: العدل في التعامل مع الناس (رد الودائع، عدم الغش في البيع).

٢ .رياضة الخاصة (المتقدمين):

- قطع التشتت: التوقف عن الانشغال بأمور تافهة (كالإفراط في المزاح أو الفضول).
- عدم التعلق بالماضي: عدم الرضا بالإنجازات الروحية السابقة (كأن تقول: "لقد صمت الشهر كله، هذا يكفي!").
- استمرار التعلُّم: تطبيق العلم حتى لا يتحول إلى مجرد معلومات مكتوبة.

٣ .رياضة خاصة الخاصة (الخواص):

- التجرد الكامل: ترك كل ما يشغل عن الله (حتى الأفكار الروحية إن أصبحت مصدر فخر!).
- التركيز على الوحدة: رؤية يد الله في كل حدث (كأن يقول القلب: "هذا الخير هو نعمة من الله").
- رفض المساومات: عدم المقايضة بين الطاعة والمعصية (مثل: "سأصلي لكن سأغتاب!").

<u>موجز ونصيحة عملية:</u>

الرياضة الروحية هي رحلة تحويل المعرفة إلى فعل:

- ابدأ بالأخلاق: اختر خُلُقًا واحدًا (كالكرم) وحاول تطبيقه أسبوعًا.
- راقب نيتك: قبل أي عمل، اسأل: "هل هذا لوجه الله أم لمدح الناس؟".
- تخلَّص من الفوضويات: قلل من عادةٍ واحدة تُضيع وقتك (كالتصفح العشوائي للإنترنت).

التدريب المستمر يصنع منك إنسانًا أفضل، خطوة بخطوة!

نص الشيخ الهروي

١٠- باب السماع

قال الله عز و جل: ﴿ولو علم الله فيهم خيرا لأسمعهم﴾(الأنفال:٢٣).
نكتة السماع حقيقة الانتباه.
وهو على ثلاثة درجات:
سماع العامة: ثلاثة أشياء: إجابة زجر الوعيد رعَةً، وإجابة دعوة الوعد جهداً، وبلوغ مشاهدة المنة استبصاراً.
وسماع الخاصة: ثلاثة أشياء: شهود المقصود في كل رمز، والوقوف على الغاية في كل حي، والخلاص من التلذذ بالتفرق.
وسماع خاصة الخاصة: سماع يغسل العلل عن الكشف، ويصل الأبد بالأزل، ويَرُدّ النهايات إلى الأول.

النصّ مكتوباً بلغة مبسّطة

١٠- باب السماع (الاستماع الواعي):

قال الله تعالى: ﴿وَلَوْ عَلِمَ اللَّهُ فِيهِمْ خَيْرًا لَّأَسْمَعَهُمْ﴾ (الأنفال: ٢٣).

السماع الحقيقي هو انتباه القلب والعقل معًا.

وهو ثلاثة مستويات:

١ .سماع العامة (المبتدئين):

- الاستجابة للتحذيرات: الخوف من عقاب الله (كالتوقف عن الذنب عند تذكيرك بالوعيد).
- الاستجابة للوعود: السعي لنيل رحمة الله (كزيادة الصدقة عند سماع آيات الجنة).
- رؤية النعم: إدراك بركات الله في حياتك (كالصحة والأمن).

٢ .سماع الخاصة (المتقدمين):

- فهم الرموز: استخلاص الحكمة من كل موقف (كأن ترى في المطر إشارةً لغفران الذنوب).
- إدراك الغاية: معرفة هدف الله من كل شيء (كالصبر في المرض لرفع الدرجات).
- التوحيد القلبي: عدم التعلق بغير الله (حتى في الأشياء الروحية!).

٣ .سماع خاصة الخاصة (الخواص):

- تطهير القلب: سماعٌ يزيل الحجب بينك وبين الله (كأن تشعر بوجوده في كل نبضة قلب).
- الاتصال الأبدي: الشعور بأنك جزء من خطة الله الأزلية (كقطرة في نهر أبدي).
- العودة للأصل: رؤية كل النهايات مرتبطة ببداية الخلق (كإدراك أن الموت بداية حقيقية).

<u>موجز ونصيحة عملية:</u>

السماع الواعي يُحوِّل الكلمات إلى أفعالٍ وحِكَم:

- استمع بتركيز: عند قراءة القرآن، تخيَّل أن الله يُخاطبك مباشرةً.
- اسأل: بعد كل موعظة، فكِّر: "ماذا يعلمني هذا عن الله؟".
- دوِّن: اكتب لحظةً واحدة يوميًّا شعرتَ فيها بمعنىً عميق من كلامٍ سمعته.

السماع الحقيقي يربطك بالله في كل تفصيلة !

٢- قسم الأبواب

وأما قسم الأبواب فهو عشرة أبواب وهي الحزن والخوف والإشفاق والخشوع والإخبات والزهد والورع والتبتل والرجاء والرغبة.

نص الشيخ الهروي

١١- باب الحزن

قال الله عز وجل: (تولوا وأعينهم تفيض من الدمع حزنا) (التوبة:٩٢).
الحزن توجع لفائت أو تأسف على ممتنع.
وله ثلاث درجات:
الدرجة الأولى، حزن العامة: وهو حزن على التفريط في الخدمة، وعلى التورط في الجفاء وعلى ضياع الأيام.
والدرجة الثانية، حزن أهل الإرادة: وهو حزن على تعلق الوقت بالتفرق وعلى اشتغال النفس عن الشهود وعلى التسلي عن الحزن.
وليست الخاصة من مقام الحزن في شيء، ولكن الدرجة الثالثة من الحزن: التحزن للعارضات دون الخواطر، ومعارضات القصود، والاعتراضات على الأحكام.

النصّ مكتوباً بلغة مبسّطة

١١- باب الحزن

قال الله تعالى: ﴿تَوَلَّوْا وَأَعْيُنُهُمْ تَفِيضُ مِنَ الدَّمْعِ حُزْنًا﴾ (التوبة: ٩٢).

الحزن هو ألمٌ على شيء فاتك أو شيء لم تستطع تحقيقه. وله ثلاث درجات:

١ .حزن العامة (العادي):
- حزنٌ بسبب:

  - التقصير في العبادات (كترك صلاة أو إهمال صدقة).
  - الوقوع في أخطاء تُبعدك عن الله (كالكذب أو الغيبة).
  - ضياع الوقت في أمور غير مفيدة.

٢ .حزن أهل الإرادة (الجادين في الطريق):

- حزنٌ بسبب:

- انشغال القلب بغير الله (حتى لو كان عملًا مباحًا).
- عدم القدرة على التركيز في العبادات (كالتفكير في الدنيا أثناء الصلاة).
- محاولة الهروب من الحزن نفسه (كالتلهي بالمسلسلات أو السفر بدل مواجهة الأخطاء).

٣ .حزن الخاصة (المُتقدّمين):

- حزنٌ نادر لا يشعر به إلا من بلغ مرتبة عالية، وهو:

- ألمٌ بسبب أي عائقٍ مؤقتٍ يقطع طريقهم إلى الله (حتى لو كان سببًا بسيطًا).
- تألمٌ عندما تُعارض نواياهم الصادقة (كأن يمنعك مرضٌ من صلاة الجماعة).
- حساسيةٌ تجاه أي نقصٍ في فهم حكمة الله (كالتساؤل: "لماذا حدث هذا؟").

<u>موجز ونصيحة عملية:</u>

الحزن الروحي ليس ضعفًا، بل دليل على حياة القلب:

- لا تخف من الحزن: دونهُ في دفترك: "أحزن لأني..."، ثم اطلب من الله الإعانة.
- حوِّل الحزن إلى فعل: إن حزنت على ضياع الوقت، خطِّط لبرنامج يوميٍ روحي.
- تأمَّل: اقرأ الآية الكريمة السابقة وفكِّر: كيف يجعلني حزني أقرب إلى الله؟

الحزن النقي يُذكِّرك بأنك لا تزال على الطريق – استمر !

نص الشيخ الهروي

١٢- باب الخوف

قال الله عز وجل: (يخافون ربهم من فوقهم)(النحل:٥٠).
الخوف هو الانخلاع عن طمأنينة الأمن بمطالعة الخبر.
وهو على ثلاث درجات:
الدرجة الأولى: الخوف من العقوبة. وهو الخوف الذي يصح به الإيمان، وهو خوف العامة، وهو يتولد من تصديق الوعيد، وذكر الجناية، ومراقبة العاقبة.
والدرجة الثانية: خوف المكر في جريان الأنفاس المستغرقة في اليقظة، المشوبة بالحلاوة.
وليس في مقام أهل الخصوص وحشة الخوف، إلا هيبة الإجلال: وهي أقصى درجة يشار إليها في غاية الخوف، وهي هيبة تعارض المكاشف أوقات المناجاة، وتصون المشاهد أحيان المسامرة، وتقصم المعاين بصدمة العزة.

النصّ مكتوباً بلغة مبسّطة

١٢- باب الخوف

قال الله تعالى: ﴿يَخَافُونَ رَبَّهُم مِّن فَوْقِهِمْ﴾ (النحل: ٥٠).

الخوف هو فقدان الشعور بالأمان بسبب تذكُّر عذاب الله. وهو ثلاثة أنواع:

١ .خوف العامة (العادي):
- الخوف من عقاب الله على الذنوب (كالنار).
- ينشأ هذا الخوف من:
  - الإيمان بوعيد الله في القرآن.
  - تذكُّر أخطائك السابقة.
  - التفكير في عواقب الأعمال يوم القيامة.

٢ .خوف الخاصة (المتقدمين):
- خوفٌ ممزوج بالرهبة واللذة الروحية، يشعر به من:

- مراقبة كل لحظة من حياته (حتى أثناء التنفس!).
- الخشية من أن تُخدعَ نفسُه بالراحة الزائفة.
- الشعور بحلاوة الإيمان مع قلقٍ دائمٍ من التقصير.

٣ .خوف خاصة الخاصة (الخواص):
- ليس خوفًا تقليديًّا، بل هيبة عظيمة لله، تظهر في:

- الشعور بالعجز أمام عظمة الله أثناء الدعاء.
- الحفاظ على إخلاص القلب حتى في لحظات الفرح.
- الانهيار الداخلي عند رؤية جمال الله وقدرته.

موجز ونصيحة عملية:

الخوف الصحي طريقٌ للتقوى:

- استغل خوفك: اكتب ذنبًا واحدًا تخشى عقابه، وخطط للتوبة منه.
- راقب نيتك: قبل أي عمل، اسأل: "هل هذا يرضي الله أم يزيد خوفي منه؟".
- اقرأ الآية يوميًّا: ﴿يَخَافُونَ رَبَّهُم مِّن فَوْقِهِمْ﴾ وفكِّر: كيف تجعل خوفك سببًا لقربك من الله؟

الخوف الحقيقي لا يُضعفك، بل يُعيد توجيه قلبك نحو الطاعة !

نص الشيخ الهروي

١٣- باب الاشفاق

قال الله عز وجل: (قالوا إنا كنا قبل في أهلنا مشفقين) (الطور:٢٦).
الإشفاق دوام الحذر مقرونا بالترحم.
وهو على ثلاث درجات:
الدرجة الأولى: إشفاق على النفس أن تجمح إلى العناد، وإشفاق على العمل أن يصير إلى الضياع، وإشفاق على الخليقة لمعرفة معاذيرها.
والدرجة الثانية: إشفاق على الوقت أن يشوبه تفرق، وعلى القلب أن يزاحمه عارض، وعلى اليقين أن يداخله سبب.
والدرجة الثالثة: إشفاق يصون سعيه من العجب، ويكف صاحبه عن مخاصمة الخلق، ويحمل المريد على حفظ الحد.

النصّ مكتوباً بلغة مبسّطة

١٣- باب الاشفاق

قال الله تعالى: ﴿قَالُوا إِنَّا كُنَّا قَبْلُ فِي أَهْلِنَا مُشْفِقِينَ﴾ (الطور: ٢٦).

الإشفاق هو خوفٌ ممزوج بالرحمة، يشعر به الإنسان تجاه نفسه والآخرين. وهو ثلاثة أنواع:

١ .إشفاق العامة (المبتدئين):
- خوفٌ على:

- النفس من التمرد على الله (كالعناد في الطاعة).
- الأعمال الصالحة من الضياع (كأن تذهب الصدقة بلا إخلاص).
- الآخرين من الوقوع في الخطأ (مع فهم أعذارهم).

٢ .إشفاق الخاصة (المتقدمين):

- خوفٌ على:

- الوقت من التشتت بين أمور الدنيا.
- القلب من انشغاله بأي شيءٍ يبعده عن الله.
- اليقين من الشكوك التي تُضعف الإيمان.

٣ .إشفاق خاصة الخاصة (الخواص):

- خوفٌ يمنع:

- العُجب بالنفس (كأن تشعر بالفخر لصلاحك!).
- المشاجرات مع الناس (حتى لو كنتَ محقًّا).
- تجاوز الحدود في العبادة (كالإفراط في الصوم حتى الإعياء).

<u>موجز ونصيحة عملية:</u>

الإشفاق توازن بين الخوف والرحمة:

-اسأل نفسك يوميًّا: "هل أخاف على إيماني كما أخاف على صحتي؟".

-اختر علاقةً واحدة: تحسَّن طريقة تعاملك فيها (كالتعاطف مع صديقٍ مقصِّر).

-اقرأ الآية: ﴿إِنَّا كُنَّا قَبْلُ فِي أَهْلِنَا مُشْفِقِينَ﴾ وتذكَّر: الخوف النافع يجعل قلبك حيًّا !

نص الشيخ الهروي

١٤- باب الخشوع

قال الله عز وجل: (ألم يأن للذين آمنوا أن تخشع قلوبهم لذكر الله وما نزل من الحق)(الحديد:١٦).

الخشوع خمود النفس وهمود الطباع لمتعاظم أو مفزع.

وهو على ثلاث درجات:

الدرجة الأولى: التذلل للأمر، والاستسلام للحكم، والاتضاع لنظر الحق.

والدرجة الثانية: ترقب آفات النفس والعمل، ورؤية فضل كل ذي فضل عليك، وتنسم نسيم الفناء.

الدرجة الثالثة: حفظ الحرمة عند المكاشفة، وتصفية الوقت من مراياة الخلق، وتجريد رؤية الفضل.

النصّ مكتوباً بلغة مبسّطة

١٤- باب الخشوع

قال الله تعالى: ﴿أَلَمْ يَأْنِ لِلَّذِينَ آمَنُوا أَنْ تَخْشَعَ قُلُوبُهُمْ لِذِكْرِ اللَّهِ وَمَا نَزَلَ مِنَ الْحَقِّ﴾ (الحديد: ١٦).

الخشوع هو سكون القلب وخضوعه أمام عظمة الله.

وهو ثلاثة أنواع:

١ .خشوع العامة (المبتدئين):

- الخضوع للأوامر: طاعة الله دون تذمر (كأداء الصلاة بخشوع).
- الاستسلام للقدر: تقبُّل ابتلاءات الحياة برضا (كفقدان مال أو صحة).
- التواضع لله: الشعور بصغار النفس أمام عظمة الخالق.

٢ .خشوع الخاصة (المتقدمين):

- مراقبة العيوب: اكتشاف نقائص النفس والأعمال (كالتفكير في نيَّة الصدقة).
- رؤية فضل الآخرين: الاعتراف بمن هم أفضل منك في العبادة أو الأخلاق.
- التأهب للقاء الله: تذكُّر الموت وزوال الدنيا (كالتفكير في الآخرة أثناء النعيم).

٣ .خشوع خاصة الخاصة (الخواص):

- حفظ الأدب مع الله: حتى في لحظات الكشف الروحي (كعدم الادعاء بالتقوى).
- تصفية الوقت من الرياء: عدم الاهتمام بمدح الناس أثناء العبادة.
- رؤية الفضل الإلهي: إدراك أن كل خيرٍ من الله وليس من نفسك.

<u>موجز ونصيحة عملية:</u>

الخشوع سرُّ التواصل مع الله:

- ابدأ بلحظة: اختر ركعة واحدة في الصلاة لتركيز القلب فيها.
- دوّن: اكتب خطأً واحدًا اكتشفته في نفسك اليوم، واطلب من الله الإعانة على تصحيحه.
- اقرأ الآية يوميًّا: ﴿أَلَمْ يَأْنِ لِلَّذِينَ آمَنُوا...﴾ واسأل: "هل قلبي خاشع حقًّا؟".

الخشوع الحقيقي يجعلك ترى الله في كل تفصيل !

نص الشيخ الهروي

١٥- باب الاخبات

قال الله عز وجل: (وبشر المخبتين)(الحج:٣٤).
الإخبات من أوائل مقام الطمأنينة، وهو ورود المأمن من الرجوع والتردد.
وهو على ثلاث درجات:
الدرجة الأولى: أن تستغرق العصمة الشهوة، وتستدرك الإدارة الغفلة، ويستهوي الطلب السلوة.
والدرجة الثانية: ان لا ينقص إرادته سبب، ولا يوحش قلبه عارض، ولا تقطع الطريق عليه فتنة.
والدرجة الثالثة: أن يستوي عنده المدح والذم، وتدوم لائمته لنفسه، ويعمى عن نقصان الخلق عن درجته.

النصّ مكتوباً بلغة مبسّطة

١٥- باب الاخبات

قال الله تعالى: ﴿وَبَشِّرِ الْمُخْبِتِينَ﴾ (الحج: ٣٤) .

الإخبات (الطمأنينة الروحية) هو استقرار القلب وهدوء النفس مع الله.

وهو ثلاثة أنواع:

١ .إخبات العامة (المبتدئين):

- قهر الشهوات: استخدام قوة الإيمان لتحويل الرغبات الدنيوية إلى طاعة (كالصوم لترويض النفس).
- علاج الغفلة: تذكير النفس بمراقبة الله عند النسيان (كالتسبيح عند التشتت).
- الانسجام مع العبادة: الاستمتاع بالطاعة بدل البحث عن الملذات المؤقتة.

٢ .إخبات الخاصة (المتقدمين):

- ثبات الإرادة: عدم تأثر العزم بالأزمات (كالمرض الذي لا يمنعك من الدعاء).
- سلامة القلب: عدم اضطراب المشاعر بالهموم (كالثقة في الله أثناء المصائب).
- عبور الفتن: تجاوز الاختبارات دون تراجع (كالصمود أمام الإغراءات).

٣ .إخبات خاصة الخاصة (الخواص):

- الاستواء بين المدح والذم: عدم التأثر بمدح الناس أو انتقادهم (فعملك لله وحده).
- النقد الذاتي الدائم: رؤية أخطائك قبل انتقاد الآخرين.
- التواضع المطلق: عدم الشعور بالتفوق حتى على من يظهر ضعفه.

موجز ونصيحة عملية:

الإخبات هو ملاذ القلب الآمن:

- ابدأ صباحك: قل: "اللهم اجعلني من المخبتين" ٣ مرات.
- دوّن إنجازًا واحدًا: حققته برضا الله (ليس لإعجاب الناس).
- اقرأ الآية يوميًّا: ﴿وَبَشِّرِ الْمُخْبِتِينَ﴾ واسأل: "هل أنا منهم؟".

الطمأنينة الحقيقية هي أن تعيش كما يريدك الله، لا كما يريدك العالم !

نص الشيخ الهروي

١٦- باب الزهد

قال الله عز وجل: (بَقِيَّتُ ٱللَّهِ خَيْرٌ لَّكُمْ)(هود:٨٦).
الزهد إسقاط الرغبة عن الشيء بالكلية.
وهو للعامة قربة، وللمريد ضرورة، وللخاصة خسّة.
وهو على ثلاث درجات:
الدرجة الأولى: الزهد في الشبهة بعد ترك الحرام؛ بالحذر من المعتبة، والأنفة من المنقصة، وكراهة مشاركة الفساق.
والدرجة الثانية: الزهد في الفضول وما زاد على المسكة والبلاغ من القوت؛ باغتنام التفرغ إلى عمارة الوقت، وحسم الجأش، والتحلي بحلية الأنبياء والصديقين.
والدرجة الثالثة: الزهد في الزهد بثلاثة أشياء: باستحقار ما زهدت فيه، واستواء الحالات عندك، والذهاب عن شهود الاكتساب ناظراً إلى وادي الحقائق.

النصّ مكتوباً بلغة مبسّطة

١٦- باب الزهد

قال الله تعالى: ﴿بَقِيَّتُ ٱللَّهِ خَيْرٌ لَّكُمْ﴾ (هود: ٨٦).

الزهد هو التخلي التام عن التعلق بالدنيا. وهو ثلاثة أنواع:

١ .زهد العامة (المبتدئين):
- تجنُّب ما هو مشبوه (حتى لو كان حلالًا) خوفًا من:
  - لوم الناس أو انتقادهم.
  - النقص في مكانتك الاجتماعية.
  - التشبه بالفسَّاق في سلوكياتهم.

٢ .زهد الخاصة (المتقدمين):

- الاكتفاء بالقليل من الطعام والملبس لـ:

- توفير الوقت للعبادة والتفكُّر.
- تقوية العزيمة وضبط النفس.
- الاقتداء بالأنبياء والصالحين في بساطة العيش.

٣ .زهد خاصة الخاصة (الخواص):

- تجاوز مفهوم الزهد نفسه عبر:

- استصغار كل ما تخلَّيت عنه (فالدنيا كلها لا تساوي عند الله جناح بعوضة!).
- عدم الاهتمام بمدح الناس أو ذمهم.
- رؤية أن كل شيء من الله، فلا تفخر بزهدك أو أعمالك.

<u>موجز ونصيحة عملية:</u>

الزهد ليس حرمانًا، بل تحرُّرٌ لروحك:

- ابدأ صغيرًا: اختر شيئًا واحدًا تُقلِّل منه (كالمبالغة في الملابس أو الطعام).
- تذكَّر الآية: ﴿بَقِيَّتُ ٱللَّهِ خَيْرٌ لَّكُمْ﴾ واسأل: "هل أفضِّل رضا الله على شهواتي؟".
- اقرأ: «ٱعْلَمُوٓاْ أَنَّمَا ٱلْحَيَوٰةُ ٱلدُّنْيَا لَعِبٌ وَلَهْوٌ وَزِينَةٌ... » (الحديد: ٢٠) وفكِّر: كيف تجعل زهدك جسرًا للقرب من الله؟

نص الشيخ الهروي

١٧- باب الورع

قال الله عز وجل: (وثيابك فطهر)(المدثر:٤).
الورع توق مستقصي على حذر، أو تحرج على تعظيم.
وهو آخر مقام الزهد للعامة، وأول مقام الزهد للمريد.
وهو على ثلاث درجات:
الدرجة الأولى: تجنب القبائح؛ لصون النفس، وتوفير الحسنات، وصيانة الإيمان.
والدرجة الثانية: حفظ الحدود عند ما لا بأس به؛ إبقاء على الصيانة والتقوى، وصعودا على الدناءة، وتخلصاً عن اقتحام الحدود.
والدرجة الثالثة: التورع عن كل داعية تدعو إلى شتات الوقت والتعلق بالتفرق، وعارض يعارض حال الجمع.

النصّ مكتوباً بلغة مبسّطة

١٧- باب الورع

قال الله تعالى: ﴿وَثِيَابَكَ فَطَهِّرْ﴾ (المدثر: ٤).

الورع هو الحذر الشديد من كل ما قد يُغضب الله، حتى في الأمور المُباحة.

وهو ثلاثة أنواع:

١ .ورع العامة (المبتدئين):

- تجنُّب الكبائر: مثل الكذب والسرقة لحماية النفس من السقوط.
- زيادة الحسنات: كالصدقة اليومية لتعويض التقصير.
- حماية الإيمان: بالابتعاد عن أماكن الفتنة (كالمجالس التي يُستهزأ فيها بالدين).

٢ .ورع الخاصة (المتقدمين):

- الحذر في الحلال: مثل عدم الإفراط في الأكل (حتى لو كان حلالًا) حفظًا للصحة والوقت.
- الالتزام بآداب الإسلام: كخفض الصوت في الأسواق تجنبًا للرياء.
- عدم تجاوز الحدود: مثل ترك النكتة الجارحة حتى لو كانت "مزحة".

٣ .ورع خاصة الخاصة (الخواص):

- التنقية الكاملة: تجنُّب كل ما يشتت القلب عن الله، حتى لو كان مباحًا (كالإقلال من استخدام وسائل التواصل الاجتماعي في الانترنت للتسلّي).
- التركيز على الوحدة مع الله: عدم الانشغال بأي شيءٍ سواه حتى في أوقات الراحة.
- عدم اقتحام الأمور المشكوك فيها: مثل ترك العمل في مجالٍ مُربحٍ لكنه يُلهي عن الصلاة.

<u>موجز ونصيحة عملية:</u>

الورع هو حراسة القلب من الخفيِّ من الذنوب:

- ابدأ بتدقيق يومي: اسأل نفسك قبل النوم: "هل فعلتُ اليوم شيئًا قد يُسخط الله؟".
- اختر عادةً واحدة: مثل تقليل الكلام غير المفيد أو مراقبة نظراتك.
- اقرأ: «وَثِيَابَكَ فَطَهِّرْ» وتذكَّر: تطهير الظاهر دليل على نقاء الباطن !

نص الشيخ الهروي

١٨- باب التبتل

قال الله عز وجل: (وتبتل إليه تبتيلا)(المزمل:٨).
التبتل الانقطاع بالكلية، وقوله (إليه) دعوة إلى التجريد المحض.
وهو على ثلاث درجات:
الدرجة الأولى: تجريد الانقطاع عن الحظوظ واللحوظ إلى العالم؛ خوفاً، أو رجاءً، أو مبالاة بحال: بحسم الرجاء بالرضى، وقطع الخوف بالتسليم، ورفض المبالاة بشهود الحقيقة.
والدرجة الثانية: تجريد الانقطاع عن التعريج على النفس؛ بمجانبة الهوى، وتنسم روح الأنس، وشيم برق الكشف.
والدرجة الثالثة: تجريد الانقطاع إلى السبق؛ بتصحيح الاستقامة، والاستغراق في قصد الوصول، والنظر إلى أوائل الجمع.

النصّ مكتوباً بلغة مبسّطة

١٨- باب التبتل

قال الله تعالى: ﴿وَتَبَتَّلْ إِلَيْهِ تَبْتِيلًا﴾ (المزمل: ٨).

التبتل هو الانفصال الكامل عن كل ما يشغل عن الله.
وهو ثلاثة مستويات:

- تبتل العامة (المبتدئين):
- قطع العلائق الدنيوية: مثل التخلي عن طلب المدح أو الثروة أو المنصب.
- الرضا بالقدر: التوقف عن الخوف من المستقبل أو الندم على الماضي.
- ترك الاهتمام بآراء الناس: التركيز على رضا الله بدلًا من إعجاب الخلق.

٢ .تبتل الخاصة (المتقدمين):

- تحرير القلب من الأهواء: مثل مقاومة الرغبة في الظهور أو التفوق على الآخرين.
- الشعور بلذة القرب من الله: كالاستمتاع بالدعاء أكثر من أي متعة دنيوية.
- رؤية علامات الله في الكون: كالتفكر في خلق السماء والأرض أثناء العبادة.

٣ .تبتل خاصة الخاصة (الخواص):

- التركيز المطلق على الله: كأن ينفصل القلب عن كل شيء سواه حتى أثناء العمل أو الكلام.
- السعي نحو الكمال الروحي: تصحيح النوايا في كل عمل، ولو كان بسيطًا.
- الاستعداد للقاء الله: العيش وكأن كل يوم هو الأخير في الدنيا.

<u>موجز ونصيحة عملية:</u>

التبتل هو رحلة تحرير القلب من كل قيد:

- خصص وقتًا يوميًا: 10 دقائق للتفكر في آية قرآنية أو دعاء خالص.
- اختر عملًا واحدًا: أخلص نيته لله تمامًا (مثل مساعدة شخص دون إخبار أحد).
- اقرأ الآية: ﴿وَتَبَتَّلْ إِلَيْهِ تَبْتِيلًا﴾ وتذكَّر: «وَمَا خَلَقْتُ الْجِنَّ وَالْإِنْسَ إِلَّا لِيَعْبُدُونِ» (الذاريات: ٥٦).

الانقطاع لله ليس هروبًا من الحياة، بل هو عيشٌ بقلبٍ حرٍّ !

نص الشيخ الهروي

١٩- باب الرجاء

قال الله عز وجل: (لقد كان لكم في رسول الله أسوة حسنة لمن كان يرجو الله واليوم الآخر)(الأحزاب:٢١).
الرجاء أضعف منازل المريد، لأنه معارضة من وجه، واعتراض من وجه.
وهو وقوع في الرعونة في مذهب هذه الطائفة، إلا ما فيه من فائدة واحدة، ولها نطق باسمه التنزيل والسنة ودخل في مسالك المحققين، وتلك الفائدة أنه يفثأ حرارة الخوف حتى لا يعدو إلى الإياس.
والرجاء على ثلاث درجات:
الدرجة الأولى: رجاء يبعث العامل على الاجتهاد، ويولد التلذذ بالخدمة، ويوقظ لسماحة الطباع بترك المناهي.
والدرجة الثانية: رجاء أرباب الرياضات، أن يبلغوا موقفا تصفو فيه هممهم؛ برفض الملذوذات، ولزوم شروط العلم، واستقصاء حدود الحمية.
والدرجة الثالثة: رجاء أرباب طيب القلوب، وهو رجاء لقاء الحق عز وجل؛ الباعث على الاشتياق، المنغص للعيش، المزهد في الخلق.

النصّ مكتوباً بلغة مبسّطة

١٩- باب الرجاء

قال الله تعالى: ﴿لَقَدْ كَانَ لَكُمْ فِي رَسُولِ اللَّهِ أُسْوَةٌ حَسَنَةٌ لِّمَن كَانَ يَرْجُو اللَّهَ وَالْيَوْمَ الْآخِرَ﴾ (الأحزاب: ٢١).

الرجاء هو تعلق القلب برحمة الله، لكنه قد يُضعف العزيمة إذا تحول إلى تواكل.

وهو ثلاثة أنواع:

١ .رجاء العامة (المبتدئين):

- الأمل في الثواب: كالاجتهاد في الصلاة والصوم طمعًا في الجنة.
- الاستمتاع بالطاعة: الشعور بالسعادة أثناء العبادة.
- التخلص من الذنوب: ترك المعاصي تدريجيًّا بدافع الأمل في المغفرة.

٢ .رجاء الخاصة (المتقدمين):

- الأمل في بلوغ المراتب الروحية: عبر:

- التخلي عن الملذات الدنيوية (كالإقلال من الطعام والكلام).
- الالتزام بآداب العلم والعمل (كطلب العلم النافع).
- مراقبة الحدود الشرعية بدقة (كعدم تجاوز وقت الصلاة).

٣ .رجاء خاصة الخاصة (الخواص):

- الشوق للقاء الله: وهو أسمى أنواع الرجاء، ويظهر في:

- اشتياق القلب الدائم لرؤية الله في الآخرة.
- عدم الاهتمام بزينة الدنيا وزخرفها.
- الشعور بأن الحياة دون القرب من الله مريرة.

موجز ونصيحة عملية:

الرجاء الصادق يوازن بين الخوف والطمع:

- ابدأ يومك بتفاؤل: قل: "اللهم إني أرجو رحمتك، وأتوب من تقصيري".
- اقرأ الآية: ﴿لَقَدْ كَانَ لَكُمْ فِي رَسُولِ اللَّهِ أُسْوَةٌ﴾ وتذكَّر: اتباع النبي صلى الله عليه وسلم هو طريق الأمل الحقيقي.
- دوِّن لحظة أمل: اكتب مرة أسبوعيًّا موقفًا شعرتَ فيه برحمة الله تغمرك.

لا تدع الرجاء يجعلك تتكاسل، بل اجعله دافعًا للعمل !

نص الشيخ الهروي

٢٠- باب الرغبة

قال الله عز وجل: (ويدعوننا رغبا ورهبا)(الأنبياء:٩٠).
الرغبة ألحَقُ بالحقيقة من الرجاء، وهي فوق الرجاء، لأن الرجاء طمع يحتاج إلى تحقيق، والرغبة سلوك على تحقيق.
والرغبة على ثلاث درجات:
الدرجة الأولى: رغبة أهل الخبر، تتولد من العلم؛ فتبعث على الاجتهاد المنوط بالشهود، وتصون السالك من وهن الفترة، وتمنع صاحبها من الرجوع إلى غثاثة الرخص.
والدرجة الثانية: رغبة أرباب الحال؛ وهي رغبة لا تبقى من المجهود إلا مبذولاً، ولا تدع للهمة ذبولاً، ولا تترك غير المقصود مأمولا.
والدرجة الثالثة: رغبة أهل الشهود؛ وهي تشرف تصحبة تقية، و تحمله همّة نقيّة، لا تبقى معه من التفرّق بقية.

النصّ مكتوباً بلغة مبسّطة

٢٠- باب الرغبة

قال الله تعالى: ﴿وَيَدْعُونَنَا رَغَبًا وَرَهَبًا﴾ (الأنبياء: ٩٠).

الرغبة هي اشتياق القلب إلى القرب من الله، وهي أعلى من مجرد الأمل لأنها فعلٌ مستمرٌ نحو الهدف.

وهي ثلاثة أنواع:

١ .رغبة العامة (أصحاب العلم):
- تنشأ من العلم بفضل الطاعة وعواقب المعصية.
- تدفعك إلى:
  - الاجتهاد في العبادة (كإطالة السجود في الصلاة).
  - تجنب الكسل الروحي (كالمحافظة على ورد يومي من الذكر).
  - عدم التعلل بأعذار ضعيفة لترك الواجبات.

٢ .رغبة الخاصة (أصحاب الحال):

- تظهر في:

- بذل كل الجهد لتحقيق الهدف (كالتضحية بالوقت والمال في سبيل الله).
- عدم تراجع الهمة حتى في أصعب الظروف.
- ترك كل ما لا يُقرِّب من الله (حتى المباحات الزائدة).

٣ .رغبة خاصة الخاصة (أصحاب الشهود):

- التفرغ الكامل لله:

- صحبةٌ روحيةٌ نقيةٌ لا تشوبها رياء.
- همةٌ عاليةٌ لا تضعف أمام الصعوبات.
- وحدةٌ مع الله تجعل القلب لا يشتاق لسواه.

<u>موجز ونصيحة عملية:</u>

الرغبة الحقيقية هي وقود السائرين إلى الله:

- خطط لهدفٍ روحاني: مثل ختم القرآن مرة شهريًّا أو إطعام محتاج كل أسبوع.
- اسأل نفسك يوميًّا: "هل فعلتُ اليوم ما يُقرِّبني من الله حقًّا؟".
- اقرأ الآية: ﴿وَإِذَا سَأَلَكَ عِبَادِي عَنِّي فَإِنِّي قَرِيبٌ﴾ (البقرة: ١٨٦) وتذكَّر: الله معك في كل خطوة !

٣- قسم المعاملات

وأما قسم المعاملات، فهو عشرة أبواب وهي:
الرعاية والمراقبة والحرمة والإخلاص والتهذيب والاستقامة والتوكل والتفويض والثقة والتسليم.

نص الشيخ الهروي

٢١- باب الرعاية

قال الله عز وجل: (فما رعوها حق رعايتها)(الحديد:٢٧).
الرعاية صون بالعناية.
وهي على ثلاث درجات:
الدرجة الأولى: رعاية الأعمال.
والدرجة الثانية: رعاية الأحوال.
والدرجة الثالثة: رعاية الأوقات.
فأما رعاية الأعمال؛ فتوفيرها بتحقيرها، والقيام بها من غير نظر إليها، وإجراؤها مجرى العلم لا على التزين بها.
وأما رعاية الأحوال؛ فهي أن يعد الاجتهاد مراياةً، والنفس تشبعاً، والحال دعوى.
وأما رعاية الأوقات؛ فأن يقف مع خطوة، ثم أن يغيب عن خطوه بالصفاء من رسمه، ثم أن يذهب عن شهود صفوه.

النصّ مكتوباً بلغة مبسّطة

٢١- باب الرعاية

قال الله تعالى: ﴿فَمَا رَعَوْهَا حَقَّ رِعَايَتِهَا﴾ (الحديد: ٢٧).

الرعاية هي حمايةٌ مدعومةٌ بالاهتمام، وهي ثلاثة أنواع:

١ .رعاية الأعمال (العبادات):

- إتقان العمل: أداء الصلاة والصدقة بإخلاص دون التفاتٍ لإعجاب الناس.
- عدم التفاخر: التعامل مع الطاعة كواجبٍ لا كمصدر فخر.
- التواضع: اعتبار الأعمال هبةً من الله، لا مجهودًا شخصيًّا.

٢ .رعاية الأحوال (الحالة القلبية):

- مراقبة النوايا: التأكد من خلو العبادة من الرياء (كالصوم لوجه الله لا لإنقاص الوزن).
- عدم الاغترار: التوقف عن الشعور بالتفوق الروحي على الآخرين.
- التخلص من الادعاء: عدم تصوير النفس كـ"شخصٍ صالح" أمام الناس.

٣ .رعاية الأوقات (إدارة الزمن):

- التركيز على اللحظة: عدم تشتيت الذهن أثناء العبادة (كالتفكير في العمل أثناء الصلاة).
- التجرد من التخطيط المفرط: الثقة بأن الله سيُصلح الأمور إذا أخلصت النية.
- العيش بسلام داخلي: نسيان الماضي والمستقبل، والاستمتاع بحاضرٍ قريبٍ من الله.

موجز ونصيحة عملية:

الرعاية الحقيقية هي أن تكون خادمًا لله في كل تفصيل:

- قبل كل عمل: اسأل: "هل هذا يُرضي الله أم أفعله لسببٍ آخر؟".
- اختر وقتًا يوميًّا: 5 دقائق لمراجعة نواياك (مثلًا بعد العصر).
- اقرأ الآية: ﴿وَاعْبُدْ رَبَّكَ حَتَّىٰ يَأْتِيَكَ الْيَقِينُ﴾ (الحجر: ٩٩) وتذكَّر: الإخلاص سرُّ القبول !

نص الشيخ الهروي

٢٢- باب المراقبة

قال الله عز وجل: (لَا يَرْقُبُونَ فِى مُؤْمِنٍ إِلًّا وَلَا ذِمَّةً)(التوبة:١٠).
المراقبة دوام ملاحظة المقصود.
وهي على ثلاث درجات:
الدرجة الأولى: مراقبة الحق في السير إليه على الدوام؛ بين تعظيم مذهل، ومداناة حاملة، وسرور باعث.
والدرجة الثانية: مراقبة نظر الحق إليك؛ برفض المعارضة، وبالإعراض عن الاعتراض، ونقض رعونة التعرض.
والدرجة الثالثة: مراقبة الأزل بمطالعة عين السبق استقبالا لعلم التوحيد، ومراقبة ظهور إشارات الأزل على أحايين الأبد، ومراقبة الخلاص من ربطة المراقبة.

النصّ مكتوباً بلغة مبسّطة

٢٢- باب المراقبة

قال الله تعالى: (لَا يَرْقُبُونَ فِى مُؤْمِنٍ إِلًّا وَلَا ذِمَّةً)(التوبة:١٠).

المراقبة هي استحضار حضور الله في كل لحظة.

وهي ثلاثة مستويات:

١ .مراقبة العامة (المبتدئين):
- الاستمرار في السير إلى الله: عبر:
- تعظيم الله في القلب (كالتفكر في عظمته أثناء الدعاء).
- الشعور بالتقصير دافعًا للاجتهاد (كزيادة الصدقات بعد تفويت صلاة).
- الفرح بالطاعة كأنها هديةٌ من الله (كالبكاء خشوعًا في الصلاة).

٢ .مراقبة الخاصة (المتقدمين):

- مراقبة نظر الله إليك: عبر:
  - ترك الاعتراض على قدر الله (كالقبول بالمرض دون تذمر).
  - تجنب الجدال العقيم الذي يُبعد عن الله.
  - التخلص من التصرفات الطائشة التي تُضعف الإيمان.

٣ .مراقبة خاصة الخاصة (الخواص):

- الارتقاء إلى أعلى المراتب:
  - رؤية حكمة الله في كل حدث (كالتفكر في خلق الكون).
  - ملاحظة علامات الأزل في الأبد (كربط الأحداث بحكمة إلهية).
  - التحرر حتى من شعور المراقبة (كأن تعيش مع الله دون وعيٍ بالذات).

موجز ونصيحة عملية:

المراقبة هي عين اليقظة الروحية:

- ابدأ بلحظات وعي: خصص دقيقتين كل ساعة لتذكُّر اسم الله "الرقيب".
- حارب التشتت: اكتب عبارة "الله يراني" على ورقة وضعها في مكانٍ بارز.
- اقرأ الآية: ﴿أَلَمْ يَعْلَمْ بِأَنَّ اللَّهَ يَرَىٰ﴾ (العلق: ١٤) وتذكَّر: الله معك في كل نفس !

نص الشيخ الهروي

٢٣- باب الحرمة

قال الله عز وجل: (وَمَن يُعَظِّمْ حُرُمَـٰتِ ٱللَّهِ فَهُوَ خَيْرٌ لَّهُۥ عِندَ رَبِّهِۦ)(الحج: ٣٠).
الحرمة هي التحرج عن المخالفات والمجاسرات.
وهي على ثلاث درجات:
الدرجة الأولى: تعظيم الأمر والنهي؛
لا خوفا من العقوبة، فيكون خصومة للنفس.
ولا طلبا لمثوبة، فيكون مسترقا للأجرة.
ولا شاهدا للجد، فيكون متدينا بالمراياة.
فإن هذه الأوصاف كلها شعب من عبادة النفس.
والدرجة الثانية: إجراء الخبر على ظاهره؛ وهو أن يبقى أعلام توحيد العامة الخبرية على ظواهرها؛
لا يتحمل البحث عنها تعسفا، ولا يتكلف لها تأويلا.
ولا يتجاوز ظواهرها تمثيلا، ولا يدعي عليها إدراكا أو توهما.
والدرجة الثالثة: صيانة الانبساط أن تشوبه جرأة، وصيانة السرور أن يداخله أمن، وصيانة الشهود أن يعارضه سبب.

النصّ مكتوباً بلغة مبسّطة

٢٣- باب الحرمة

قال الله تعالى: ﴿ وَمَن يُعَظِّمْ حُرُمَـٰتِ ٱللَّهِ فَهُوَ خَيْرٌ لَّهُۥ عِندَ رَبِّهِۦ﴾ (الحج: ٣٠).

الحرمة هي احترامٌ عميقٌ لحدود الله، وتجنُّب كل ما يُخالفها.
وهي ثلاثة أنواع:

١ .حرمة العامة (المبتدئين):
- تعظيم أوامر الله ونواهيه:
- ليس خوفًا من العقاب (كمن يصلي خوفًا من النار).

- ولا طمعًا في الثواب (كمن يتصدق طمعًا في الجنة).
- ولا ليراه الناس (كمن يصوم ليُمدح).

- الغاية هنا: الإخلاص لله وحده دون شوائب النفس.

٢ .حرمة الخاصة (المتقدمين):
- التعامل مع النصوص الشرعية ببساطة:

- عدم تحميل النصوص معانيَ معقدةً بعيدًا عن ظاهرها (كالتأويلات المتكلفة).
- الابتعاد عن التمثيل المبالغ فيه (كوصف الجنة والنار بتفاصيل لم يرد بها نص).
- عدم الادعاء بفهمٍ خاصٍ للدين دون دليل.

٣ .حرمة خاصة الخاصة (الخواص):
- حماية القلب من الانحرافات الخفية:

- عدم السماح للثقة بالنفس بأن تتحول إلى جرأةٍ على الله (كالتسويف في التوبة).
- عدم تحوُّل الفرح بالطاعة إلى أمانٍ زائفٍ من الحساب.
- عدم تشتيت الشهود الروحي (كالتفكير في الدنيا أثناء الذكر).

<u>موجز ونصيحة عملية:</u>

الحرمة الحقيقية هي احترام الله في السر والعلن:

- حاسِب نفسك: قبل أي عمل، اسأل: "هل هذا يُعظِّم حدود الله أم يتجاوزها؟".
- اقرأ النصوص ببساطة: لا تبحث عن تعقيداتٍ فلسفية في الآيات والأحاديث.
- دوِّن: اكتب ثلاثة أمورٍ تُقدِّسها في حياتك (كالصلاة في وقتها، بر الوالدين).
- التقديس ليس خوفًا، بل هو حبٌ واحترامٌ لصاحب الجلالة !

نص الشيخ الهروي

٢٤- باب الإخلاص

قال الله عز وجل: (ألا لله الدين الخالص)(الزمر:٣).
الإخلاص تصفية العمل من كل شوب.
وهو على ثلاث درجات:
الدرجة الأولى: إخراج رؤية العمل من العمل، والخلاص من طلب العوض على العمل، والنزول عن الرضى بالعمل.
والدرجة الثانية: الخجل من العمل مع بذل المجهود، وتوفير الجهد بالاحتماء من الشهود، ورؤية العمل في نور التوفيق من عين الجود.
والدرجة الثالثة: إخلاص العمل بالخلاص من العمل؛ تدعه يسير مسير العلم، وتسير أنت مشاهداً للحكم، حرا من رق الرسم.

النصّ مكتوباً بلغة مبسّطة

٢٤- باب الإخلاص

قال الله تعالى: ﴿أَلَا لِلَّهِ الدِّينُ الْخَالِصُ﴾ (الزمر: ٣).

الإخلاص (النية الخالصة لله) هو تنقية الأعمال من أي شائبةٍ غير الله.

وهو ثلاثة مستويات:

١ .إخلاص العامة (المبتدئين):

- عدم ربط العمل بنفسك: أداء العبادة دون التفكير في مدح الناس أو الفخر بها.
- عدم انتظار مقابل: الصدقة دون تمني الشكر أو الدعاء لك.
- عدم الرضا عن العمل: اعتبار الطاعة هبةً من الله، لا إنجازًا شخصيًّا.

٢ .إخلاص الخاصة (المتقدمين):

- الخجل من العمل: الشعور بالتقصير حتى مع بذل الجهد (كمن يصوم ويقول: "لعل الله يتقبل").
- إخفاء العمل: فعل الخير سرًّا (كإطعام محتاج دون إخبار أحد).
- رؤية التوفيق من الله: الاعتراف أن نجاح العمل بفضل الله، لا بقدراتك.

٣ .إخلاص خاصة الخاصة (الخواص):

- التحرر من رقابة الذات: العبادة كأنها جزء من طبيعتك (كالتنفس لا تفكر فيه!).
- العيش كمشاهدٍ لحكم الله: ترك الأعمال تسير بقدرة الله، دون تدخل الأنا.
- التجرد من الصورة الروحية: عدم الادعاء بالتقوى حتى لو كنتَ تفعل الخير دائمًا.

<u>موجز ونصيحة عملية:</u>

الإخلاص هو سرُّ قبول الأعمال:

- قبل أي عمل: اسأل: "لو لم يرني أحد، هل سأفعله بنفس الجودة؟".
- اختر عملًا سريًّا: مثل مساعدة جارٍ دون أن يعلم.
- اقرأ الآية: ﴿وَمَا أُمِرُوا إِلَّا لِيَعْبُدُوا اللَّهَ مُخْلِصِينَ﴾ (البينة: ٥) وتذكَّر: الله يرى ما تخفيه القلوب !

نص الشيخ الهروي

٢٥- باب التهذيب

قال الله عز وجل: (فَلَمَّآ أَفَلَ قَالَ لَآ أُحِبُّ ٱلۡـَٔافِلِينَ)(الأنعام:٧٦).
التهذيب محنة أهل البدايات، وهو شريعة من شرائع الرياضة.
وهو على ثلاث درجات:
الدرجة الأولى: تهذيب الخدمة؛ أن لا تخالجها جهالة، ولا تسوقها عادة، ولا تقف عندها همة.
والدرجة الثانية: تهذيب الحال؛ وهو أن لا يجمح الحال إلى علم، ولا يخضع لرسم، ولا يلتفت إلى حظ.
والدرجة الثالثة: تهذيب القصد؛ وهو تصفيته من ذل الإكراه، وتحفظه من مرض الفتور، ونصرته على منازعات العلم.

النصّ مكتوباً بلغة مبسّطة

٢٥- باب التهذيب

قال الله تعالى: ﴿ فَلَمَّآ أَفَلَ قَالَ لَآ أُحِبُّ ٱلۡـَٔافِلِينَ ﴾ (الأنعام: ٧٦).

التهذيب هو تدريب النفس على التخلص من العادات السيئة والانحرافات.

وهو ثلاثة أنواع:

١ .تهذيب العبادات:

- تحسين جودة العبادة:

- عدم أدائها بجهل (كالصلاة دون فهم معاني الأذكار).
- عدم تحويلها إلى روتين ممل (كالتسبيح بلا تركيز).
- عدم التوقف عن تطويرها (كزيادة الخشوع في الصلاة).

٢ .تهذيب الحالة القلبية:
- ضبط المشاعر الروحية:

- عدم تحوُّل الفرح بالطاعة إلى كبرياء (كالتفاخر بالصيام).
- عدم التقيُّد بالشكليات (كالتركيز على شكل الصلاة دون جوهرها).
- عدم الانشغال بمصالح شخصية أثناء العبادة (كالدعاء للنجاح الدنيوي فقط).

٣ .تهذيب النوايا:
- تنقية القصد الداخلي:

- التخلص من الإجبار في الطاعة (كالصدقة بدافع الضغط الاجتماعي).
- الحماية من الكسل الروحي (كترك الوِرد اليومي لانشغال بسيط).
- تجنُّب الجدالات العقيمة التي تُضعف الإيمان (كالنقاشات حول أمور غيبية بلا فائدة).

موجز ونصيحة عملية:

التهذيب هو رحلة تحويل العادات إلى عبادة:

- قيم نفسك يوميًّا: اسأل: "هل تحسَّنت عباداتي اليوم أم بقيت على حالها؟".
- حوِّل عادةً واحدة: مثل استبدال التصفح العشوائي في الانترنت بقراءة آيتين قبل النوم.
- اقرأ الآية ﴿ قَدْ أَفْلَحَ مَن زَكَّىٰهَا ﴾ (الشمس: ٩) وتذكَّر: النجاح في تزكية النفس هو أعظم الفلاح !

نص الشيخ الهروي

٢٦- باب الاستقامة

قال الله عز وجل: (فاستقيموا إليه)(فصلت:٦).
قوله عز وجل (إليه) إشارة إلى عين التفريد.
والاستقامة روح تحيى بها الأحوال، كما تربو للعامة عليها الأعمال.
وهي برزخ بين أوهاد التفرق وروابي الجمع.
وهي على ثلاث درجات:
الدرجة الأولى: الاستقامة على الاجتهاد في الاقتصاد، لا عادياً رسم العلم، ولا متجوزا حد الإخلاص، ولا مخالفا نهج السنة.
والدرجة الثانية: استقامة الأحوال؛ وهي شهود الحقيقة لا كسباً، ورفض الدعوى لا علماً، والبقاء مع نور اليقظة لا تحفظاً.
والدرجة الثالثة: استقامة بترك رؤية الاستقامة، وبالغيبة عن تطلب الاستقامة، بشهود إقامة الحق وتقويمه عز اسمه.

النصّ مكتوباً بلغة مبسّطة

٢٦- باب الاستقامة

قال الله تعالى: ﴿فَاسْتَقِيمُوا إِلَيْهِ﴾ (فصلت: ٦).

الاستقامة هي الثبات على طريق الله دون انحراف.

الاستقامة روحٌ تُحيي الحالات القلبية، فكما تنمو أعمال العامة الظاهرة، تنمو بها الأحوال الباطنة. وهي جسرٌ بين وديان التشتت (الانحرافات) وروابي القرب من الله (الاتصال الروحي الآمن).

وهي ثلاثة أنواع:

١ .استقامة المبتدئين (الاعتدال في العبادة):
- التزام الاعتدال:

- لا تُبالغ في العبادات (كصيام أيام متتالية دون قدرة).
- لا تتجاوز حدود الإخلاص (كطلب مدح الناس).
- التزم بالسنة النبوية دون ابتداع (كالصلاة كما علّمنا النبي صلى الله عليه وسلم).

٢ .استقامة المتقدمين (سلامة القلب):
- التجرد من الادعاءات:

- اشهد الحقائق الإيمانية بقلب نقي (كأن تعبد الله كأنك تراه).
- ارفض التظاهر بالتقوى (كعدم الادعاء بمعرفة غيبية).
- ابقَ مع نور اليقظة الداخلية (راقب أفكارك السلبية واقطعها).

٣ .استقامة الخواص (التجرد الكامل):
- التحرر من رؤية الذات:

- انسَ أنك "مستقيم" (عِشْ لله دون وعي بذاتك).
- توقف عن السعي وراء الشعور بالكمال (فالكمال لله وحده).
- اشهد أن الله هو المُقيم لك (التوكل المطلق عليه).

<u>موجز ونصيحة عملية:</u>
الاستقامة ليست كمالًا، بل ثباتٌ على المبدأ:

- ابدأ يومك بدعاء: "اللهم ثبت قلبي على دينك".
- التزم بعادة صغيرة: حافظ على ركعتي الضحى يوميًّا.
- اقرأ الآية: ﴿ إِنَّ ٱلَّذِينَ قَالُواْ رَبُّنَا ٱللَّهُ ثُمَّ ٱسْتَقَٰمُواْ﴾ (فصلت: ٣٠) وفكِّر: الثواب العظيم للثابتين!

نص الشيخ الهروي

٢٧- باب التوكل

قال الله عز وجل: (وعلى الله فتوكلوا إن كنتم مؤمنين)(المائدة:٢٣).
التوكل كِلَةُ الأمر كُلّه إلى مالكه، والتعويل على وكالته.
وهو من أصعب منازل العامة عليهم، وأوهى السبل عند الخاصة؛ لأن الحق قد وكل الأمور كلها إلى نفسه، وأيْأسَ العالم من ملك شيء منها.
وهو على ثلاث درجات، كلها تسير مسير العامة:
الدرجة الأولى: التوكل مع الطلب، ومعاطاة السبب؛ على نية شغل النفس، ونفع الخلق، وترك الدعوى.
والدرجة الثانية: التوكل مع إسقاط الطلب، وغض العين عن السبب؛ اجتهادا في تصحيح التوكل، وقمع تشرف النفس، وتفرغاً إلى حفظ الواجبات.
والدرجة الثالثة: التوكل مع معرفة التوكل، النازعة إلى الخلاص من علة التوكل؛ وهو أن يعلم أن ملكه الحق تعالى للأشياء ملكة عزة لا يشاركه فيها مشارك فيكل شركته إليه.
فإن من ضرورة العبودية أن يعلم العبد أن الحق هو مالك الأشياء وحده.

النصّ مكتوباً بلغة مبسّطة

٢٧- باب التوكل

قال الله عز وجل: ﴿وَعَلَى اللَّهِ فَتَوَكَّلُوا إِنْ كُنْتُمْ مُؤْمِنِينَ﴾ (المائدة: ٢٣).

التوكل هو إيكالُ كلِّ الأمور إلى الله مالكها الحقيقي، والاعتماد الكامل على تدبيره وحكمته.

هذا الباب صعبٌ على عامة الناس، لأنه يتطلب تسليمًا تامًّا، بينما يرى المخلصون (الخاصة) أن التوكل سهلٌ؛ لأن الله وحده هو المتحكم في الكون، ولا قدرة لأحدٍ غيره على التصرف في أمرٍ من الأمور.

والتوكل ثلاث درجات، جميعها تصلح لعامة الناس:

الدرجة الأولى:
التوكل مع السعي والحرص على الأسباب الظاهرة (كالعمل والعلاج)، لكن بنية إشغال النفس وإفادة الآخرين، دون ادعاء أن السعي هو سبب النجاح.

الدرجة الثانية:
التوكل مع ترك التعلق بالطلب (أي عدم التوسل إلى الله بخشية)، وعدم الالتفات للأسباب؛ لتدريب النفس على التسليم، وتفريغ القلب للعبادة وواجبات الإيمان.

الدرجة الثالثة:
التوكل مع اليقين بأن الله هو المالك الحقيقي لكل شيء، فلا يحتاج العبد حتى إلى "التفكير" في التوكل؛ لأنه يعلم أن الله مُدبِّرٌ لا يُشارِكُه أحد، فيستريح قلبه من هَمِّ التدبير.

فالعبودية الحقيقية تعني إدراك أن الله هو المُتَصَرِّفُ الوحيد في الخلق، وأن البشر لا يملكون شيئًا.

موجز المعاني ونصيحة عملية:

- التوكل ليس مجرد كلمة، بل هو ثقةٌ تُغَذِّيها اليقين بأن الله كافٍ لعبده.
- ابدأ بتدريب نفسك على التسليم في المواقف الصغيرة: كأن تقول عند الخروج من البيت: "حسبي الله"، أو تترك القلق عند فقدان فرصةٍ ظاهرًا. تذكَّر قول الله: ﴿فَإِذَا عَزَمْتَ فَتَوَكَّلْ عَلَى اللَّهِ﴾ (آل عمران: ١٥٩).
- لا تيأس إن وجدت نفسك تتعلق بالأسباب؛ الروحُ تحتاج إلى تدريب.
- اقرأ القرآن بتأمل، خاصة آيات التوكل مثل: ﴿وَمَنْ يَتَوَكَّلْ عَلَى اللَّهِ فَهُوَ حَسْبُهُ﴾ (الطلاق: ٣)، وسلِّم قلبك لله خطوةً خطوةً.

-

نص الشيخ الهروي

٢٨- باب التفويض

قال الله عز وجل حاكيا عن مؤمن آل فرعون: (وأفوض أمري إلى الله إن الله بصير بالعباد)(غافر:٤٤).

التفويض ألطف إشارة وأوسع معنى من التوكل؛ فإن التوكل بعد وقوع السبب، والتفويض قبل وقوعه وبعده، وهو عين الاستسلام، والتوكل شعبة منه.

وهو على ثلاث درجات:

الدرجة الأولى: أن تعلم أن العبد لا يملك قبل عمله استطاعة؛ فلا يأمن من مكر، ولا ييأس من معونة، ولا يعول على نية.

والدرجة الثانية: معاينة الاضطرار؛ فلا ترى عملا منجيا، ولا ذنبا مهلكا، ولا سببا حاملاً.

والدرجة الثالثة: شهودك انفراد الحق؛ بملك الحركة والسكون، والقبض والبسط، ومعرفته بتصريف التفرقة والجمع.

النصّ مكتوباً بلغة مبسّطة

٢٨- باب التفويض

قال الله عز وجل: ﴿وَأُفَوِّضُ أَمْرِي إِلَى اللَّهِ إِنَّ اللَّهَ بَصِيرٌ بِالْعِبَادِ﴾ (غافر: ٤٤).

التفويض هو تسليمُ الأمر كُلِّه لله بلا تردد، وهو أرقى من التوكل؛ لأن التوكل يَتبع الأسباب الظاهرة، أما التفويض فهو استسلامٌ مطلقٌ قبل الأسباب وبعدها، وهو جوهرُ الاستقامة الروحية.

وله ثلاث درجات :

الدرجة الأولى:

أن تعترف أنك لا تملك حقيقةً قدرةً على ضمان نتائج أعمالك، فلا تَغترَّ بجهودك (كأن تظن أن عملك يحميك من قَدَر الله)، ولا تَقنَطْ من رحمته إن فشلت، ولا تَعتمدْ على مجرد نواياك.

الدرجة الثانية:
أن تدرك عجزك الكامل، فلا ترى عملاً يُنجيك (كأن تظن الصلاة تُغني عن تقوى القلب)، ولا ذنبًا يُهلكك (لأن المغفرة بيد الله)، ولا سبَبًا يَحملك على الطمع في النتائج.

الدرجة الثالثة:
أن تشهدَ بقلبك أن الله وحده هو مُدبِّرُ حالات "التفرقة" و"الجمع" الروحية؛
فـ"التفرقة" هي شعورك بالبُعد عن الله (كالحيرة أو الضيق)، و"الجمع" هي ذوقك القرب منه (كالطمأنينة)، وهو الذي يُقلِّبك بينهما لِيُصفِّي إيمانك.

<u>موجز المعاني ونصيحة عملية:</u>

- التفويض هو أن تَخلعَ يدَك من التصرف، وتَرى الله هو الفاعل الحقيقي في كل شيء.
- ابدأ يومك بقول: "حسبي الله ونعم الوكيل"، وتأمَّل قول الله: ﴿وَمَا تَشَاءُونَ إِلَّا أَنْ يَشَاءَ اللَّهُ﴾ (الإنسان: ٣٠).
- إذا مررتَ بضيقٍ روحي (تفرقة)، فاعلم أنها مرحلةٌ لتنقية قلبك، وإذا ذقتَ سكينةً (جمع)، فاعلم أنها هبةٌ منه.
- اقرأ سورة الفاتحة بتدبُّرٍ، وكرِّر: "إياك نعبد وإياك نستعين"، وثق أن الله يُديرُ أحوالك بحكمةٍ لا تُدركها.

نص الشيخ الهروي

٢٩- باب الثقة

قال الله عز وجل: (فإذا خفت عليه فألقيه في اليم)(القصص:٧).
الثقة سواد عين التوكل، ونقطة دائرة التفويض وسويداء قلب التسليم
وهي على ثلاث درجات:
الدرجة الأولى درجة الإياس؛ وهو إياس العبد من مقاواة الأحكام، ليقعد عن منازعة الأقسام، وليتخلص من قحة الإقدام.
والدرجة الثانية: درجة الأمن؛ وهو أمن العبد من فوت المقدور، وانتقاص المسطور؛ فيظفر بروح الرضى، وإلا فبغنى اليقين، وإلا فبظلف الصبر.
والدرجة الثالثة: معاينة أولية الحق؛ ليتخلص من محن القصود، وتكاليف الحمايات، والتعريج على مدارج الوسائل.

النصّ مكتوباً بلغة مبسّطة

٢٩- باب الثقة

قال الله عز وجل: ﴿فَإِذَا خِفْتِ عَلَيْهِ فَأَلْقِيهِ فِي الْيَمِّ﴾ (القصص: ٧).

الثقة هي روح التوكل، وأساس التفويض، وجوهر التسليم لله.
فهي ليست مجرد طمأنينة، بل يقينٌ بأن ما قَدَّره الله هو الخير، حتى لو خَفِيَ الحكمة.

وللثقة ثلاث درجات:

الدرجة الأولى (اليأس من المقاومة):
أن تيأسَ من قدرتك على تغيير قضاء الله، فتُوقِفَ الجدال مع الأقدار، وتتخلَّص من تهور التصرفات التي تُعارض حكمته.

الدرجة الثانية (الأمان من الخوف):
أن تشعرَ بأمانٍ تامٍ من ضياع ما كتبه الله لك، فإما أن تنالَ راحة الرضا، أو غنى اليقين بأن الله كافيك، أو صبرًا ثابتًا كالجبل.

الدرجة الثالثة (مشاهدة تدبير الله):
أن ترى بعين القلب أن الله هو المدبر الأول لكل شيء، فتَخرُجَ من حيرة الخطط البشرية، ولا تتعب نفسك بالاعتماد على الوسائل، بل تترك الأمر له وحده.

<u>موجز المعاني ونصيحة عملية:</u>

- الثقة الحقيقية هي أن تعيشَ وكأنك رأيتَ يدَ الله تعمل في كل تفصيل.
- ابدأ بتطبيقها في مواقف بسيطة: إذا شعرت بالقلق على رزقٍ أو صحةٍ، ردد: "حسبي الله لا إله إلا هو عليه توكلت"، وتأمّل قوله تعالى: ﴿وَمَن يَتَوَكَّلْ عَلَى اللَّهِ فَهُوَ حَسْبُهُ﴾ (الطلاق: ٣).
- لا تُرهق نفسك بالخطط المبالغ فيها؛ فالله يقول: ﴿وَكَفَى بِاللَّهِ وَكِيلًا﴾ (النساء: ٨١).
- اقرأ سورة القصص بتدبُّر، وتذكَّر أن أم موسى ألقت بابنها في اليم بثقةٍ عمياء، فحفظه الله. الثقةُ تحتاج إلى تمرينٍ يومي، فاجعل قلبك مرسىً لإيمانك.

نص الشيخ الهروي

٣٠- باب التسليم

قال الله عز وجل: (فلا وربك لا يؤمنون حتى يحكموك فيما شجر بينهم ثم لا يجدوا في أنفسهم حرجا مما قضيت ويسلموا تسليماً)(النساء:٦٥).
وفي التسليم والثقة والتفويض ما في التوكل من الاعتلال، وهو من أعلى درجات سبيل العامة.
وهو على ثلاث درجات:
الدرجة الأولى: تسليم ما يزاحم العقول مما يشق على الأوهام من الغيب، والإذعان لما يغالب القياس من سير الدول والقسم، والإجابة لما يفزع المريد من ركوب الأحوال.
والدرجة الثانية: تسليم العلم إلى الحال، والقصد إلى الكشف، والرسم إلى الحقيقة.
والدرجة الثالثة: تسليم ما دون الحق إلى الحق، مع السلامة من رؤية التسليم، بمعاينة تسليم الحق إياك إليه.

النصّ مكتوباً بلغة مبسّطة

٣٠- باب التسليم

قال الله عز وجل: ﴿فَلَا وَرَبِّكَ لَا يُؤْمِنُونَ حَتَّى يُحَكِّمُوكَ فِيمَا شَجَرَ بَيْنَهُمْ ثُمَّ لَا يَجِدُوا فِي أَنْفُسِهِمْ حَرَجًا مِمَّا قَضَيْتَ وَيُسَلِّمُوا تَسْلِيمًا﴾ (النساء: ٦٥).

التسليم هو ذروة الاستجابة لله، وهو يشترك مع الثقة والتفويض في جوهر الاعتماد على الله، لكنه أعلى درجات السالكين من العامة.

وله ثلاث مراحل:

الدرجة الأولى:
قبول ما يُعارض العقل البشري (كأمور الغيب)، والخضوع للأقدار التي لا تُفسَّر بالمنطق (كتقلبات الزمن)، والاستجابة للتوجيهات الروحية حتى لو كانت مُخيفة (كالدعوة للتضحية).

الدرجة الثانية:
التخلي عن الاعتماد على المعرفة النظرية لصالح الاختبار القلبي (كاستبدال الجدل بالخشوع)، وترك التمسك بالشكليات الدينية لصالح الحقائق الروحية (كالانتقال من الصورة إلى الجوهر).

الدرجة الثالثة:
أن تذوب إرادتك في إرادة الله، فلا ترى حتى أنك "مُسَلِّم"، لأنك تشهد أن الله هو الذي سلَّمك إليه، فأنت مُجرد مرآةٍ لإرادته.

<u>موجز المعاني ونصيحة عملية:</u>
التسليم هو أن ترميَ وراءك كل "لماذا؟" و"كيف؟".

- ابدأ بتدريب نفسك على قَبول الأقدار المؤلمة بقلبٍ هادئ، وتأمَّل قول الله: ﴿وَمَا كَانَ لِمُؤْمِنٍ وَلَا مُؤْمِنَةٍ إِذَا قَضَى اللَّهُ وَرَسُولُهُ أَمْرًا أَنْ يَكُونَ لَهُمُ الْخِيَرَةُ مِنْ أَمْرِهِمْ﴾ (الأحزاب: ٣٦).
- إذا واجهتك محنةٌ لا تُحتمل، تذكَّر قصة النبي يونس في بطن الحوت، حين نادى في الظلمات: ﴿لَّا إِلَـٰهَ إِلَّا أَنتَ سُبْحَانَكَ إِنِّي كُنتُ مِنَ الظَّالِمِينَ﴾ (الأنبياء: ٨٧)، فاستجاب الله له وأنقذه.
- التسليم يحتاج إلى تمرينٍ يومي: اختم صلاتك بقول: "ربِّ لا تكلني إلى نفسي طرفة عين"، وثق أن الله يكتب لك الخير حيثما اتجهت.

٤- قسم الأخلاق

وأما قسم الأخلاق فهو عشرة أبواب وهي الصبر والرضى والشكر والحياء والصدق والإيثار والخلق والتواضع والفتوة والانبساط.

نص الشيخ الهروي

٣١- باب الصبر

قال الله عز وجل: (واصبر وما صبرك إلا بالله)(النحل:١٢٧).
الصبر حبس النفس على جزع كامن عن الشكوى. وهو أيضا من أصعب المنازل على العامة، وأوحشها في طريق المحبة، وأنكرها في طريق التوحيد. وهو على ثلاث درجات:
الدرجة الأولى: الصبر عن المعصية بمطالعة الوعيد؛ إبقاء على الإيمان، وحذرا من الجزاء. وأحسن منها الصبر عن المعصية حياء.
والدرجة الثانية: الصبر على الطاعة؛ بالمحافظة عليها دواماً، وبرعايتها إخلاصاً، وبتحسينها علماً.
والدرجة الثالثة: الصبر في البلاء؛ بملاحظة حسن الجزاء، وانتظار روح الفرج، وتهوين البلية بعد أيادي المنن، وتذكر سوالف النعم.
وفي هذه الدرجات الثلاث من الصبر نزلت (اصبروا) يعني في البلاء و(صابروا) يعني عن المعصية (ورابطوا)(الأنعام:٢٠٠)، يعني على الطاعة.
وأضعف الصبر: الصبر لله، وهو صبر العامة.
وفوقه الصبر بالله: وهو صبر المريد.
وفوقهما الصبر على الله: وهو صبر السالك.

النصّ مكتوباً بلغة مبسّطة

٣١- باب الصبر

قال الله عز وجل: ﴿وَاصْبِرْ وَمَا صَبْرُكَ إِلَّا بِاللَّهِ﴾ (النحل: ١٢٧).

الصبر هو ضبطُ النفس عن الشكوى رغم الألم الداخلي. وهو من أصعب المراحل على عامة الناس، ويبدو كطريقٍ موحشٍ في الطريق الى المحبة والتوحيد.
وله ثلاث درجات:

<u>الدرجة الأولى (الصبر عن المعصية):</u>
الامتناع عن الذنوب خوفًا من عقاب الله، أو حياءً منه. هذا الصبر يحمي الإيمان ويُبقي على سلامة القلب.

الدرجة الثانية (الصبر على الطاعة):

المثابرة على العبادات بانتظام (كالصلاة والصوم)، مع إخلاص النية، وتعلُّم تفاصيلها لتحسين أدائها.

الدرجة الثالثة (الصبر في البلاء):

تقبُّل الابتلاءات بثلاثة مفاتيح:

- تذكُّر ثواب الصبر العظيم.
- انتظار فرج الله مع اليقين بقدومه.
- مقارنة البلاء بالنعم السابقة لتهوين المصيبة.

وفي القرآن إشارة لهذه الدرجات:

"اصبروا" (في البلاء)

"صابروا" (عن المعصية)

"رابطوا" (على الطاعة)   (الأنعام:٢٠٠)

مستويات الصبر:

-الصبر لله (العامة): الصبر خوفًا من العقاب أو طمعًا في الثواب.

-الصبر بالله (المريدون): الصبر باستعانة بقوة الله ورحمته.

-الصبر على الله (السالكون): الصبر بمعرفة أن البلاء نفسه نعمةٌ من الله لترقية الروح.

موجز المعاني ونصيحة عملية:

الصبر ليس مجرد "انتظار"، بل هو مدرسةٌ لتربية الإيمان. ابدأ بتدريب نفسك على:

- الدرجة الأولى: تجنُّب ذنبٍ واحدٍ يوميًا (كالغيبة) مع تذكُّر عذاب النار.
- الدرجة الثانية: أَدِّ صلاة الفجر بانتظام، وحسِّن وضوءك أو خشوعك.
- الدرجة الثالثة: إذا أصابك همٌّ، اكتب قائمةً بنعم الله عليك، وتأمَّل قوله: ﴿إِنَّ مَعَ الْعُسْرِ يُسْرًا﴾ (الشرح: ٦).

الصبر يحتاج إلى مراقبة القلب: قل دائمًا: "اللهم أعني على ذكرك وشكرك وحسن عبادتك".

نص الشيخ الهروي

٣٢- باب الرضى

قال الله عز وجل: (إرجعي إلى ربك راضية مرضية)(الفجر:٢٨).
لم يدع في هذه الآية للمتسخط إليه سبيلا، وشرط للقاصد الدخول في الرضى.
والرضى اسم للوقوف الصادق حيث ما وقف العبد، لا يلتمس متقدما ولا متأخرا، ولا يستزيد مزيدا، ولا يستبدل حالا.
وهو من أوائل مسالك أهل الخصوص، وأشقها على العامة.
وهو على ثلاث درجات:
الدرجة الأولى: رضى العامة؛ وهو الرضى بالله ربّاً، بسخط عبادة ما دونه. وهذا قطب رحى الإسلام، وهو يطهر من الشرك الأكبر.
وهو يصح بثلاث شرائط: أن يكون الله عز وجل أحب الأشياء إلى العبد، وأولى الأشياء بالتعظيم، وأحق الأشياء بالطاعة.
والدرجة الثانية: الرضى عن الله عز وجل. وبهذا الرضى نطقت آيات التنزيل؛ وهو الرضى عنه في كل ما قضى، وهذا من أوائل مسالك أهل الخصوص.
ويصح بثلاث شرائط: باستواء الحالات عند العبد، وبسقوط الخصومة مع الخلق، وبالخلاص من المسألة والإلحاح.
والدرجة الثالثة: الرضى برضى الله. فلا يرى العبد لنفسه سخطا ولا رضى، فيبعثه على ترك التحكم وحسم الاختيار، وإسقاط التمييز ولو أدخل النار.

النصّ مكتوباً بلغة مبسّطة

٣٢- باب الرضى

قال الله عز وجل: ﴿ارْجِعِي إِلَى رَبِّكِ رَاضِيَةً مَرْضِيَّةً﴾ (الفجر: ٢٨).

الرضى هو القناعة الكاملة بقضاء الله دون تذمر أو طلب تغيير، وهو طريقٌ مُغلق أمام الشكوى، وشرطٌ أساسي للسالكين نحو الله.
الرضى ثلاث درجات:

الدرجة الأولى (رضى العامة):
- الرضا بالله ربًّا واحدًا، ورفض عبادة غيره.

- يشترط لتحقيقه:
  - أن يكون الله أحبَّ شيءٍ إلى قلبك.
  - أن تُعظِّمه فوق كل شيء.
  - أن تُطيعه قبل كل شيء.
- هذا الرضى يُطهِّر القلب من الشرك الأكبر (عبادة غير الله).

الدرجة الثانية (الرضى عن الله):

- الرضا بكل ما قدَّره الله، سواءً كان خيرًا أو شرًا في ظاهره.
- يشترط لتحقيقه:
  - التساوي عندك بين النعم والابتلاءات.
  - عدم الخصام مع الناس على أقدار الله.
  - التوقف عن طلب تغيير القضاء.
- هذا الرضى هو بداية طريق الخواص (المقرَّبين).

الدرجة الثالثة (الرضى برضى الله):

- أن تَذوب إرادتك في إرادة الله، فلا تطلب ما يرضيك، بل ما يرضيه.
- هنا، لا تهتمُّ حتى بدخول الجنة أو النار؛ لأن رضى الله هو غايتك الوحيدة.

موجز المعاني ونصيحة عملية:

الرضى ليس استسلامًا سلبيًا، بل هو قوةُ قلبٍ تُريك الجمال في كل قضاء. ابدأ بتدريب نفسك على:

-الدرجة الأولى: كرِّر يوميًا: "رضيتُ بالله ربًا، وبالإسلام دينًا"، وتأمَّل قول الله: ﴿وَمَنْ يُسْلِمْ وَجْهَهُ إِلَى اللَّهِ وَهُوَ مُحْسِنٌ فَقَدِ اسْتَمْسَكَ بِالْعُرْوَةِ الْوُثْقَى﴾ (لقمان: ٢٢).

-الدرجة الثانية: إذا أصابك مكروه، قل: "الحمد لله على كل حال"، واقرأ قصة النبي أيوب الذي قال: ﴿ أَنِّي مَسَّنِيَ ٱلضُّرُّ وَأَنتَ أَرۡحَمُ ٱلرَّٰحِمِينَ ﴾ (الأنبياء: ٨٣).

-الدرجة الثالثة: خصص وقتًا يوميًا لتلاوة آية ﴿رَضِيَ اللَّهُ عَنْهُمْ وَرَضُوا عَنْهُ﴾ (المائدة: ١١٩)، وتأمل معنى الرضى المتبادل بينك وبين الله. اسأل نفسك: "هل أفعالي تُرضي الله؟". حوِّلْ هذا التساؤل إلى مرآةٍ تُصحِّح بها نواياك قبل أعمالك.

نص الشيخ الهروي

٣٣- باب الشكر

قال الله عز وجل: (وقليل من عبادي الشكور)(سبأ:١٣).
الشكر اسم لمعرفة النعمة لأنها السبيل إلى معرفة المنعم، ولهذا المعنى سمي الله تعالى الإسلام والإيمان في القرآن شكراً.
ومعاني الشكر ثلاثة أشياء: معرفة النعمة، ثم قبول النعمة، ثم الثناء بها.
وهو أيضا من سبل العامة. وهو على ثلاث درجات:
الدرجة الأولى: الشكر في المحاب؛ وهذا شكر شاركت المسلمين فيه اليهود والنصارى والمجوس، ومن سعة بر البارئ أنه عده شكرا ووعد عليه الزيادة وأوجب له المثوبة.
والدرجة الثانية: الشكر في المكاره؛ وهذا ممن يستوى عنده الحالات إظهار الرضى، وممن يميز بين الأحوال كظم الشكوى ورعاية الأدب وسلوك مسلك العلم، وهذا الشاكر أول من يدعى إلى الجنة.
والدرجة الثالثة: أن لا يشهد العبد إلا المنعم. فإذا شهد المنعم عبودة استعظم منه النعمة، وإذا شهده حبا استحلى منه الشدة، وإذا شهده تفريدا لم يشهد منه شدة ولا نعمة.

النصّ مكتوباً بلغة مبسّطة

٣٣- باب الشكر

قال الله عز وجل: ﴿وَقَلِيلٌ مِنْ عِبَادِيَ الشَّكُورُ﴾ (سَبَأ: ١٣).

الشكر هو معرفةُ النعمة واعترافٌ بأنها هِبةٌ من الله، وهو طريقٌ لمعرفة المُنعِم سبحانه.

وله ثلاثة أركان:
معرفة النعمة: إدراك أن كل ما تملكه هو مِن فضل الله.
قبول النعمة: استخدامها في طاعة الله.
الثناء بها: حمد الله عليها بالقلب واللسان والعمل.

وهو ثلاثة أنواع:

الدرجة الأولى (الشكر في النعم):

- شكر الله على الخيرات الظاهرة (كالصحة والمال).
- يشترك فيه حتى غير المسلمين، والله يقبله ويُضاعف ثوابه.

الدرجة الثانية (الشكر في المصائب):

- شكر الله على الابتلاءات بتسليم القلب وعدم الشكوى.
- هنا يظهر المؤمنُ رضاه بقضاء الله، ويكتم ألمه حفاظًا على أدب العبودية.
- هؤلاء الشاكرون هم أول مَن يُدعى إلى الجنة.

الدرجة الثالثة (الشكر بالقلب لا بالحدث):

- أن ترى الله هو المُنعِم الحقيقي في كل حال، فلا تنشغل بالنعمة أو المصيبة، بل بمن وهبها.
- هنا يذوب قلبك في محبة الله، فلا فرق عندك بين الرخاء والشدّة؛ لأن كِلَيْهما مِن حكمته.

<u>موجز المعاني ونصيحة عملية:</u>

الشكر الحقيقي هو أن ترى يدَ الله في كل شيء. ابدأ يومك بـ "الحمد لله الذي بنعمته تتم الصالحات"، وخُذْ خطواتٍ عملية:

- الدرجة الأولى: اكتب ثلاث نِعَمٍ جديدةٍ تشكر الله عليها كل يوم.
- الدرجة الثانية: إذا أصابك همٌّ، قل: "الحمد لله على كل حال"، وتأمّل قول الله: ﴿لَئِنْ شَكَرْتُمْ لَأَزِيدَنَّكُمْ﴾ (إبراهيم: ٧).
- الدرجة الثالثة: حوِّلْ نظرتك للأحداث؛ فبدلًا من قول "لماذا أصابني هذا؟"، قل: "ما الحكمة التي يريدها الله مني هنا؟".

نص الشيخ الهروي

٣٤- باب الحياء

قال عز وجل: (ألم يعلم بأن الله يرى)(العلق:١٤).
الحياء من أوائل مدارج أهل الخصوص؛ يتولد من تعظيم منوط بود.
وهو على ثلاث درجات:
الدرجة الأولى: حياء يتولد من علم العبد بنظر الحق إليه؛ فيجذبه إلى تحمل المجاهدة، ويحمله على استقباح الجناية، ويسكته عن الشكوى.
والدرجة الثانية: حياء يتولد من النظر في علم القرب؛ فيدعوه إلى ركوب المحبة، ويربطه بروح الأنس، ويكره إليه ملابسة الخلق.
والدرجة الثالثة: حياء يتولد من شهود الحضرة؛ وهي التي تشوبها هيبة، ولا تقاويها تفرقة، ولا يوقف لها على غاية.

النصّ مكتوباً بلغة مبسّطة

٣٤- باب الحياء

قال الله عز وجل: ﴿أَلَمْ يَعْلَمْ بِأَنَّ اللَّهَ يَرَى﴾ (العلق: ١٤).

الحياء هو خُلقٌ يمنعك من فعل القبيح خوفًا من نظرة الله إليك، وهو مفتاحُ طريق المقرَّبين إلى الله.

الحياء ثلاث درجات:

الدرجة الأولى (حياء المراقبة):

- ينشأ من إدراكك أن الله يراك دائمًا، فيدفعك لتجنب المعاصي، ويُقبّحُ في عينيك فعلَ الذنب، ويُسكِتُ لسانك عن الشكوى.

الدرجة الثانية (حياء القرب):

- ينشأ من شعورك بصلتك الوثيقة بالله، فيجعلك تُفضِّلُ عزلتَك مع حبّهِ على مخالطة الناس، ويملأ قلبك طمأنينةً وأنسًا به.

الدرجة الثالثة (حياء الشهود):

- ينشأ من إحساسك بالهيبة الإلهية في حضور الله، فلا تستطيع وصفه، ولا تقوى على مفارقته، ولا تعرف له نهايةً.

موجز المعاني ونصيحة عملية:

الحياءُ هو جدارٌ واقٍ بينك وبين المعاصي. ابدأ بتدريب نفسك:

- الدرجة الأولى: قُلْ قبل أي فعل: "الله يراني"، وتأمَّل قول الله: ﴿إِنَّ اللَّهَ كَانَ عَلَيْكُمْ رَقِيبًا﴾ (النساء: ١).
- الدرجة الثانية: خصص وقتًا يوميًّا للخلوة مع الله (كصلاة الضحى أو الدعاء)، وحاول أن تشعر بوجودِه معك.
- الدرجة الثالثة: اقرأ سورة "الملك" قبل النوم، وتذكَّر عظمة الله في خلق السماوات، واسأله: "اللهم ارزقني حياءً يمنعني من معصيتك".

نص الشيخ الهروي

٣٥- باب الصدق

قال الله عز وجل: (فإذا عزم الأمر فلو صدقوا الله لكان خيرا لهم)(محمد:٢١).
الصدق اسم لحقيقة الشيء بعينه حصولا ووجودا.
وهو على ثلاث درجات:
الدرجة الأولى: صدق القصد. وبه يصح الدخول في هذا الشأن، ويتلافى به كل تفريط، ويتدارك كل فائت، ويعمر كل خراب.
وعلامة هذا الصادق أن لا يحتمل داعية تدعو إلى نقض عهد، ولا يصبر على صحبة ضِدّ، ولا يقعد عن الجد بحال.
والدرجة الثانية: أن لا يتمنى الحياة إلا للحق، ولا يشهد من نفسه إلا أثر النقصان، ولا يلتفت إلى ترفيه الرخص.
والدرجة الثالثة: الصدق في معرفة الصدق. فإن الصدق لا يستقيم في علم الخصوص إلا على حرف واحد، وهو أن يتفق رضى الحق بعمل العبد أو حاله أو وقته، وإتيان العبد وقصده، فيكون العبد راضيا مرضيا، فأعماله إذا مرضية، وأحواله صادقة، وقصوده مستقيمة.
وإن كان العبد كسي ثوبا معارا؛ فأحسن أعماله ذنب، وأصدق أحواله زور، وأصفى قصوده قعود.

النصّ مكتوباً بلغة مبسّطة

٣٥- باب الصدق

قال الله عز وجل: ﴿فَإِذَا عَزَمَ الْأَمْرُ فَلَوْ صَدَقُوا اللَّهَ لَكَانَ خَيْرًا لَهُمْ﴾ (محمد: ٢١).

الصدق هو أن تكون أفعالك ونواياك مُطابقة لحقيقة إيمانك بالله، وهو أساس كل خير.

الصدق ثلاث درجات:

الدرجة الأولى (صدق النية):

- أن تنوي بعملك وجه الله فقط، دون رياء أو طمع دنيوي.
- علامة صاحبها: لا يخون عهده، ولا يصاحب من يضلُّه، ولا يتوقف عن السعي في الخير.

الدرجة الثانية (صدق التجرُّد):

- أن تعيشَ للحق فقط، وتَعترفَ دائمًا بقصورك، ولا تتهاونَ في التزاماتك الدينية.

الدرجة الثالثة (صدق التطابق):

- أن تتوافق أعمالك وأحوالك مع رضى الله تمامًا، حتى يصير رضاه هو دافعك الوحيد.
- هنا، حتى أفضل أعمالك قد تراها ناقصةً لأنك تُدرك أن الكمال لله وحده.

<u>موجز المعاني ونصيحة عملية:</u>

الصدقُ الحقيقي هو أن ترى الله في كل حركةٍ وسكنة. ابدأ بتدريب نفسك على:

- الدرجة الأولى: اسأل نفسك قبل أي عمل: "لماذا أفعل هذا؟"، وتأمَّل قول الله: ﴿ وَٱلَّذِى جَآءَ بِٱلصِّدْقِ وَصَدَّقَ بِهِۦٓ أُوْلَـٰٓئِكَ هُمُ ٱلْمُتَّقُونَ﴾ (الزمر: ٣٣).
- الدرجة الثانية: اكتبْ يوميًّا خطأً واحدًا اعترفتَ به، واستغفر منه.
- الدرجة الثالثة: حوِّلْ همَّك من "كيف يُرضيني الناس؟" إلى "كيف أُرضي الله؟".

نص الشيخ الهروي

٣٦- باب الإيثار

قال الله عز وجل: (ويؤثرون على أنفسهم ولو كان بهم خصاصة)(الحشر:٩).
الإيثار تخصيص واختيار. والأثرة تحسن طوعاً، وتصح كرهاً.
وهو على ثلاث درجات:
الدرجة الأولى: أن تؤثر الخلق على نفسك فيما لا يحرم عليك ديناً، ولا يقطع عليك طريقاً، ولايفسد عليك وقتاً.
ويستطاع هذا بثلاثة أشياء: بتعظيم الحقوق، ومقت الشح، والرغبة في مكارم الأخلاق.
والدرجة الثانية: إيثار رضى الله تعالى على رضى غيره؛ وإن عظمت فيه المحن، وثقلت به المؤن، وضعفت عنه الطول والبدن.
ويستطاع هذا بثلاثة أشياء: بطيب العود، وحسن الإسلام، وقوة الصبر.
والدرجة الثالثة: إيثار إيثار الله تعالى؛ فإن الخوض في الإيثار دعوى في الملك، ثم ترك شهود رؤيتك إيثار الله، ثم غيبتك عن الترك.

النصّ مكتوباً بلغة مبسّطة

٣٦- باب الإيثار

قال الله عز وجل: ﴿وَيُؤْثِرُونَ عَلَى أَنْفُسِهِمْ وَلَوْ كَانَ بِهِمْ خَصَاصَةٌ﴾ (الحشر: ٩).
الإيثار هو تقديمُ غيرك على نفسك في الخير، حتى لو كنتَ في حاجةٍ إليه.
وهو ثلاث درجات:

الدرجة الأولى (إيثار الناس):
- تقديم مصلحة الآخرين على نفسك في الأمور المباحة، بشرط ألا:
  - تُخالفَ شرعًا.
  - تُضيّعَ وقتك أو طاقتك.
- يُكتسب هذا بثلاثة أمور:
  - احترام حقوق الناس.
  - كراهية البخل.
  - الرغبة في اكتساب الأخلاق العظيمة.

الدرجة الثانية (إيثار رضى الله):

- تقديم رضى الله على رضى الناس، حتى لو تسبَّبَ لك في مشقَّةٍ أو خسارةٍ دنيوية.

- يُكتسب هذا بثلاثة أمور:

- نقاء القلب من الأنانية.
- فهم حقيقة الإسلام (الاستسلام الكامل لله).
- قوة الصبر على التحديات.

الدرجة الثالثة (إيثار الإيثار نفسه):

- أن تدرك أن امتلاكك لأي شيء هو وهمٌ، فكل شيء ملكٌ لله. حتى عندما تُؤثِرُ غيرك، فأنت مجرد وسيطٍ لإرادة الله.
- هنا لا ترى نفسك "مُؤثِرًا"، بل تشهد أن الله هو المُؤثِر الحقيقي. تختفي ذاتك، فلا تطلب ثوابًا ولا تخشى لومًا، لأنك تعلم أن الفعل لله وحده.

<u>موجز المعاني ونصيحة عملية:</u>

الإيثارُ الحقيقي هو أن تنسى نفسك في سبيل الله والآخرين. ابدأ بتدريب نفسك على:

- الدرجة الأولى: تبرَّعْ بشيءٍ تحتاجه أنت (كطعامٍ أو وقت) لشخصٍ أكثر حاجةً، وتذكَّر قول الله: ﴿وَمَا تُقَدِّمُوا لِأَنْفُسِكُمْ مِنْ خَيْرٍ تَجِدُوهُ عِنْدَ اللَّهِ﴾ (البقرة: ١١٠).
- الدرجة الثانية: اخترْ قرارًا يُرضي الله حتى لو أغضب الناس (كرفض رشوةٍ أو دفاعٍ عن مظلوم)، وتأمَّل قوله تعالى: ﴿وَاللَّهُ يُحِبُّ الْمُحْسِنِينَ﴾ (آل عمران: ١٣٤).
- الدرجة الثالثة: تأمَّل قوله: ﴿وَلِلَّهِ مُلْكُ السَّمَاوَاتِ وَالْأَرْضِ﴾ (آل عمران: ١٨٩). اسأل نفسك: "هل أنا أملك شيئًا حتى أُوثِر به؟".

نص الشيخ الهروي

٣٧- باب الخُلُق

قال الله عز وجل: (وإنك لعلى خلق عظيم)(القلم:٤).
الخلق ما يرجع إليه المتكلف من نعته.
واجتمعت كلمة الناطقين في هذا العلم أن التصوف هو الخُلق، وجماع الكلام فيه يدور على قطب واحد، وهو بذل المعروف وكف الأذى.
وإنما يدرك إمكان ذلك قي ثلاثة أشياء: في العلم، والجود، والصبر.
وهو على ثلاث درجات:
الدرجة الأولى: أن تعرف مقام الخلق، أنهم بأقدارهم مربوطون، وفي طاقتهم محبوسون، وعلى الحكم موقوفون. فتستفيد بهذه المعرفة ثلاثة أشياء: أمن الخلق منك حتى الكلب، ومحبة الخلق إياك، ونجاة الخلق بك.
والدرجة الثانية: تحسين خُلُقك مع الحق، وتحسينه منك أن تعلم أن كل ما يأتي منك يوجب عذراً، وكل ما يأتي من الحق يوجب شكراً، وأن لا ترى له من الوفاء بدّاً.
والدرجة الثالثة: التخلّق بتصفية الخُلُق، ثم الصعود عن تفرق التخلّق، ثم التخلق بمجاوزة الأخلاق.

النصّ مكتوباً بلغة مبسّطة

٣٧- باب الخُلُق

قال الله عز وجل: ﴿وَإِنَّكَ لَعَلَى خُلُقٍ عَظِيمٍ﴾ (القلم: ٤).

الخُلُق هو أساس التصوف، ويُختصر في فعل الخير واجتناب الأذى.

وهو مبني على ثلاثة أركان:
العلم بأصول الأخلاق، والجود بالعطاء، والصبر على المشاق.

الخُلُق ثلاث درجات:

الدرجة الأولى (فهم طبيعة الناس):

- إدراك أن الناس محدودون بأقدارهم وقدراتهم، فلا تحمل عليهم فوق طاقتهم.
- ثمرات هذه الدرجة:

- أمان الناس من أذاك.
- حبهم لك.
- كونك سببًا في هدايتهم.

الدرجة الثانية (تحسين الخُلُق مع الله):

- أن تعترف أن كل تقصير منك يحتاج إلى استغفار، وكل نعمة من الله تحتاج إلى شكر.
- هنا تصل إلى حالةٍ من الرضا الدائم بقضاء الله، فلا ترى لنفسك فضلًا في الطاعة.

الدرجة الثالثة (تجاوز الخُلُق الاعتيادي):

- تصل إلى مرحلةٍ تصفو فيها أخلاقك تمامًا، فلا تحتاج إلى مجاهدةٍ لفعل الخير، بل يصير جزءًا من كيانك.
- بعدها ترتفع عن التصنُّع في الأخلاق، وتتجاوز المفاهيم التقليدية للخير والشر؛ لأن أفعالك تنبع من اتصالك بالله مباشرةً.

<u>موجز المعاني ونصيحة عملية:</u>

الأخلاق الحسنة هي مرآة الإيمان. ابدأ بتدريب نفسك على:

- الدرجة الأولى: تعامَلْ بلطفٍ مع شخصٍ يُزعجك، وتذكَّر قول النبي ﷺ: "إنما بُعثت لأتمم مكارم الأخلاق".
- الدرجة الثانية: اكتبْ كل ليلةٍ خطأً واحدًا اعترفتَ به، ونعمةً واحدةً شكرتَ الله عليها.
- الدرجة الثالثة: صلِّ ركعتين بنية تحسين الخُلُق، واقرأ سورة "الحجرات" بتدبُّر، خاصة قوله تعالى: ﴿ إِنَّ أَكْرَمَكُمْ عِندَ ٱللَّهِ أَتْقَىٰكُمْ﴾ (الحجرات: ١٣).

نص الشيخ الهروي

٣٨- باب التواضع

قال الله عز وجل: (وعباد الرحمن الذين يمشون على الأرض هونا)(الفرقان:٦٣).
التواضع أن يتضع العبد لصولة الحق.
وهو على ثلاث درجات:
الدرجة الأولى: التواضع للدين. وهو أن لا يعارض بمعقول منقولا، ولا يتهم على الدين دليلا، ولا يرى إلى الخلاف سبيلا.
ولا يصح ذلك له إلا بأن يعلم أن النجاة في البصيرة، والاستقامة بعد الثقة، وأن البينة وراء الحجة.
والدرجة الثانية: أن ترضى بمن رضى الحق لنفسه عبداً، من المسلمين أخاً،
وأن لا ترد على عدوك حقاً، وتقبل من المعتذر معاذيره.
والدرجة الثالثة: أن تتضع للحق، فتنزل عن رأيك في الخدمة، ورؤية حقك في الصحبة، وعن رسمك في المشاهدة.

النصّ مكتوباً بلغة مبسّطة

٣٨- باب التواضع

قال الله عز وجل: ﴿وَعِبَادُ الرَّحْمَٰنِ الَّذِينَ يَمْشُونَ عَلَى الْأَرْضِ هَوْنًا﴾ (الفرقان: ٦٣).

التواضع هو الخضوع الكامل لحُكم الله، وعدم التفاخر بالذات أو الجدال بغير حكمة.

وهو ثلاث درجات:

الدرجة الأولى (التواضع للدين):
- التسليم الكامل لأحكام الشرع دون معارضة النصوص الدينية بالرأي الشخصي أو المنطق.
- يشترط لتحقيقه:

- الإيمان بأن النجاة في اتباع الوحي، لا في الجدال.
- الثقة بأن الاستقامة طريقُ الأمان.
- فهم أن الحقائق الإلهية تفوق حجج البشر.

الدرجة الثانية (التواضع مع الخَلق):

- تقبُّل الآخرين كما هم:

- رضا بما رضيه الله لهم من منزلة.
- عدم ردِّ الإساءة بمثلها، وقبول اعتذار المُخطئ.
- التعامل بلطف حتى مع الخصوم، لأنهم عباد الله.

الدرجة الثالثة (التواضع مع الحق):

- التخلي عن الأنانية تمامًا:

- ترك التمسك بالرأي الشخصي في خدمة الله.
- عدم المطالبة بحقوقك في العلاقات الإنسانية.
- نسيان الذات أثناء العبادة، فلا ترى نفسك "صاحب فضل".

موجز المعاني ونصيحة عملية:

التواضعُ هو تاجُ المؤمن. ابدأ بتدريب نفسك على:

- الدرجة الأولى: اقرأ آية ﴿يَمْشُونَ عَلَى الْأَرْضِ هَوْنًا﴾ يوميًا، وتخيل كيف تمشي بخشوعٍ كأنك تحمل كتابًا مقدسًا على رأسك.
- الدرجة الثانية: إذا أساء إليك أحد، قل: "اللهم اغفر له، فهو لا يعلم"، وتذكَّر قول النبي ﷺ: "مَنْ تَوَاضَعَ لِلَّهِ رَفَعَهُ اللَّهُ".
- الدرجة الثالثة: اختم يومك بسؤال: "هل فعلتُ اليوم شيئًا لوجه الله فقط؟"، واقرأ سورة "لقمان" بتدبُّر، خاصة قوله تعالى: ﴿وَلَا تُصَعِّرْ خَدَّكَ لِلنَّاسِ وَلَا تَمْشِ فِي الْأَرْضِ مَرَحًا﴾ (لقمان: ١٨).

نص الشيخ الهروي

٣٩- باب الفتوة

قال الله عز وجل: (إِنَّهُمْ فِتْيَةٌ ءَامَنُواْ بِرَبِّهِمْ وَزِدْنَـٰهُمْ هُدًى)(الكهف:١٣).
نكتة الفتوة أن لا تشهد لك فضلاً، ولا ترى لك حقاً.
وهي على ثلاث درجات:
الدرجة الأولى: ترك الخصومة، والتغافل عن الزلة، ونسيان الأذية.
والدرجة الثانية: أن تقرب من يقصيك، وتكرم من يؤذيك، وتعتذر إلى من يجنى عليك. سماحاً لا كظماً، وبراحا لا مصابرة.
والدرجة الثالثة: أن لا تتعلق في المسير بدليل، ولا تشوب إجابتك بعوض، ولا تقف في شهودك على رسم.
واعلم أن من أحوج عدوه إلى شفاعة، ولم يخجل من المعذرة إليه، لم يشم رائحة الفتوة.
ثم في علم الخصوص، من طلب نور الحقيقة على قدم الاستدلال، لم يحل له دعوى الفتوة أبداً.

النصّ مكتوباً بلغة مبسّطة

٣٩- باب الفتوة

قال الله عز وجل: ﴿إِنَّهُمْ فِتْيَةٌ ءَامَنُواْ بِرَبِّهِمْ وَزِدْنَـٰهُمْ هُدًى﴾ (الكهف: ١٣).

الفتوة هي روح النبل الروحي، وتعني التجرُّد من الأنانية وعدم المطالبة بحقوقك.

الفتوة ثلاث درجات:

الدرجة الأولى (التسامح البسيط):

- تجنُّب الخصومات، وتجاهل أخطاء الآخرين، ونسيان الأذى الذي تعرَّضتَ له.

الدرجة الثانية (التسامح الفعَّال):

- تقرُّبٌ ممن يبتعد عنك، وإكرامٌ لمن يؤذيك، واعتذارٌ لمن يظلمك – ليس كتمًا للغضب، بل نقاءً في القلب.

الدرجة الثالثة (التجرُّد الكامل):

- الاستغناء عن الدليل العقلي المجرد (الاعتماد على المنطق البشري دون الوحي أو توجيه الشيخ)، وعدم انتظار مقابلٍ لأعمالك، وعدم التقيُّد بالشكليات في عبادة الله.

تحذيرات:

- من احتاج إلى وسيطٍ (شفيع) ليُصالح عدوَّه أو يقبل اعتذاره، وَمَنْ كَانَ الْاعْتِذَارُ عَلَيْهِ صَعْبًا، فهو لم يفهم الفتوة الحقيقية.
- من سعى لفهم الحقائق الإلهية بالمنطق المجرد (بدون توجيه روحي أو اتّباع الوحي)، لا يستحق أن يدَّعي الفتوة.

موجز المعاني ونصيحة عملية:

الفتوةُ هي أن تَعِيشَ كـ"فتى الكهف" – مُخلصًا لإيمانك بلا تردد. ابدأ بتدريب نفسك على:

- الدرجة الأولى: اكتب ثلاثة مواقف غضبتَ فيها مؤخرًا، وحلِّلها بعين التسامح.
- الدرجة الثانية: قدِّم هديةً رمزيةً لشخصٍ أساء إليك، وتأمَّل قول الله: ﴿وَلَا تَسْتَوِي الْحَسَنَةُ وَلَا السَّيِّئَةُ ادْفَعْ بِالَّتِي هِيَ أَحْسَنُ﴾ (فصلت: ٣٤).
- الدرجة الثالثة: صلِّ ركعتين بنية التجرُّد من حب الظهور، واقرأ قصة "أصحاب الكهف" بتدبُّر.

نص الشيخ الهروي

٤٠- باب الانبساط

قال الله عز وجل حاكيا عن كليمة عليه السلام: (أتهلكنا بما فعل السفهاء منا إن هي إلا فتنتك تضل بها من تشاء وتهدي من تشاء)(الأعراف:١٥٥).

الانبساط إرسال السجية والتحاشي من وحشة الحشمة. وهو السير مع الجبلة.

وهو على ثلاث درجات:

الدرجة الأولى: الانبساط مع الخلق. وهو أن لا تعتز لهم ضنا على نفسك، أو شحا على حظك، وتسترسل لهم في فضلك، وتسعهم بخلقك، وتدعهم يطؤونك، والعلم قائم، وشهودك المعنى دائم.

والدرجة الثانية: الانبساط مع الحق. وهو أن لا يجنبك خوف، ولا يحجبك رجاء، ولا يحول بينك وبينه آدم وحواء.

والدرجة الثالثة: الانبساط في الانطواء عن الانبساط. وهو رحب الهمة لانطواء انبساط العبد في بسط الحق جل جلالة.

النصّ مكتوباً بلغة مبسّطة

٤٠- باب الانبساط

قال الله عز وجل: ﴿أَتَهْلِكُنَا بِمَا فَعَلَ السُّفَهَاءُ مِنَّا إِنْ هِيَ إِلَّا فِتْنَتُكَ تُضِلُّ بِهَا مَنْ تَشَاءُ وَتَهْدِي مَنْ تَشَاءُ﴾ (الأعراف: ١٥٥).

الانبساط هو انفتاحُ القلب وصفاؤه، وعدم التكلُّف في التعامل مع الخلق أو مع الله.

وهو ثلاثة أنواع:

الدرجة الأولى (الانبساط مع الخلق):

- التعامل ببساطةٍ وسماحةٍ مع الناس دون أنانيةٍ أو خوفٍ من النقص.
- أن تمنح الآخرين من وقتك ومواردك بلا تردد، وتتقبَّل أخطاءهم، وتبقى مُطمئنًّا أن الله هو الرزاق.

الدرجة الثانية (الانبساط مع الحق):

- التحرُّر من قيود الخوف من العقاب أو الطمع في الثواب، والاتصال بالله بحريةٍ كأنك تُحدِّث صديقًا حميمًا.
- هنا لا يحجُبُك عن الله شيء، حتى الأسباب المادية أو العلاقات البشرية.

الدرجة الثالثة (الانبساط في الانطواء):

- الوصول إلى حالةٍ من السلام الداخلي حيث لا تحتاج إلى بذل جهدٍ للانفتاح، لأن قلبك مُتَّصلٌ بالله دائمًا.
- هنا تختفي الحدود بين "الانبساط" و"الانطواء"، فأنت في سكينةٍ مع الله دون حاجةٍ إلى مظاهر.

<u>موجز المعاني ونصيحة عملية:</u>

الانبساط هو أن تعيشَ بقلبٍ خفيفٍ كالفراشة. ابدأ بتدريب نفسك على:

- الدرجة الأولى: ساعد شخصًا غريبًا دون انتظار شكر، وتأمَّل قول الله: ﴿وَمَا تُنفِقُوا مِنْ خَيْرٍ يُوَفَّ إِلَيْكُمْ﴾ (البقرة: ٢٧٢).
- الدرجة الثانية: صلِّ ركعتين بنية التقرُّب إلى الله، واقرأ دعاء: "اللهم اجعلني من الذين إذا أَنعَمتَ عليهم شكروا، وإذا ابتليتَهم صبروا".
- الدرجة الثالثة: اقرأ سورة "الرعد" بتدبُّر، خاصة قوله تعالى: ﴿الَّذِينَ آمَنُوا وَتَطْمَئِنُّ قُلُوبُهُم بِذِكْرِ اللَّهِ ۗ أَلَا بِذِكْرِ اللَّهِ تَطْمَئِنُّ الْقُلُوبُ﴾ (الرعد: ٢٨)، وكرِّر يوميًّا: "حسبي الله ونعم الوكيل" ١٠٠ مرة.

٥- قسم الأصول

وأما قسم الأصول فهو عشرة أبواب وهي:
القصد والعزم والإرادة والأدب واليقين والأنس والذكر والفقر والغنى ومقام المراد.

نص الشيخ الهروي

٤١- باب القصد

قال الله عز وجل: (ومن يخرج من بيته مهاجرا إلى الله ورسوله ثم يدركه الموت فقد وقع أجره على الله)(النساء:١٠٠).
القصد: الإزماع على التجرد للطاعة وهو على ثلاث درجات:
الدرجة الأولى: قصد يبعث على الارتياض، ويخلص من التردد، ويدعو إلى مجانبة الأغراض.
والدرجة الثانية: قصد لا يلتقي سببا إلا قطعه، ولا يدع حائلا إلا منعه، ولا تحاملا إلا سهله.
والدرجة الثالثة: قصد استسلام لتهذيب العلم، وقصد إجابة لوطئ الحكم، وقصد اقتحام في بحر الفناء.

النصّ مكتوباً بلغة مبسّطة

٤١- باب القصد

قال الله عز وجل: ﴿وَمَنْ يَخْرُجْ مِنْ بَيْتِهِ مُهَاجِرًا إِلَى اللَّهِ وَرَسُولِهِ ثُمَّ يُدْرِكْهُ الْمَوْتُ فَقَدْ وَقَعَ أَجْرُهُ عَلَى اللَّهِ﴾ (النساء: ١٠٠).

القصد هو العزمُ الصادق على طاعة الله.
وهو ثلاثة مستويات:

١ .الدرجة الأولى (القصد التمهيدي):

- بدايةُ تشكيل النية الخالصة، والتدريب على ترك التردد، والابتعاد عن الأهداف الدنيوية.
- مثل: أن تنوي الصيام لوجه الله، وتتجنب المباهاة بذلك.

٢ .الدرجة الثانية (القصد الجاد):

- عزمٌ لا يعترف بالعوائق، يُزيل الصعاب، ويُسهِّل التحديات.
- مثل: الاستمرار في العبادة رغم المشاغل، ورفض التأجيل بحججٍ واهية.

٣ .الدرجة الثالثة (القصد الكامل):

- استسلامٌ تامٌّ لإرادة الله، واستجابةٌ فوريةٌ لأمره، وانغماسٌ في محبته حتى تذوب الأنانية.
- هنا يصل العبد إلى حالةٍ يشعر فيها أن أفعاله ليست إلا انعكاسًا لإرادة الله.

<u>موجز المعاني ونصيحة عملية:</u>

القصدُ الحقيقي هو أن تتحول نيتك إلى بوصلةٍ توجه كل خطواتك نحو الله. ابدأ بتدريب نفسك على:

- الدرجة الأولى: اكتب نيةً واحدةً صادقةً كل صباح (كمساعدة محتاج أو قراءة قرآن)، وتأمل قوله تعالى: ﴿وَمِنَ النَّاسِ مَنْ يَشْرِي نَفْسَهُ ابْتِغَاءَ مَرْضَاتِ اللَّهِ﴾ (البقرة: ٢٠٧).
- الدرجة الثانية: إذا فكرت في تأجيل عملٍ صالح، قل: "اللهم أعني على ذِكرك وشكرك وحُسن عبادتك"، وافعلهُ فورًا.
- الدرجة الثالثة: خصص ٥ دقائق يوميًا للجلوس في صمت، واسأل نفسك: "هل ما أفعله الآن يُرضي الله؟"، واقرأ سورة "العنكبوت" بتدبر، خاصة قوله: ﴿ وَمَن جَـٰهَدَ فَإِنَّمَا يُجَـٰهِدُ لِنَفْسِهِۦٓ﴾ (العنكبوت: ٦).

نص الشيخ الهروي

٤٢- باب العزم

قال الله عز وجل: (فإذا عزمت فتوكل على الله)(آل عمران:١٥٩).
العزم تحقيق القصد طوعاً أو كرهاً.
وهو على ثلاث درجات:
الدرجة الأولى: إباء الحال على العلم، بشَيْم برق الكشف، واستدامة نور الأنس، والإجابة لإماتة الهوى.
والدرجة الثانية: الاستغراق في لوائح المشاهدة، واستنارة ضياء الطريق، واستجماع قوى الاستقامة.
والدرجة الثالثة: معرفة علة العزم، ثم العزم على التخلص من العزم، ثم الخلاص من تكاليف ترك العزم، فإن العزائم لم تورث أربابها ميراثا أكرم من وقوفهم على علل العزائم.

النصّ مكتوباً بلغة مبسّطة

٤٢- باب العزم

قال الله عز وجل: ﴿فَإِذَا عَزَمْتَ فَتَوَكَّلْ عَلَى اللَّهِ﴾ (آل عمران: ١٥٩).

العزم هو التحقيق العملي للنية، سواءً برغبةٍ أو بغيرها.

وهو ثلاث درجات:

١ .الدرجة الأولى (العزم الأساسي):

- رفض الركود الروحي والسعي نحو المعرفة الإلهية.
- الحفاظ على نور الإيمان في القلب.
- مقاومة الأهواء الشخصية بقوة الإرادة.

٢ .الدرجة الثانية (العزم المتقدّم):

- الانغماس الكامل في مراقبة آيات الله في الكون.
- استنارة البصيرة لرؤية طريق الحق بوضوح.
- جمع قوى النفس للثبات على الاستقامة.

٣ .الدرجة الثالثة (العزم الكامل):

- فهم الدوافع الخفية وراء عزمك (مثل الرغبة في الثواب أو الخوف من العقاب).
- التحرر من الحاجة إلى "العزم" كجهدٍ بشري، والاعتماد الكلي على توفيق الله.
- الوصول إلى مرحلةٍ حيث الأفعال تنبع تلقائيًّا من الاستسلام التام لإرادة الله، دون حاجةٍ إلى تكلف.

<u>موجز المعاني ونصيحة عملية:</u>
العزم الحقيقي هو أن تتحول إرادتك إلى جسرٍ بينك وبين الله.
ابدأ بتدريب نفسك على:

- الدرجة الأولى: خصص ٥ دقائق صباحًا لقراءة آية ﴿فَإِذَا عَزَمْتَ فَتَوَكَّلْ عَلَى اللَّهِ﴾(آل عمران:١٥٩)، واكتب قرارًا واحدًا ستلتزم به اليوم (كترك غيبة أو مساعدة محتاج).
- الدرجة الثانية: صلِّ ركعتين بنية طلب الثبات، وتأمل قول الله: ﴿ وَٱلَّذِينَ جَٰهَدُواْ فِينَا لَنَهۡدِيَنَّهُمۡ سُبُلَنَا﴾ (العنكبوت: ٦٩).
- الدرجة الثالثة: اسأل نفسك قبل أي عمل: "هل هذا الفعل لوجه الله أم لشهوة نفسي؟"، واقرأ سورة "الشرح" بتدبر.

نص الشيخ الهروي

٤٣- باب الإرادة

قال الله عز وجل: (قل كل يعمل على شاكلته)(الإسراء:٨٤).
الإرادة من قوانين هذا العلم وجوامع أبنيته، وهي الإجابة لدواعي الحقيقة طوعاً.
وهي على ثلاث درجات:
الدرجة الأولى: ذهاب عن العادات بصحبة العلم، وتعلق بأنفاس السالكين مع صدق القصد، وخلع كل شاغل من الإخوان، ومشتت من الأوطان.
والدرجة الثانية: تقطّعٌ بصحبة الحال، وترويح الأنس، والسير بين القبض والبسط.
والدرجة الثالثة: ذهولٌ مع صحة الاستقامة، وملازمة الرعاية على تهذيب الأدب.

النصّ مكتوباً بلغة مبسّطة

٤٣- باب الإرادة

قال الله عز وجل: ﴿قُلْ كُلٌّ يَعْمَلُ عَلَىٰ شَاكِلَتِهِ﴾ (الإسراء: ٨٤).

الإرادة هي القوة الدافعة نحو الحق.

وهي ثلاث مراحل:

١ .الدرجة الأولى (الإرادة التأسيسية):

- التخلص من العادات السيئة بمرافقة العلم النافع.
- الارتباط بالصالحين بنية صادقة، وقطع العلاقات المشتتة عن الطريق.

٢ .الدرجة الثانية (الإرادة المتقدمة):

- تجاوز التعلق بالحالات الروحية المؤقتة (كالفرح أو الحزن).
- التمتع بالأنس مع الله في كل الظروف، والتوازن بين الشدائد والنعم.

٣ .الدرجة الثالثة (الإرادة الكاملة):

- الاندماج الكامل في عبادة الله مع الحفاظ على الاستقامة.
- صقل الأخلاق باستمرار، حتى تصير الأفعال انعكاسًا طبيعيًّا للإيمان.

<u>موجز المعاني ونصيحة عملية:</u>

الإرادة الحقيقية هي أن تتحول رغباتك إلى وقودٍ للتقرب إلى الله.
ابدأ بتدريب نفسك على:

- الدرجة الأولى: اكتب عادةً واحدةً تريد تركها (كالتأخر عن الصلاة)، واربطها بعملٍ إيجابي (كقراءة آية يوميًّا). تأمل قوله تعالى: ﴿إِنَّ اللَّهَ لَا يُغَيِّرُ مَا بِقَوْمٍ حَتَّى يُغَيِّرُوا مَا بِأَنْفُسِهِمْ﴾ (الرعد: ١١).
- الدرجة الثانية: إذا شعرت بضيقٍ روحي، صلِّ ركعتين وردِّد: "يا مُقَلِّبَ القلوب ثَبِّتْ قَلْبِي عَلَى دِينِكَ".
- الدرجة الثالثة: اختتم يومك بسؤال: "هل أخلاقي اليوم رضيتُ عنها؟"، واقرأ سورة "القصص" بتدبُّر، خاصة قوله: ﴿وَمَا تَوْفِيقِي إِلَّا بِاللَّهِ﴾ (القصص: ٥٦).

نص الشيخ الهروي

٤٤- باب الأدب

قال الله عز وجل: (وَٱلۡحَٰفِظُونَ لِحُدُودِ ٱللَّهِ)(التوبة:١١٢).
الأدب حفظ الحد بين الغلو والجفاء بمعرفة ضرر العدوان.
وهو على ثلاث درجات:
الدرجة الأولى: منع الخوف أن يتعدى إلى الإياس، وحبس الرجاء أن يخرج إلى الأمن، وضبط السرور أن يضاهي الجرأة.
والدرجة الثانية: الخروج من الخوف إلى ميدان القبض، والصعود عن الرجاء إلى ميدان البسط، والترقي عن السرور إلى ميدان المشاهدة.
والدرجة الثالثة: معرفة الأدب، ثم الغنى عن التأدب بتأديب الحق، ثم الخلاص من شهود أعباء الأدب.

النصّ مكتوباً بلغة مبسّطة

٤٤- باب الأدب

قال الله عز وجل: ﴿ وَٱلۡحَٰفِظُونَ لِحُدُودِ ٱللَّهِ﴾ (التوبة: ١١٢).

الأدب هو الحفاظ على التوازن بين الإفراط (المبالغة) والتفريط (التقصير)، بمعرفة مخاطر تجاوز الحدود.

وهو ثلاث درجات:

١ .الدرجة الأولى (ضبط المشاعر):

- منع الخوف من التحول إلى يأس.
- كبح الأمل الزائد من أن يصير غرورًا.
- التحكم في الفرح لئلا يؤدي إلى تهور.

٢ .الدرجة الثانية (الارتقاء الروحي):

- تحويل الخوف إلى خشوعٍ لله (القبض).
- رفع الأمل إلى ثقةٍ في رحمة الله (البسط).
- ترقية الفرح إلى تأملٍ في عظمة الخالق (المشاهدة).

٣ .الدرجة الثالثة (الأدب التلقائي):

- فهم قواعد الأدب دون تكلف.
- الوصول إلى مرحلةٍ تصبح فيها الأخلاق جزءًا من كيانك، كهديةٍ من الله.
- التحرر من الشعور بثقل الالتزام، لأن الأدب يصير طبيعةً لا مجهودًا.

موجز المعاني ونصيحة عملية:

الأدب الحقيقي هو أن تكون أفعالك مرآةً لقلبك النقي.

ابدأ بتدريب نفسك على:

- الدرجة الأولى: راقب مشاعرك اليومية، واسأل: "هل خوفي من الله يدفعني للأمل أم اليأس؟" وتأمل قوله تعالى: ﴿وَاتَّقُوا اللَّهَ وَيُعَلِّمُكُمُ اللَّهُ﴾ (البقرة: ٢٨٢).
- الدرجة الثانية: صلِّ ركعتين شكرًا على نعمة التوازن، واقرأ سورة "الحشر" بتدبر، خاصة: ﴿لَا تَكُونُوا كَالَّذِينَ نَسُوا اللَّهَ فَأَنسَاهُمْ أَنفُسَهُمْ﴾ (الحشر: ١٩).
- الدرجة الثالثة: اكتب ثلاث صفاتٍ أخلاقيةٍ تحبها في نفسك، واشكر الله عليها قبل النوم.

نص الشيخ الهروي

٤٥- باب اليقين

قال الله عز وجل: (وَفِى ٱلْأَرْضِ ءَايَـٰتٌ لِّلْمُوقِنِينَ)(الذاريات:٢٠).
اليقين مركب الآخذ في هذا الطريق، وهو غاية درجات العامة، وقيل أول خطوة الخاصة، وهو على ثلاث درجات:
الدرجة الأولى: علم اليقين. وهو قبول ما ظهر من الحق، وقبول ما غاب للحق، والوقوف على ما قام بالحق.
والدرجة الثانية: عين اليقين. وهو الغنى بالاستدراك عن الاستدلال، وعن الخبر بالعيان، وخرق الشهود حجاب العلم.
والدرجة الثالثة: حق اليقين. وهو إسفار صبح الكشف، ثم الخلاص من كلفة اليقين، ثم الفناء في حق اليقين.

النصّ مكتوباً بلغة مبسّطة

٤٥- باب اليقين

قال الله عز وجل: ﴿ وَفِى ٱلْأَرْضِ ءَايَـٰتٌ لِّلْمُوقِنِينَ﴾ (الذاريات: ٢٠).

اليقين هو الثقةُ الراسخة بالله التي تُحوِّل الإيمانَ إلى حقيقةٍ ملموسة.

وهو ثلاث مراحل:

١ .المرحلة الأولى (علم اليقين):

- الإيمان بالحقائق الظاهرة (كوجود الله من خلال خلقه) والباطنة (كالبعث والجزاء).
- مثل: تصديق أن القلب ينبض بإرادة الله، حتى لو لم تُرَ يدُه مباشرةً.

٢ .المرحلة الثانية (عين اليقين):

- الانتقال من الإيمان النظري إلى المشاهدة القلبية، كمن يرى النار فيعلم حرارتها دون لمسها.
- هنا يذوب الشك، ويصير الإيمان كالضوء يُنير كل شكوكك.

٣ .المرحلة الثالثة (حق اليقين):

- الوصول إلى حقيقة الإيمان كتجربةٍ وجودية، حيث يغمرك حضور الحقِ حتى تفنى إرادتك في إرادته.
- هنا تشعر أن كل ذرة في الكون تُسبِّح الله، فتصير أنت جزءًا من هذه التسبيحة.

<u>موجز المعاني ونصيحة عملية:</u>

اليقينُ هو أن ترى يدَ الله في كل شيء.

ابدأ رحلتك بالتدرج:

- المرحلة الأولى: تأمَّل آيةً كونيةً يوميًا (كالسماء أو النبات)، وردِّد: " رَبَّنَا مَا خَلَقْتَ هَٰذَا بَاطِلًا " (آل عمران: ١٩١).
- المرحلة الثانية: خصص ١٠ دقائق يوميًا للتفكُّر في أسماء الله الحسنى، وكيف تظهر في حياتك.
- المرحلة الثالثة: اقرأ سورة "الذاريات" بتدبُّر، وتخيَّل أنك تسمع تسبيح كل شيء حولك، وقل: "اللهم اجعلني من المُوقِنين."

نص الشيخ الهروي

٤٦- باب الأنس

قال الله عز وجل: (وإذا سألك عبادي عني فإني قريب)(البقرة:١٨٦).
الأنس عبارة عن روح القرب وهو على ثلاث درجات
الدرجة الأولى: الأنس بالشواهد؛ وهو استحلاء الذكر، والتغذي بالسماع، والوقوف على الإشارات.
والدرجة الثانية: الأنس بنور الكشف؛ وهو أنس شاخص عن الأنس الأول،
تشوبه صولة الهيمان، ويضربه موج الفناء.
وهذا الذي غلب قوما على عقولهم، وسلب قوما طاقة الاصطبار، وحل عنهم قيود العلم. وفي هذا ورد الخبر بهذا الدعاء: (أسألك شوقا إلى لقائك من غير ضراء مضرة ولا فتنة مضلة).
والدرجة الثالثة: أنس اضمحلال في شهود الحضرة؛ لا يعبر عن عينه، ولا يشار إلى حده، ولا يوقف على كنهه.

النصّ مكتوباً بلغة مبسّطة

٤٦- باب الأنس

قال الله عز وجل: ﴿وَإِذَا سَأَلَكَ عِبَادِي عَنِّي فَإِنِّي قَرِيبٌ﴾ (البقرة:١٨٦).

الأنس هو روح القرب من الله، وينقسم إلى ثلاث درجات:

الدرجة الأولى: الأنس بالشواهد

وهو أن يجد القلب لذة في ذِكر الله، ويتغذّى بسماع كلامه، ويتأمل الإشارات الإلهية في الكون والحياة. مثلما يفرح الطفل بلعبته، يفرح المؤمن بذِكر ربه.

الدرجة الثانية: الأنس بنور الكشف

هنا يبدأ القلب يرى بنور الإيمان أشياء خفيّة، لكن هذه المرحلة يصاحبها اضطرابٌ روحيٌّ وشعورٌ بالذوبان في محبة الله. يُصبح العقل عاجزًا عن التحليل، ويضعف الصبر، وتختفي قيود العلوم الظاهرية. وفي هذه المناسبة يُذكر الدعاء: "اللهم ارزقني شوقًا إلى لقائك دون معاناة أو ضلال ."

الدرجة الثالثة: أنس اضمحلال في شهود الحضرة
هنا يصل المؤمن إلى حالةٍ يفنى فيها شعورُه بذاته أمام عظمة الله، فلا يستطيع وصفَها بكلمات، ولا تحديدَها بحدود، ولا إدراكَ سرِّها. إنها هِبةٌ إلهيةٌ تَمنحُ القلبَ سكينةً لا تُقاس.

<u>الموجز والنصيحة العملية:</u>
الأنس بالله رحلةٌ روحية تبدأ بالذِّكر، ثم ترتقي بنور الإيمان، حتى تصل إلى السكينة المطلقة.

نصيحتنا لك:
-داوِم على الذكر (أَقِلّ الكلام إلا في الخير، واجعل لسانك رطبًا بذكر الله).
-تأمّل آيات القرآن، مثل: ﴿ ٱلَّذِينَ ءَامَنُواْ وَتَطْمَئِنُّ قُلُوبُهُم بِذِكْرِ ٱللَّهِۗ أَلَا بِذِكْرِ ٱللَّهِ تَطْمَئِنُّ ٱلْقُلُوبُ﴾ (الرعد:٢٨).
-لا تستعجل النتائج؛ فطريق القرب خطوةٌ خطوة. كلما زاد حبُّك لله، زاد أنسُك به.

نص الشيخ الهروي

٤٧- باب الذكر

قال الله عز وجل: (واذكر ربك إذا نسيت)(الكهف:٢٤).
يعني إذا نسيت غيره ونسيت نفسك في ذكرك، ثم نسيت ذكرك في ذكرك، ثم نسيت في ذكر الحق إياك كل ذكر.
والذكر هو التخلص من الغفلة والنسيان.
وهو على ثلاث درجات:
الدرجة الأولى: الذكر الظاهر، من ثناء، أو دعاء، أو رعاء.
والدرجة الثانية: الذكر الخفي؛ وهو الخلاص من الفتور، والبقاء مع الشهود، ولزوم المسامرة.
والدرجة الثالثة: الذكر الحقيقي؛ وهو شهود ذكر الحق إياك، والتخلص من شهود ذكرك، ومعرفة افتراء الذاكر في بقائه مع ذكره.

النصّ مكتوباً بلغة مبسّطة

٤٧- باب الذكر

قال الله عز وجل: ﴿وَاذْكُرْ رَّبَّكَ إِذَا نَسِيتَ﴾ (الكهف:٢٤).

الذكر هو الخلاص من الغفلة والنسيان، وله ثلاث درجات:

الدرجة الأولى: الذكر الظاهر

وهو التلفظ بالثناء على الله، أو الدعاء، أو قراءة القرآن. مثلما ينادي المسافر دليله في الطريق، ينادي المؤمنُ ربَّه بلسانه ليبقى متصلاً به.

الدرجة الثانية: الذكر الخفي

هنا يصبح الذكر سريًّا في القلب؛ حيث يترك المؤمنُ الكسلَ الروحي، ويظلّ واعيًا لوجود الله في كل لحظة، كمن يسامر صديقًا عزيزًا دون انقطاع.

الدرجة الثالثة: الذكر الحقيقي

هنا يدرك المؤمن أن الله هو مَنْ يذكره ويُحيط به بعنايته قبل أن يذكره هو. فيختفي شعورُه بذِكره الشخصي، ويدرك أن كلَّ ذكرٍ صادرٍ منه هو في الحقيقة هبةٌ من الله.

<u>الموجز والنصيحة العملية:</u>

الذكر هو سلاحٌ ضد النسيان وغذاءٌ للروح.
نصيحتنا لك:

- اجعل ذكر الله عادةً يومية (في الصباح، المساء، وأثناء العمل).
- تأمّل معنى الآية: ﴿ يَٰٓأَيُّهَا ٱلَّذِينَ ءَامَنُواْ ٱذۡكُرُواْ ٱللَّهَ ذِكۡرًا كَثِيرًا﴾ (الأحزاب:٤١).
- لا تقتصر على الذكر اللساني؛ بل اجعله ينبع من قلبك. كلما عمقْتَ حضورَك مع الله، زادتْ حلاوةُ الذكر.

نص الشيخ الهروي

٤٨- باب الفقر

قال الله عز وجل: (۞ يَٰٓأَيُّهَا ٱلنَّاسُ أَنتُمُ ٱلْفُقَرَآءُ إِلَى ٱللَّهِ)(فاطر:١٥).
الفقر اسم للبراءة من رؤية الملكة.
وهو على ثلاث درجات:
الدرجة الأولى: فقر الزهاد؛ وهو نفض اليدين من الدنيا ضبطا أو طلبا، وإسكات اللسان عنها ذما أو مدحا، والسلامة منها طلبا أو تركا.وهذا هو الفقر الذي تكلموا في شرفه.
والدرجة الثانية: الرجوع إلى السبق بمطالعة الفضل، وهو يورث الخلاص من رؤية الأعمال، ويقطع شهود الأحوال، ويمحص من أدناس مطالعة المقامات.
والدرجة الثالثة: صحة الاضطرار، والوقوع في يد التقطع الوحداني، والاحتباس في قيد التجريد، وهذا فقر الصوفية.

النصّ مكتوباً بلغة مبسّطة

٤٨- باب الفقر

قال الله عز وجل: ﴿ يَٰٓأَيُّهَا ٱلنَّاسُ أَنتُمُ ٱلْفُقَرَآءُ إِلَى ٱللَّهِ﴾ (فاطر:١٥).

الفقر هو التحرر من وَهْمِ التملك والاستغناء عن الله.

وله ثلاث درجات:

الدرجة الأولى: فقر الزاهدين

وهو ترك التعلق بالدنيا، سواء بالامتلاك أو بالرغبة فيها، وعدم الحديث عنها مدحًا أو ذمًّا، والبحث عن السلامة منها. مثلما يترك المسافرُ أمتعته ليخفف حمله، يترك الزاهدُ الدنيا ليتفرغ لله.

الدرجة الثانية: الرجوع إلى فضل الله

هنا يتوقف المؤمن عن الاعتماد على أعماله، ويدرك أن كلَّ فضلٍ هو من الله. تزول عنه غشاوةُ الاعتزاز بمنزلته الروحية، وينصرف قلبه عن مراقبة الأحوال أو المقامات. كمن ينسى جهده في الرحلة ليتذكر دائمًا دليلَه الحكيم.

الدرجة الثالثة: الفقر الحقيقي (فقر الصوفية)

هنا يصل المؤمن إلى حالةٍ من الاضطرار الكامل إلى الله، حيث يُفنى عن إرادته ويُحاط بتجريدٍ إلهيٍّ يجعله يعيش في قبضة الله وحده. كطفلٍ صغيرٍ يثق بأمه تمامًا، لا يملك شيئًا سوى الثقة بالرحمن.

<u>الموجز والنصيحة العملية:</u>

الفقر إلى الله هو سرُّ التحرر من الأوهام والوصول إلى اليقين.

نصيحتنا لك:

- تذكّر دائمًا: ﴿وَاللَّهُ الْغَنِيُّ وَأَنتُمُ الْفُقَرَاءُ﴾ (محمد:٣٨).
- لا تَغْتَرَّ بجهودك؛ فكلُّ خيرٍ هو هبةٌ من الله.
- اقترب من الله بالشكر، وليس بالادِّعاء. كلما ازددت فقرًا إليه، ازددت غنىً برحمته.

نص الشيخ الهروي

٤٩- باب الغنى

قال الله عز وجل: (وَوَجَدَكَ عَآيِلًا فَأَغۡنَىٰ)(الضحى: ٨).

الغنى اسم للملك التام.

وهو على ثلاث درجات:

الدرجة الأولى: غنى القلب؛ وهو سلامته من السبب، ومسالمته الحكم، وخلاصة من الخصومة.

والدرجة الثانية: عنى النفس؛ وهو استقامتها على المرغوب، وسلامتها من المسخوط، وبراءتها من المراياة.

والدرجة الثالثة: الغنى بالحق. وهو على ثلاث مراتب:

المرتبة الأولى، شهود ذكره إياك؛ والثانية، دوام مطالعة أوليته؛ والثالثة، الفوز بوجوده.

النصّ مكتوباً بلغة مبسّطة

٤٩- باب الغنى

قال الله عز وجل: ﴿وَوَجَدَكَ عَآيِلًا فَأَغۡنَىٰ﴾ (الضحى: ٨).

الغنى هو التمكُّن الحقيقي الذي ينبع من القرب من الله.

وله ثلاث درجات:

الدرجة الأولى: غنى القلب

وهو تحرُّر القلب من التعلق بالأسباب المادية، وقبوله لقضاء الله دون اعتراض، وخلوُّه من الجدال. مثلَ المُزارعِ الذي يزرع أرضَه باجتهاد، ثم يترك النموَّ لرحمة الله، لا يقلق إن تأخر المطر أو قلَّ، لأنه يعلم أن الرزق بيد الله وحده.

الدرجة الثانية: غنى النفس

هنا تستقيم النفس على طاعة الله، فتترك ما يُسخطه، وتُخلص في أعمالها دون رياء. كالتاجر الأمين الذي يكتفي بربحه الحلال دون خداع.

الدرجة الثالثة: الغنى بالحق

وهي أعلى المراتب، وتنقسم إلى ثلاث مراحل:

- المرحلة الأولى: أن تشعر بأن الله يذكرك ويرعاك في كل لحظة.
- المرحلة الثانية: أن تتأمل دائمًا أن الله هو الأول الذي لا شيء قبله.
- المرحلة الثالثة: أن تذوب في شعورك بوجود الله وحضوره، فتَغْنى به عن كل شيء.

الموجز والنصيحة العملية:

الغنى الحقيقي ليس في المال، بل في القرب من الله ورضاه. نصيحتنا لك:

- تذكَّر دائمًا: ﴿وَمَا مِن دَابَّةٍ فِي الْأَرْضِ إِلَّا عَلَى اللَّهِ رِزْقُهَا﴾ (هود:٦).
- اعمل بجدٍّ كالمُزارع، لكن ثِقْ بأن النتائج بيد الله.
- اقرأ القرآن بتدبُّر، خاصة قوله تعالى: ﴿فَإِنَّ مَعَ الْعُسْرِ يُسْرًا﴾ (الشرح:٦).

كلما ازددت ثقةً بالله، ازداد غناك الروحي.

نص الشيخ الهروي

٥٠- باب مقام المراد

قال الله عز وجل: (وما كنت ترجو أن يلقى إليك الكتاب)(القصص:٨٦).
أكثر المتكلمين في هذا العلم جعلوا المراد والمريد اثنين، وجعلوا مقام المراد فوق مقام المريد.
وإنما أشاروا باسم المراد إلى الضنائن الذين ورد فيهم الخبر.
وللمراد ثلاث درجات:
الدرجة الأولى: أن يعصم العبد وهو يستشرف للجفاء اضطراراً؛ بتنغيص الشهوات، وتعويق الملاذ، وسد مسالك المعاطب عليه إكراهاً.
والدرجة الثانية: أن يضع عن العبد عوار النقص، ويعافيه من سمة اللائمة، ويملكه عواقب الهفوات. كما فعل بسليمان في قتل الخيل، حمله على الريح الرخاء والعاصف فأغناه عن الخيل؛ وفعل بموسى حين ألقى الألواح وأخذ برأس أخيه، لم يعتب عليه كما عتب على آدم ونوح وداود ويونس.
والدرجة الثالثة: اجتباء الحق عبده، واستخلاصه إياه بخالصته؛ كما ابتدأ موسى وهو خرج يقتبس نارا، فاصطنعه لنفسه، وأبقى منه رسما معاراً.

النصّ مكتوباً بلغة مبسّطة

٥٠- باب مقام المراد

قال الله عز وجل: ﴿وَمَا كُنتَ تَرْجُو أَن يُلْقَىٰ إِلَيْكَ الْكِتَابُ﴾ (القصص:٨٦).

مقام المراد هو منزلةُ المُختارين من عباد الله الذين يمنحهم الله رعايةً خاصةً تفوق منزلة السالكين العاديين.

وهذا المقام له ثلاث درجات:

الدرجة الأولى: الحفظ الإلهي
يحفظ الله عبده من الانحراف رغم تعرُّضه لشدائد تدفعه نحو الغفلة، مثل تقليل شهواته، أو تعطيل ملذاته، أو إغلاق طرق الفتن أمامه قسرًا. كمَن يُنقذ من الغرق بقوةٍ إلهيةٍ وهو على شفا الهلاك.

الدرجة الثانية: التكريم والتسديد
يزيل الله عن عبده نقائصه، ويُعافيه من الذنوب، ويمنحه القدرة على تدارك أخطائه. كمَا فعل مع سليمان حين استبدل له الخيلَ بالريح المسخَّرة، أو كما عفا عن موسى حين ألقى الألواح دون لومٍ شديدٍ، دلالةً على رفعة منزلته.

الدرجة الثالثة: الاصطفاء الإلهي
هنا يختار الله عبدًا ويُصفِّيه ليكون خاصًّا به، كمَا اصطفى موسى حين خرج لِيَقْتَبِسَ نارًا فجعله نبيًّا، أو كمَن يُهديه الله إلى طريقٍ لا يَسلكه إلا المُقرَّبون.

الموجز والنصيحة العملية:

مقام المراد هِبةٌ إلهيةٌ تُذكِّرنا بأن الله يختار من يشاء برحمته. نصيحتنا لك:
- تأمّل قوله تعالى: ﴿وَإِذَا سَأَلَكَ عِبَادِي عَنِّي فَإِنِّي قَرِيبٌ﴾ (البقرة:١٨٦).
- لا تيأس من رحمة الله؛ فاصطفاؤه لعباده ليس محصورًا في زمنٍ أو شخص.
- اطلب الإخلاص في عبادتك، وثق أن الله يُصلحُ قلوبَ المُتقين.

٦- قسم الأودية

وأما قسم الأودية فهو عشرة أبواب وهي:
الإحسان والعلم والحكمة والبصيرة والفراسة والتعظيم والإلهام والسكينة والطمأنينة والهمة.

نص الشيخ الهروي

٥١- باب الإحسان

قال الله عز وجل: (هَلْ جَزَآءُ ٱلْإِحْسَـٰنِ إِلَّا ٱلْإِحْسَـٰنُ)(الرحمن:٦٠).
قد ذكرنا في صدر الكتاب أن الإحسان اسم جامع نبوي يجمع أبواب الحقائق وهو (أن تعبد الله كأنك تراه).
وهو على ثلاث درجات:
الدرجة الأولى: الإحسان في القصد؛ بتهذيبه علما، وإبرامه عزما، وتصفيته حالا.
والدرجة الثانية: الإحسان في الأحوال؛ وهو أن تراعيها غيرةً، وتسترها تظرّفاً، وتصححها تحقيقا.
والدرجة الثالثة: الإحسان في الوقت؛ وهو أن لا تزايل المشاهدة أبدا، ولا تلحظ لهمتك أمدا، وتجعل هجرتك إلى الحق سرمدا.

النصّ مكتوباً بلغة مبسّطة

٥١- باب الإحسان

قال الله عز وجل: ﴿هَلْ جَزَآءُ ٱلْإِحْسَـٰنِ إِلَّا ٱلْإِحْسَـٰنُ﴾ (الرحمن:٦٠).

الإحسان هو أعلى مراتب العبادة، كما عرَّفه النبي صلى الله عليه وسلم: «أن تعبد الله كأنك تراه».

وهو ثلاثة درجات:

الدرجة الأولى: الإحسان في النية
وهي تنقيةُ القصدِ من الشوائب بالعلم (معرفة طريق الحق)، والعزمِ (إرادة الخير)، وتصفيةِ القلبِ من الأهواء. مثل عاملٍ يبني بيتًا بإتقانٍ لأنه يريد رضا الله، لا مدح الناس.

الدرجة الثانية: الإحسان في الأحوال
هنا يراقب المؤمنُ مشاعره وأفعاله بدقة؛ فيخفي فضائلَه خوفًا من الرياء، ويُصلح أخطاءه بصدق، ويحافظ على خشوعه كأنه أمام الله دائمًا. كمن يُنظِّف ثوبَه من الغبار كل يومٍ ليظل نقيًّا.

الدرجة الثالثة: الإحسان في الزمن
وهي أن يعيش المؤمنُ كلَّ لحظةٍ في حضور الله، لا يغيب عن ذكره طرفةَ عين، ويجعل سعيه الدائمَ نحو التقرب منه. كمسافرٍ لا يتوقف عن السير حتى يبلغ القمة.

<u>الموجز والنصيحة العملية:</u>
الإحسان طريقُ الكمالِ الإيماني. نصيحتنا لك:
- تأمّل قوله تعالى: ﴿وَأَحْسِنُوا إِنَّ اللَّهَ يُحِبُّ الْمُحْسِنِينَ﴾ (البقرة:١٩٥).
- ابدأ بنيّتك؛ أصلحها قبل كل عمل.
- حاسب نفسك يوميًّا: هل فعلت اليوم شيئًا لوجه الله فقط؟

نص الشيخ الهروي

٥٢- باب العلم

قال الله عز وجل: (وَعَلَّمْنَـٰهُ مِن لَّدُنَّا عِلْمًا)(الكهف:٦٥).
العلم ما قام بدليل ورفع الجهل.
وهو على ثلاث درجات:
الدرجة الأولى: علم جليّ؛ يقع بعيان، أو استفاضة صحيحة، أو صحة تجربة قديمة.
والدرجة الثانية: علم خفي؛ ينبت في الأسرار الطاهرة، من الأبدان الزاكية، بماء الرياضة الخالصة. ويظهر في الأنفاس الصادقة لأهل الهمة العالية، في الأحايين الخالية، في الأسماع الصاحية.وهو علم يُظهر الغائب، ويغيّب الشاهد، ويشير إلى الجمع.
والدرجة الثالثة: علم لدني؛ إسناده وجوده، وإدراكه عيانه، ونعته حكمه، ليس بينه وبين الغيب حجاب.

النصّ مكتوباً بلغة مبسّطة

٥٢- باب العلم

قال الله عز وجل: ﴿وَعَلَّمْنَـٰهُ مِن لَّدُنَّا عِلْمًا﴾ (الكهف:٦٥).

العلم هو نورٌ يُزيل الجهل، ويقوم على الأدلة، وينقسم إلى ثلاث درجات:

الدرجة الأولى: العلم الظاهر
وهو ما يُدرَك بالحواس أو التجربة أو النقل الموثوق، مثل معرفة الطالب بخصائص النبات من خلال المختبر، أو فهم التاريخ من كتبٍ صحيحة.

الدرجة الثانية: العلم الخفي
ينمو هذا العلم في القلب النقي عبر المجاهدة الروحية، ويظهر لأصحاب الهمم العالية في لحظات الخلوة. كفلاحٍ يزرع البذور بصبرٍ فيترقب نموَّها، يُدرك بالبصيرة ما لا تراه العين، ويُفرّق بين الحق والباطل.

الدرجة الثالثة: العلم اللدني

هبةٌ إلهيةٌ مباشرةٌ من الله، لا تحتاج إلى وساطةٍ أو أدلة. مثل مرآةٍ صافيةٍ تعكس نور الشمس دون عوائق، يُشرق هذا العلم في القلب المطهَّر فيكشف الأسرار الإلهية.

الموجز والنصيحة العملية:

العلم طريقٌ لمعرفة الله وتزكية النفس. نصيحتنا لك:

- تأمّل قوله تعالى: ﴿وَقُل رَّبِّ زِدْنِي عِلْمًا﴾ (طه:١١٤).
- اطلب العلم النافع بقلبٍ خالصٍ، ولا تقف عند الظاهر بل ابحث في الأسرار.
- نقّ قلبك بالعبادة؛ فالعلم الإلهي يُمنح للأرواح الطاهرة.

نص الشيخ الهروي

٥٣- باب الحكمة

قال الله عز وجل: (يؤتي الحكمة من يشاء ومن يؤت الحكمة فقد أوتي خيرا كثيرا)(البقرة:٢٦٩).
الحكمة اسم لإحكام وضع الشيء في موضعه.
وهي على ثلاث درجات:
الدرجة الأولى: أن تعطي كل شيء حقه، ولا تعديه حده، ولا تعجّله وقته.
والدرجة الثانية: أن تشهد نظر الله في وعيده، وتعرف عدله في حكمه، وتلحظ برّه في منعه.
والدرجة الثالثة: أن تبلغ في استدلالك البصيرة، وفي إرشادك الحقيقة، وفي إشارتك الغاية.

النصّ مكتوباً بلغة مبسّطة

٥٣- باب الحكمة

قال الله عز وجل: ﴿يُؤْتِي الْحِكْمَةَ مَن يَشَاءُ ۚ وَمَن يُؤْتَ الْحِكْمَةَ فَقَدْ أُوتِيَ خَيْرًا كَثِيرًا﴾ (البقرة:٢٦٩).

الحكمة هي وضع الأشياء في مواضعها الصحيحة بحكمةٍ إلهية.

وتنقسم إلى ثلاث درجات:

الدرجة الأولى: الحكمة في التصرُّف

أن تعطي كلَّ شيءٍ حقَّه دون إفراطٍ أو تفريط، وتنتظر الوقت المناسب لِفعله. مثل مزارعٍ يزرع بذوره في فصل الربيع، ولا يسرع بحصادها قبل نضجها.

الدرجة الثانية: الحكمة في الفهم

أن تدرك حكمة الله في تحذيراته، وعدله في قضائه، ورحمته حتى في منعه. كطبيبٍ حكيمٍ يمنع المريضَ من طعامٍ ضارٍّ رغم رغبته فيه، لأنه يعلم أن المنعَ رحمة.

الدرجة الثالثة: الحكمة في الإرشاد

أن تصل ببصيرتك إلى حقائق الأمور، وتُرشد الآخرين إليها بأسلوبٍ واضح، وتُشاركهم الهدف الأسمى من الحياة: عبادة الله. كمعلّمٍ يشرح الدرسَ بطرقٍ مختلفة حتى يفهمه كلُّ تلميذ.

<u>الموجز والنصيحة العملية:</u>

الحكمةُ كنزٌ يجمع بين الفهم والعمل. نصيحتنا لك:

- تأمّل قوله تعالى: ﴿ادْعُ إِلَىٰ سَبِيلِ رَبِّكَ بِالْحِكْمَةِ﴾ (النحل:١٢٥).
- اسأل الله الحكمة في كل قرار، وافهم أن تأخير الشيء قد يكون خيرًا.
- تعلّم من تجاربك؛ فالحكيم مَن يُصحّح مساره بعد كل خطأ.

نص الشيخ الهروي

٥٤- باب البصيرة

قال الله عز وجل: (قل هذه سبيلي ادعو إلى الله على بصيرة أنا ومن اتبعني)(يوسف:١٠٨).
البصيرة ما يخلصك من الحيرة،
وهو على ثلاث درجات:
الدرجة الأولى: أن تعلم أن الخبر القائم بتمهيد الشريعة يصدر عن عين لا تخاف عواقبها، فترى من حقه أن تلذّه يقينا، وتغضب له غيرة.
والدرجة الثانية: أن تشهد في هداية الحق وإضلاله إصابة العدل، وفي تلوين أقسامه رعاية البر، وتعاين في جذبه حبل الوصال.
والدرجة الثالثة: بصيرة تفجر المعرفة، وتثبت الإشارة، وتنبت الفراسة.

النصّ مكتوباً بلغة مبسّطة

٥٤- باب البصيرة

قال الله عز وجل: ﴿قُلْ هَٰذِهِ سَبِيلِي أَدْعُو إِلَى اللَّهِ عَلَىٰ بَصِيرَةٍ أَنَا وَمَنِ اتَّبَعَنِي﴾ (يوسف:١٠٨).

البصيرة هي النور الذي يُزيل الحيرة.

وتنقسم إلى ثلاث درجات:

الدرجة الأولى: البصيرة في اليقين
أن تثق في أحكام الشريعة ثقةً تامّةً كأنك ترى نتائجها أمامك، فتسعد بطاعتها وتنفر من معصيتها. مثل قبطان السفينة الذي يتبع البوصلة بدقةٍ لأنه يعلم أنها الطريق الآمن.

الدرجة الثانية: البصيرة في العدل الإلهي

أن تفهم أن هداية الله أو ابتلاءَه له حكمةٌ ورحمةٌ، حتى لو خفيت عليك الآن. كطبيبٍ يُجري عمليةً مؤلمةً لإنقاذ المريض، فالألم مؤقتٌ والشفاء دائمٌ.

الدرجة الثالثة: البصيرة في المعرفة

أن تُدرك الحقائق الخفية بنور الإيمان، وتستدل على الأسرار الإلهية بقلبٍ نقيٍّ، وتُميّز بين الحق والباطل بفراسةٍ إلهيةٍ. مثل منارةٍ تُنير الطريق للسفن في الظلام.

الموجز والنصيحة العملية:

البصيرةُ هِبةٌ تُنير طريقَ القلبِ إلى الله. نصيحتنا لك:

- تأمّل قوله تعالى: ﴿أَفَلَمْ يَسِيرُوا فِي الْأَرْضِ فَتَكُونَ لَهُمْ قُلُوبٌ يَعْقِلُونَ بِهَا﴾ (الحج:٤٦).
- اطلب البصيرةَ بالدعاء، وثق أن كلَّ ابتلاءٍ خلفه حكمةٌ.
- عليك بتنقية قلبك بالذكر؛ فالبصيرةُ تُولَدُ في القلوبِ الطاهرة.

نص الشيخ الهروي

٥٥- باب الفراسة

قال الله عز وجل: (إِنَّ فِى ذَٰلِكَ لَـَٔايَـٰتٍ لِّلْمُتَوَسِّمِينَ)(الحجر:٧٥).
التوسم التفرس. وهو استئناس حكم غيب، من غير استدلال بشاهد، ولا اختبار بتجربة.
وهي على ثلاث درجات:
الدرجة الأولى: فراسة طارئة نادرة، تسقط على لسان وحشي في العمر مرة، لحاجة سمع مريد صادق إليها، لا يوقف على مخرجها، ولا يوبه بصاحبها. وهذا شيء لا يلخّص من الكهانة وما ضاهاها؛ لأنها لم تشر، عن عين ولم تصدر عن علم، ولم تسق بوجود.
والدرجة الثانية: فراسة تُجنى من غرس الإيمان، وتطلع من صحة الحال، وتلمع من نور الكشف.
والدرجة الثالثة: فراسة سرية، لم تجتلبها روية، على لسان مصطنع، تصريحا أو رمزا.

النصّ مكتوباً بلغة مبسّطة

٥٥- باب الفراسة

قال الله عز وجل: ﴿إِنَّ فِى ذَٰلِكَ لَـَٔايَـٰتٍ لِّلْمُتَوَسِّمِينَ﴾ (الحجر:٧٥).

الفِراسة هي إدراكُ الحقائق الخفية بنور الإيمان، دون حاجةٍ إلى أدلةٍ مادية أو تجارب.

وهي ثلاث درجات:

الدرجة الأولى: الفِراسة العابرة
هِبَةٌ نادرةٌ تُلهمُ القلبَ فجأةً لضرورةٍ روحية، كأن يوجَّه شخصٌ لقول كلمةٍ تُنقذ مُستمعًا صادقًا، دون معرفةٍ بمصدرها. هذه ليست كهانةً؛ لأنها تأتي من الله، لا من تنجيم أو ادعاء.

الدرجة الثانية: الفِراسة المُستنبتة

تنمو مع قوة الإيمان وصِدق الحال، وتظهر مع نور الكشف الإلهي. كفلاحٍ خبيرٍ يتنبأ بموعد المطر من خلال علاماتٍ خفيةٍ في الطبيعة.

الدرجة الثالثة: الفِراسة السرية

هِبةٌ إلهيةٌ خالصةٌ لا تحتاج إلى تأملٍ أو رمز، تُكشَفُ للقلب النقي مباشرةً. كمرآةٍ صافيةٍ تعكس الحقيقة دون تشويش.

<u>الموجز والنصيحة العملية:</u>

الفِراسةُ نافذةُ الروحِ إلى الحقائق الإلهية. نصيحتنا لك:

- تأمّل قوله تعالى: ﴿وَتِلْكَ ٱلْأَمْثَٰلُ نَضْرِبُهَا لِلنَّاسِ لَعَلَّهُمْ يَتَفَكَّرُونَ﴾ (الحشر: ٢١).
- طهِّر قلبك بالذكر والعبادة؛ فالفِراسةُ تُمنحُ للأرواحِ المُطَهَّرة.
- لا تخلط بين الفِراسة والتنجيم؛ فالأولى هِبةٌ إلهيةٌ، والثاني منهيٌّ عنه.

نص الشيخ الهروي

٥٦- باب التعظيم

قال الله عز وجل: (مالكم لا ترجون لله وقارا)(نوح:١٣).
التعظيم معرفة العظمة مع التذلل لها.
وهو على ثلاث درجات:
الدرجة الأولى: تعظيم الأمر والنهي؛ وهو أن لا يعارضا بترخص جاف، ولا يعرّضا لتشديد غال، ولا يحملا على علة توهن الانقياد.
والدرجة الثانية: تعظيم الحكم؛ أن يبغى له عوج، أو يدافع بعلم، أو يرضى بعوض.
والدرجة الثالثة: تعظيم الحق؛ وهو أن لا تجعل دونه سببا. أو ترى عليه حقا، أو تنازع له اختيارا.

النصّ مكتوباً بلغة مبسّطة

٥٦- باب التعظيم

قال الله عز وجل: ﴿مَّا لَكُمْ لَا تَرْجُونَ لِلَّهِ وَقَارًا﴾ (نوح:١٣).

التعظيم هو الخضوع لعظمة الله مع معرفتها.

وله ثلاث درجات:

الدرجة الأولى: تعظيم الأمر والنهي
طاعة أوامر الله ونواهيه بلا تساهلٍ يضعفها، ولا تشديدٍ يُثقلها، ولا حججٍ تُضعف الانقياد. مثل طالبٍ يلتزم بقوانين المدرسة بدقةٍ دون تفريطٍ أو تعسُّف.

الدرجة الثانية: تعظيم الحكم الإلهي

القبول بقضاء الله دون محاولة تحريفه بالجدل، أو رفضه بالعلم المحدود، أو طلب بديلٍ عنه. كمريضٍ يثق في خطة الطبيب رغم صعوبتها، لأنه يعلم أنها لصالحه.

الدرجة الثالثة: تعظيم الحق المطلق

أن تجعل الله هو الغاية دون وسيط، ولا تدعي لنفسك حقًّا في اختيارٍ يخالف مشيئته. كابنٍ يطيع والديه تمامًا لأنه يرى في طاعتهما طاعةً لله.

الموجز والنصيحة العملية:

التعظيمُ دليلُ الإيمانِ العميقِ بالله. نصيحتنا لك:

- تأمّل قوله تعالى: ﴿وَمَا قَدَرُوا اللَّهَ حَقَّ قَدْرِهِ﴾ (الأنعام:٩١).
- حافِظ على الصلاة؛ فهي أعظم مظهرٍ لتعظيم الله.
- اسأل نفسك يوميًّا: هل أخذتُ رخصَ الشرعِ بغير حاجةٍ؟ هل قبلتُ قضاءَ الله برضىً؟

نص الشيخ الهروي

٥٧- باب الإلهام

قال الله عز وجل: (قَالَ ٱلَّذِي عِندَهُۥ عِلۡمٞ مِّنَ ٱلۡكِتَٰبِ أَنَا۠ ءَاتِيكَ بِهِۦ قَبۡلَ أَن يَرۡتَدَّ إِلَيۡكَ طَرۡفُكَ) (النمل: ٤٠).

الإلهام مقام المحدَّثين، وهو فوق الفراسة؛ لأن الفراسة ربما وقعت نادرة، أو استصعبت على صاحبها وقتا، واستعصت عليه، والإلهام لا يكون إلا في مقام عتيد.

وهو على ثلاث درجات:

الدرجة الأولى: إلهام نبأ يقع وحيا قاطعا، مقرونا بسماع أو مطلقا.

والدرجة الثانية: إلهام يقع عينا، وعلامة صحته أنه لا يخرق سترا، ولا يجاوز حدا، ولا يخطئ أبدا.

والدرجة الثالثة: إلهام يجلو عين التحقيق صرفا، وينطق عن عين الأزل محضا.

وللإلهام غاية تمتنع عن الإشارة إليها.

النصّ مكتوباً بلغة مبسّطة

٥٧- باب الإلهام

قال الله عز وجل: ﴿قَالَ ٱلَّذِي عِندَهُۥ عِلۡمٞ مِّنَ ٱلۡكِتَٰبِ أَنَا۠ ءَاتِيكَ بِهِۦ قَبۡلَ أَن يَرۡتَدَّ إِلَيۡكَ طَرۡفُكَ﴾ (النمل: ٤٠).

الإلهام هو هِبةٌ إلهيةٌ تُكشَفُ للقلوب الطاهرة، تفوق الفِراسةَ في الدقة والثبات.

وتنقسم إلى ثلاث درجات:

الدرجة الأولى: إلهام الخبر اليقيني

وهو وحيٌ واضحٌ يصل إلى القلب فجأةً، سواءً بصوتٍ مسموعٍ أو إدراكٍ داخليٍّ.

مثل طبيبٍ يُلهَمُ بتشخيص مرضٍ صعبٍ دون تحاليل.

الدرجة الثانية: إلهام الرؤية الصادقة

يُظهر اللهُ للعبد حقائقَ لا تُناقضُ الشرعَ، ولا تتعدى حدودَ الأدبِ مع الله، ولا تخطئُ أبدًا. كقائدٍ يرى طريقَ النجاةِ في ظلامِ الأزماتِ بوحيٍ إلهيٍّ.

الدرجة الثالثة: إلهام الحقائق الأزلية

كشفٌ إلهيٌّ يُزيلُ الشكوكَ، ويُظهرُ الأسرارَ الكونيةَ التي خَلقها اللهُ منذ الأزل. مثل عالِمٍ يكتشفُ قانونًا في الطبيعةِ كان خفيًّا على الجميع.

الموجز والنصيحة العملية:

الإلهامُ هِبةٌ تُمنحُ للأرواحِ المُخلصةِ. نصيحتنا لك:

- تأمّل قوله تعالى: ﴿وَاتَّقُوا اللَّهَ وَيُعَلِّمُكُمُ اللَّهُ﴾ (البقرة:٢٨٢).
- طهّر قلبك بالصلاة والصدقة؛ فالإلهامُ لا ينزلُ إلا على النفوسِ الزكيةِ.
- لا تخلط بين الإلهامِ والأوهام؛ تأكَّدْ أن ما يصلُك لا يُخالفُ الشرعَ.

نص الشيخ الهروي

٥٨- باب السكينة

قال الله عز وجل: (هو الذي أنزل السكينة في قلوب المؤمنين)(الفتح:٤).
اسم السكينة لثلاثة أشياء:
أولها: سكينة بني إسرائيل التي أعطوها في التابوت. قال أهل التفسير هي ريح هفافة وذكروا صفتها وفيها ثلاثة أشياء: هي لانبيائهم معجزة، ولملوكهم كرامة، وهي آية النصرة تخلع قلوب العدو بصوتها رعبا إذ التقى الصفان للقتال.
والسكينة الثانية: التي تنطق على ألسن المحدّثين ليست هي شيئا يُملك، إنما هي شيء من لطائف صنيع الحق، يلقى على لسان المحدَّث الحكمة، كما يلقى الملك الوحي على قلوب الأنبياء، وتنطق المحدثين بنكت الحقائق مع ترويح الاسرار وكشف الشُّبه.
والسكينة الثالثة: هي التي أنزلت في قلب النبي صلى الله عليه و سلم وقلوب المؤمنين، وهي شيء يجمع نورا، وقوة، وروحا؛ يسكن إليه الخائف، ويتسلى به الحزين والضجر، ويستكين له العصي والجري والأبي. وأما سكينة الوقار التي تراها نعتا أربابها، فإنها ضياء تلك السكينة الثالثة التي ذكرناها، وهي على ثلاث درجات:
الدرجة الأولى: سكينة الخشوع عند القيام بالخدمة؛ رعاية، وتعظيما، وحضورا.
والدرجة الثانية: السكينة عند المعاملة؛ بمحاسبة النفس، وملاطفة الخلق، ومراقبة الحق.
والدرجة الثالثة: السكينة التي تُثبِت الرضى بالقِسم، وتمنع من الشطح الفاحش، وتقف صاحبها على حد الرتبة.

النصّ مكتوباً بلغة مبسّطة

٥٨- باب السكينة

قال الله عز وجل: ﴿هُوَ الَّذِي أَنزَلَ السَّكِينَةَ فِي قُلُوبِ الْمُؤْمِنِينَ﴾ (الفتح:٤).

السكينةُ نفحةٌ إلهيةٌ تُهدّئُ القلوبَ وتُقوّيها، وهي ثلاثة أنواع:

السكينة الأولى: مَثَلُها سكينة بني إسرائيل

ريحٌ لطيفةٌ أُنزلت في التابوت كمعجزةٍ للأنبياء، وعزوةٍ للملوك، وآيةٍ للنصر تُرعب الأعداء. مثل جنديٍ يشعرُ بقوةٍ خفيةٍ تمنحهُ الشجاعةَ في المعركة.

السكينة الثانية: سكينة المُحدَّثين

حكمةٌ إلهيةٌ تُلقى على ألسنةِ الصالحين، فتكشفُ الحقائقَ وتُزيحُ الشكوكَ دون أن يمتلكوها. كعالمٍ يُلهَمُ بفهمٍ عميقٍ لأسرار الكون دون دراسةٍ مسبقةٍ.

السكينة الثالثة: سكينة المؤمنين

نورٌ وقوةٌ تُنزلُ الطمأنينةَ في القلوب،
وتنقسم إلى ثلاث درجات:

- الدرجة الأولى: سكينة الخشوع في العبادة، كالمصلّي الذي ينسى الدنيا ويندمجُ في مناجاة ربه.
- الدرجة الثانية: سكينة التعامل مع الناس بالعدل واللطف، كصديقٍ يصبرُ على زلات الآخرين ويُحسنُ الظنَّ بهم.
- الدرجة الثالثة: سكينة الرضى بقضاء الله، كأبٍ يفقدُ عملَه فيرضى بحكمة الله ويبحثُ عن فرصٍ جديدةٍ بثقةٍ.

الموجز والنصيحة العملية:

السكينةُ مفتاحُ القلبِ المطمئنِ. نصائحنا لك:

- تأمّل قوله تعالى: ﴿ٱلَّذِينَ ءَامَنُواْ وَتَطۡمَئِنُّ قُلُوبُهُم بِذِكۡرِ ٱللَّهِ﴾ (الرعد:٢٨).
- أكثِرْ من الذكر؛ فهو يُنزل السكينةَ ويُذهب الهمَّ.
- تعاملْ بتواضعٍ مع الناس، وارضَ بتدبير الله حتى في الشدائد.

نص الشيخ الهروي

٥٩- باب الطمأنينة

قال الله عز وجل: (يَٰٓأَيَّتُهَا ٱلنَّفۡسُ ٱلۡمُطۡمَئِنَّةُ)(الفجر:٢٧).
الطمأنينة سكون يقويه أمن صحيح شبيه بالعيان.
وبينه وبين السكينة فرقان:
أحدهما، أن السكينة صولة تورث خمود الهيبة أحيانا، والطمأنينة سكون أمنٍ فيه استراحة أنس.
والثاني، أن السكينة تكون نعتا وتكون حينا بعد حين، والطمأنينة نعت لا يزايل صاحبه.
وهي على ثلاث درجات:
الدرجة الأولى: طمأنينة القلب بذكر الله؛ وهي طمأنينة الخائف إلى الرجاء، والضجر إلى الحكم، والمبتلي إلى المثوبة.
والدرجة الثانية: طمأنينة الروح في القصد إلى الكشف، وفي الشوق إلى العدة، وفي التفرقة إلى الجمع.
والدرجة الثالثة: طمأنينة شهود الحضرة إلى اللطف، وطمأنينة الجمع إلى البقاء، وطمأنينة المقام إلى نور الأزل.

النصّ مكتوباً بلغة مبسّطة

٥٩- باب الطمأنينة

قال الله عز وجل: ﴿يَٰٓأَيَّتُهَا ٱلنَّفۡسُ ٱلۡمُطۡمَئِنَّةُ﴾ (الفجر:٢٧).

الطمأنينة هي سكينةٌ دائمةٌ تنبع من ثقة القلب بالله، تختلف عن السكينة المؤقتة التي قد تزول.

وهي ثلاث درجات:

الدرجة الأولى: طمأنينة القلب

يشعر المؤمنُ بالراحة والثقة لأن ذِكر الله يملأ قلبه، فيتحول خوفه إلى أمل، وتعبُه إلى رضًا، وابتلاؤه إلى ثقةٍ بالثواب. مثل طفلٍ يهدأ عند احتضان والديه.

الدرجة الثانية: طمأنينة الروح

تسمو الروحُ بالسعي نحو فهم أسرار الخلق، والشوق للقاء الله، والجمع بين الظاهر والباطن في الإيمان. كباحثٍ يدرس الكونَ بصبرٍ لاكتشاف حكمة الله فيه.

الدرجة الثالثة: طمأنينة القرب من الله

يشهد القلبُ لطفَ الله الخفيّ، ويستقر في نور وجوده الأزليّ، كسفينةٍ تسبح في محيطٍ هادئٍ لا تعكّر أمواجه ظروفُ الدنيا.

الموجز والنصيحة العملية:

الطمأنينةُ ثمرةُ الإيمانِ العميقِ بالله. نصائحنا لك:

- تأمّل قوله تعالى: ﴿ ٱلَّذِينَ ءَامَنُواْ وَتَطۡمَئِنُّ قُلُوبُهُم بِذِكۡرِ ٱللَّهِۗ﴾ (الرعد:٢٨).
- خُذْ بِأسباب الطمأنينة: حافظ على الذكر، واستشعر حكمة الله في كل شيء.
- ثِقْ بأن الابتلاء مؤقتٌ، وأن الراحةَ الحقيقيةَ في القرب من الله.

نص الشيخ الهروي

٦٠- باب الهمة

قال الله عز وجل: (ما زاغ البصر وما طغى)(النجم:١٧).
الهمة ما يملك الانبعاث للمقصود صرفاً، لا يتمالك صاحبها ولا يلتفت عنها.
وهي على ثلاث درجات:
الدرجة الأولى: همة تصون القلب من خسة الرغبة في الفاني، وتحمله على الرغبة في الباقي، وتصفية من كدر التواني.
والدرجة الثانية: همة تورث أنفة من المبالاة بالعلل، والنزول على العمل، والثقة بالأمل.
والدرجة الثالثة: همة تصاعد عن الأحوال والمقامات، وتزرى بالأعواض والدرجات، وتنحو عن النعوت نحو الذات.

النصّ مكتوباً بلغة مبسّطة

٦٠- باب الهمة

قال الله عز وجل: ﴿مَا زَاغَ الْبَصَرُ وَمَا طَغَىٰ﴾ (النجم:١٧).

الهِمَّةُ هي العزيمةُ التي تُوجِّه القلبَ نحو الله دون ترددٍ أو انحراف.

وتنقسم إلى ثلاث درجات:

الدرجة الأولى: هِمَّة التطهير
تُنقي القلبَ من التعلق بالدنيا الفانية، وتدفعه لطلب الباقي عند الله، وتُخلِّصه من كسل الروح. كمُسافرٍ يرمي أمتعته الزائدة ليَخِفَّ في سيره نحو هدفه.

الدرجة الثانية: هِمَّة الثبات
تمنحُ صاحبَها عزيمةً لا تُهزم أمام المصاعب، وثقةً بوعد الله، واستعدادًا للتضحية من أجل الحق. كجنديٍّ يسير في طريقٍ وعرٍ وهو واثقٌ من نصر قادم.

الدرجة الثالثة: هِمَّة التجرُّد

تعلو بالقلب فوق كلِّ منصبٍ أو مرتبةٍ دنيوية، فلا يهتم إلا بقرب الله. كطائرٍ يحلِّق في السماء لا يلتفت لِما تحته.

الموجز والنصيحة العملية:

الهِمَّةُ سرُّ الارتقاءِ الروحيِّ. نصائحنا لك:

- تأمّل قوله تعالى: ﴿فَبِمَا رَحْمَةٍ مِّنَ اللَّهِ لِنتَ لَهُمْ وَلَوْ كُنتَ فَظًّا غَلِيظَ الْقَلْبِ لَانفَضُّوا مِنْ حَوْلِكَ﴾ (آل عمران:١٥٩).
- حدِّد هدفك الأسمى: اجعل رضا الله غايتك الأولى في كل عمل.
- لا تستسلم لليأس؛ فالهِمَّةُ العالية تُحوِّل العقباتِ إلى سلالمٍ للقرب من الله.

٧- قسم الأحوال

وأما قسم الأحوال فهو عشرة أبواب وهي:
المحبة والغيرة والشوق والقلق والعطش والوجد والدهش والهيمان والبرق والذوق.

نص الشيخ الهروي

٦١- باب المحبة

قال الله عز وجل: (من يرتد منكم عن دينه فسوف يأتي الله بقوم يحبهم ويحبونه)(المائدة:٥٤).
المحبة تعلق القلب بين الهمة والأنس، في البذل والمنع، على الإفراد.
والمحبة أول أودية الفناء، والعقبة التي ينحدر منها على منازل المحو، وهي آخر منزل تلقى فيه مقدمة العامة ساقة الخاصة. وما دونها أغراض لأعواض.
والمحبة هي سمة الطائفة وعنوان الطريقة ومعقد النسبة.
وهي على ثلاث درجات:
الدرجة الأولى: محبة تقطع الوساوس، وتلذّ الخدمة، وتسلي عن المصائب.وهي محبة تنبت من مطالعة المنة، وتثبت باتباع السنة، وتنمو على الإجابة للفاقة.
والدرجة الثانية: محبة تبعث على إيثار الحق على غيره، وتلهج اللسان بذكره، وتعلق القلب بشهوده.وهي محبة تظهر من مطالعة الصفات، والنظر في الآيات، والارتياض بالمقامات.
والدرجة الثالثة: محبة خاطفة تقطع العبارة، وتدقق الإشارة، ولا تنتهي بالنعوت.
وهذه المحبة هي قطب هذا الشأن، وما دونها محاب نادت عليها الألسن، وادعتها الخليقة، وأوجبتها العقول.

النصّ مكتوباً بلغة مبسّطة

٦١- باب المحبة

قال الله عز وجل: ﴿مَن يَرْتَدَّ مِنكُمْ عَن دِينِهِ فَسَوْفَ يَأْتِي اللَّهُ بِقَوْمٍ يُحِبُّهُمْ وَيُحِبُّونَهُ﴾ (المائدة:٥٤).

المحبة هي أعلى درجات القرب من الله، تُوجِّه القلبَ إليه في السراء والضراء.
وتنقسم إلى ثلاث درجات:

الدرجة الأولى: محبة البداية

تُخلص القلبَ من الشكوك، وتجعل العبادةَ لذيذةً، وتُسهِّل تحمُّلَ المصاعب. تنمو هذه المحبة بتذكُّر نعم الله، واتباع سنَّة النبي، صلى الله عليه و سلم، والاستجابة لنداء الفقراء. مثل مسافرٍ يجدُ لذةً في السير نحو هدفه رغم التعب.

الدرجة الثانية: محبة العمق

تدفعُك لتفضيل رضا الله على كل شيء، فلا يلهج لسانك إلا بذكره، ولا يشتاق قلبك إلا لرؤية آياته. تنمو بتأمُّل صفات الله، ودراسة آياته في الكون، والاجتهاد في العبادة. كشاعرٍ يُغرم بمعشوقته فيذكرها في كل لحظة.

الدرجة الثالثة: محبة الذروة

محبةٌ تفوق الوصف، لا تُعبَّر بكلماتٍ ولا تُحدُّ بإشارات، كضوءٍ ساطعٍ يُعمي العينَ عن رؤية ما سواه. هذه المحبة هي قِبلَةُ الروح، وعلامةُ القرب الحقيقي من الله.

<u>الموجز والنصيحة العملية:</u>

المحبةُ طريقُ القلبِ إلى الله. نصائحنا لك:

- تأمّل قوله تعالى: ﴿وَٱلَّذِينَ ءَامَنُوٓاْ أَشَدُّ حُبّٗا لِّلَّهِۗ﴾ (البقرة:١٦٥).
- اجعل حبَّ الله أولويتك: اذكره دائمًا، واخدم خلقه، وابحث عن رضاه في كل عمل.
- لا تيأس إن لم تصل إلى الدرجة الثالثة؛ فالمحبةُ تُزرعُ بالصبرِ والإخلاص.

نص الشيخ الهروي

٦٢- باب الغيرة

قال الله عز وجل، حاكيا عن سليمان عليه السلام: (ردوها علي فطفق مسحا بالسوق والأعناق)(ص:٣٣).

الغيرة سقوط الاحتمال ضنّا، والضيق عن الصبر نفاسة.

وهي على ثلاث درجات:

الدرجة الأولى: غيرة العابد على ضائع يسترد ضياعه ، ويستدرك فواته، ويتدارك تواه.

والدرجة الثانية: غيرة المريد على وقت فات، وهي غيرة قاتلة؛ فإن الوقت وحي الغضب، أبيّ الجانب، بطيء الرجوع.

والدرجة الثالثة: غيرة العارف على عين غطاها غينٌ، وسر غشيه رينٌ، ونفس علق برجاء، أو التفت إلى عطاء.

النصّ مكتوباً بلغة مبسّطة

٦٢- باب الغيرة

قال الله عز وجل: ﴿رُدُّوهَا عَلَيَّ ۖ فَطَفِقَ مَسْحًا بِالسُّوقِ وَالْأَعْنَاقِ﴾ (ص:٣٣).

الغيرة في طريق الله هي شعورٌ مقدسٌ صادر عن حب الله، يُحرِّك القلبَ لحماية الإيمان وتصحيح الأخطاء.

وتنقسم إلى ثلاث درجات:

الدرجة الأولى: غيرة العابد على ضياع الطاعات

كمن يفقدُ مالًا ثمينًا فيبذل جهده لاستعادته، هكذا يغار المؤمنُ على وقته الضائع في المعاصي ويُسرعُ للتوبة. مثل تاجرٍ يُصلحُ متجره بعد حريقٍ ليعودَ للعمل.

الدرجة الثانية: غيرة المريد على الوقت الضائع

ألمٌ عميقٌ لضياع لحظاتٍ كان يمكن أن تُستثمر في العبادة أو الخير. هذه الغيرة تُذكِّرُنا بأن الوقت كنزٌ لا يعود. كطالبٍ يندمُ على إهمال دراسته فيُضاعفُ جهده قبل الامتحان.

الدرجة الثالثة: غيرة العارف على القلوب الغافلة

غيرةُ المربي الروحيِّ على مَن أغفلوا ذكر الله، فيسعى لتنقية قلوبهم من الشوائب. كطبيبٍ يُجري عمليةً دقيقةً لإنقاذ مريضٍ من مرضٍ خفيٍّ.

الموجز والنصيحة العملية:

الغيرةُ المقدسةُ وقودٌ لإصلاح النفس والغير. نصيحتنا لك:

- تأمّل قوله تعالى: ﴿قَدۡ كَانَتۡ لَكُمۡ أُسۡوَةٌ حَسَنَةٞ فِيٓ إِبۡرَٰهِيمَ﴾ (الممتحنة: ٤).
- احرص على وقتك؛ فهو رأس مالِك في طريق الله.
- لا تيأس من إصلاح نفسك أو غيرك؛ فالغيرةُ الإيمانيةُ تبدأ بخطوةٍ صادقةٍ.

نص الشيخ الهروي

٦٣- باب الشوق

قال الله عز وجل: (مَن كَانَ يَرۡجُواْ لِقَآءَ ٱللَّهِ فَإِنَّ أَجَلَ ٱللَّهِ لَأٓتٖۚ)(العنكبوت:٥).

الشوق هبوب القلب إلى غائب. وفي مذهب هذه الطائفة علة الشوق عظيمة، فإن الشوق إنما يكون إلى غائب، ومذهب هذه الطائفة إنما قام على المشاهدة، ولهذه العلة لم ينطق القرآن باسمه.

ثم هو على ثلاث درجات:

الدرجة الأولى: شوق العابد إلى الجنة؛ ليأمن الخائف، ويفرح الحزين، ويظفر الآمل.

والدرجة الثانية: شوق إلى الله عز وجل؛ زرعه الحب الذي نبت على حافات المنن، فعلق قلبه بصفاته المقدسة، فاشتاق إلى معاينة لطائف كرمه، وآيات بره، وأعلام فضله. وهذا الشوق تفثأه المبار، وتخالجه المسار، ويقاويه الاصطبار.

والدرجة الثالثة: نار أضرمها صفو المحبة؛ فنغصت العيش، وسلبت السلوة، ولم ينهنهها مُعِزّ دون اللقاء.

النصّ مكتوباً بلغة مبسّطة

٦٣- باب الشوق

قال الله عز وجل: ﴿ مَن كَانَ يَرۡجُواْ لِقَآءَ ٱللَّهِ فَإِنَّ أَجَلَ ٱللَّهِ لَأٓتٖۚ ﴾ (العنكبوت:٥).

الشوق في طريق الصوفية هو اشتياقٌ خاصٌّ، لكنه يحمل "عِلَّة" (تناقضًا ظاهريًّا)؛ لأن الشوق في اللغة يكون لِغائبٍ، بينما مذهبهم قائمٌ على "المشاهدة" (الإحساس بوجود الله الدائم). لذلك لم يرد لفظ "الشوق" في القرآن تجاه الله، بل ورد "المحبة"، لأن الله حاضرٌ لا يغيب عن قلب المؤمن.

يُعبَّر عن هذا الشوق الروحي بثلاث درجات:

الدرجة الأولى: شوق العابد إلى الجنة

بحث المؤمن هنا عن الأمان من الخوف، والفرح بعد الحزن، وتحقيق الأمل بالثواب. مثل مسافرٍ يتوق إلى وطنه بعد غياب طويل.

الدرجة الثانية: شوق القلب إلى الله

ينمو هذا الشوق من حب صفات الله العظيمة، فيشتاق القلب لرؤية كرمه في الكون، لكنه يدرك أن الله قريبٌ لا يغيب. مثل تلميذٍ يشتاق لمعلمه الحاضر دائمًا ليستفيد من حكمته.

الدرجة الثالثة: شوق النار

اشتياقٌ كالنار يُذيب لذة الدنيا، لكنه ليس لغياب الله، بل لشدة القرب منه! كعاشقٍ يشتاق لمحبوبه رغم وجوده معه، لأن القرب يزيد الشوق.

<u>الموجز والنصيحة العملية:</u>

الشوقُ الروحيُّ دليلٌ على حبِّ الله، لا على غيابه. نصيحتنا لك:

- تأمّل قوله تعالى: ﴿وَهُوَ مَعَكُمْ أَيْنَ مَا كُنتُمْ﴾ (الحديد: ٤).
- حوّل شوقك إلى عملٍ: أكثر من الذكر، فالله أقربُ إليك من حبل الوريد.
- لا تفهم الشوقَ بمعناه المادي؛ فالله حاضرٌ، وشوقك إليه دليلُ اتصالِ قلبك به.

نص الشيخ الهروي

٦٤- باب القلق

قال الله عز وجل، حاكيا عن موسى عليه السلام: (وعجلت إليك رب لترضى)(طه:٨٤).
القلق تحريك الشوق بإسقاط الصبر.
وهو على ثلاث درجات:
الدرجة الأولى: قلق يُضيّق الخلق، ويبغض الخَلْق، ويلذّذ الموت.
والدرجة الثانية: قلق يغالب العقل، ويخلي السمع، ويصاول الطاقة.
والدرجة الثالثة: قلق لا يرحم أبداً، ولا يقبل أمدا، ولا يُبقي أحدا.

النصّ مكتوباً بلغة مبسّطة

٦٤- باب القلق

قال الله عز وجل: ﴿وَعَجِلْتُ إِلَيْكَ رَبِّ لِتَرْضَىٰ﴾ (طه:٨٤).

القلق في طريق السائرين إلى الله هو اضطرابٌ نابعٌ من شوقٍ عارمٍ لِلِقاء الله، يُضعف الصبرَ ويُحرك القلبَ بلا هدوء.

وهو ثلاث درجات:

الدرجة الأولى: قلق الفراق
يشعر المؤمنُ بضيقٍ يجعله ينفر من الناس، ويَملُّ من الدنيا، حتى يرى الموتَ راحةً من هذا الألم. مثل حيوانٍ محبوسٍ في قفصٍ يائسٍ من الخلاص.

الدرجة الثانية: قلق العجز
هنا يُصاب العقلُ بالارتباك، وتُصعَبُ سماعُ النصائح، وتنفدُ الطاقةُ في صراعٍ داخليٍّ. كمن يُحاصَر في عاصفةٍ لا يَهدأ فيها باله.

الدرجة الثالثة: قلق النار

قلقٌ لا يُرحم، كالنارِ التي لا تُطفأ، يَأكل القلبَ ولا يتركُ له مجالًا للراحة أو الأمل. كسفينةٍ تُحطمها الأمواجُ دون توقفٍ.

الموجز والنصيحة العملية:

القلقُ الروحيُّ علامةٌ على شوقِ القلبِ إلى الله، لكنه يحتاجُ إلى توجيه. نصائحنا لك:

- تأمّل قوله تعالى: ﴿فَإِنَّ مَعَ الْعُسْرِ يُسْرًا . إِنَّ مَعَ الْعُسْرِ يُسْرًا﴾ (الشرح:٥-٦).
- استعن بالصبر والصلاة: فهما مفتاحُ تهدئةِ القلق.
- لا تبتعد عن الناس: شاركهم همومك، واستفد من حكمتهم.

نص الشيخ الهروي

٦٥- باب العطش

قال الله عز وجل، حاكيا عن خليله عليه السلام: (فَلَمَّا جَنَّ عَلَيۡهِ ٱلَّيۡلُ رَءَا كَوۡكَبٗاۖ قَالَ هَٰذَا رَبِّي)(الأنعام:٧٦).
العطش كناية عن غلبة ولوع بمأمول.
وهو على ثلاث درجات:
الدرجة الأولى: عطش المريد إلى شاهد يرويه، أو إشارة تشفيه، أو عطفة تؤويه.
والدرجة الثانية: عطش السالك إلى أجل يطويه، ويوم يريه ما يغنيه، ومنزل يستريح فيه.
والدرجة الثالثة: عطش المحب إلى جلوة ما دونها سحاب علة، ولا يغطيها حجاب تفرقة، ولا يعرّج دونها على انتظار.

النصّ مكتوباً بلغة مبسّطة

٦٥- باب العطش

قال الله عز وجل: ﴿ فَلَمَّا جَنَّ عَلَيۡهِ ٱلَّيۡلُ رَءَا كَوۡكَبٗاۖ قَالَ هَٰذَا رَبِّي﴾ (الأنعام:٧٦).

العطشُ الروحيُّ هو اشتياقٌ شديدٌ لِلقُربِ من الله، كظمَانٌ لا يَرتوي إلا بِرِضاه.

وهو ثلاث درجات:

الدرجة الأولى: عطش المبتدئ

يبحث المؤمنُ هنا عن دليلٍ يهديه، أو كلمةٍ تُطمئنه، أو ملجأٍ يحميه. كطالبٍ ينتظرُ نتائجَ امتحانٍ بفارغ الصبر.

الدرجة الثانية: عطش السالك

يشتاقُ القلبُ إلى يومٍ يَكشفُ اللهُ له عن أسرارٍ تُغنيه، أو مرحلةٍ يجدُ فيها راحةً مِن تعبِ الطريق. كمسافرٍ في صحراءٍ يتوقُ لِرؤيةِ واحةٍ تَروي ظمأه.

الدرجة الثالثة: عطش العاشق

شوقٌ لا يُحجَبُ بغيومِ الشكوك، ولا يُفصَلُ عنه بحواجزِ الأوهام، ولا يرضى بغيرِ اللقاءِ الكاملِ مع الله. كعاشقٍ لا يهدأُ حتى يَلتقيَ مَحبوبَه.

<u>الموجز والنصيحة العملية :</u>

العطشُ الروحيُّ دليلُ حياةِ القلبِ. نصائحنا لك:

- تأمّل قوله تعالى: ﴿أَلَا بِذِكْرِ اللَّهِ تَطْمَئِنُّ الْقُلُوبُ﴾ (الرعد:٢٨).
- لا تُطفئ عطشَكَ بالدُّنيا: ابحث عن الله في الصلاةِ والتفكُّر.
- اصبر على الطريق: العطشُ الشديدُ يسبقُ الوصولَ إلى النبعِ العذبِ.

نص الشيخ الهروي

٦٦- باب الوجد

قال الله عز وجل: (وربطنا على قلوبهم إذ قاموا)(الكهف:١٤).
الوجد لهب يتأجج من شهود عارض مقلق.
وهو على ثلاث درجات:
الدرجة الأولى: وجد عارض يستفيق له شاهد السمع، أو شاهد البصر، أو شاهد الفكر، أبقى على صاحبه أثرا أو لم يبق.
والدرجة الثانية: وجد يستفيق له الروح بلمع نور أزلي، أو سماع نداء أولي، أو جذب حقيقي، إن أبقى على صاحبه لباسه، وإلا أبقى عليه نوره.
والدرجة الثالثة: وجد يخطف العبد من يد الكونين، ويمحص معناه من درن الحظ، ويسلبه من رق الماء والطين، إن سلبه أنساه اسمه، وإن لم يسلبه أعاره رسمه.

النصّ مكتوباً بلغة مبسّطة

٦٦- باب الوجد

قال الله عز وجل: ﴿وَرَبَطْنَا عَلَىٰ قُلُوبِهِمْ إِذْ قَامُوا﴾ (الكهف:١٤).

الوجد هو اشتعالٌ روحيٌّ يحدث عند تجلّي الحقائق الإلهية، يُحرِّك القلبَ ويُصفِّيه.

وهو ثلاث درجات:

الدرجة الأولى: وجد عابر
تأثُّرٌ مؤقتٌ بسماع آيةٍ، أو رؤية منظرٍ عظيمٍ، أو فكرةٍ عميقةٍ تُلهب المشاعر. مثل مَن يبكي عند سماع قرآنٍ مؤثِّرٍ، ثم يعود لحالته الطبيعية.

الدرجة الثانية: وجد النور الأزلي
إشراقٌ روحيٌّ يُحيط بالقلبِ كنورٍ قديمٍ، أو نداءٍ داخليٍّ يَجذبُه نحو الله، أو قوةٍ تُطهِّره من الشوائب. كشجرةٍ تُنقّى من الأوراق الميتة لتنمو من جديد.

الدرجة الثالثة: وجد التجرُّد

انفصالٌ كاملٌ عن الدنيا، حيثُ ينسى العبدُ نفسَه ويذوبُ في شهود الله. كطائرٍ يتحرر من قفصه ويطيرُ في السماء بلا قيود.

<u>الموجز والنصيحة العملية :</u>

الوجدُ نفحةٌ إلهيةٌ تُذكِّرُك بقرب الله. نصائحنا لك:

- تأمّل قوله تعالى: ﴿أَلَا بِذِكْرِ اللَّهِ تَطْمَئِنُّ الْقُلُوبُ﴾ (الرعد:٢٨).
- استثمِر هذه اللحظات: صلِّ، ادعُ، واقرأ القرآن عندما تشعر بوجدٍ روحيٍّ.
- لا تَخشَ الانفصالَ عن الدنيا: فالتجرُّدُ الحقيقيُّ يجعلك أقربَ إلى الله.

نص الشيخ الهروي

٦٧- باب الدهش

قال الله عز وجل: (فلما رأينه أكبرنه)(يوسف:٣١).
الدهش بهتة تأخذ العبد إذ فجأه ما يغلب عقله، أو صبره، أو علمه.
وهو على ثلاث درجات:
الدرجة الأولى: دهشة المريد؛ عند صولة الحال على علمه، والوجد على طاقته، والكشف على همته.
والدرجة الثانية: دهشة السالك؛ عند صولة الجمع على رسمه، والسبق على وقته، والمشاهدة على روحه.
والدرجة الثالثة: دهشة المحب؛ عند صولة الاتصال على لطف العطية، وصوله نور القرب على نور العطف، وصولة شوق العيان على شوق الخبر.

النصّ مكتوباً بلغة مبسّطة

٦٧- باب الدهش

قال الله عز وجل: ﴿فَلَمَّا رَأَيْنَهُ أَكْبَرْنَهُ﴾ (يوسف:٣١).

الدهش هو ذهولٌ يُصيبُ القلبَ عند مواجهةِ عظمة الله التي تفوقُ العقلَ والصبرَ والعلم.

وهو ثلاث درجات:

الدرجة الأولى: دهشة المريد
يشعرُ السالكُ بالعجزِ حين تفوقُ تجربةٌ روحيةٌ علمَه، أو تُنهكُ قواه، أو تُذهلُ عزيمتَه. كطالبٍ يسمعُ نظريةً علميةً معقدةً لأول مرةٍ فيَذهلُ من عظمة الخلق.

الدرجة الثانية: دهشة السالك

هنا تُحاطُ الروحُ بلمحةٍ من نورِ الله فتَنسى الزمانَ والمكانَ، وتذوبُ في الشهودِ. كمن يرى البحرَ لأول مرةٍ فيَغيبُ عن كلِّ شيءٍ إلا عظمةِ الأمواجِ.

الدرجة الثالثة: دهشة المحب

ذهولٌ يمحو الحدودَ بين العبدِ وربِّه، ليس باتحادٍ، بل بإدراكِ قربٍ لا يُوصف. كطفلٍ يُهدى له كنزٌ ثمينٌ فيَجمُدُ من الفرحِ دون أن يستطيعَ الكلامَ.

الموجز والنصيحة العملية:

الدهشُ دليلُ عجزِ العقلِ عن إدراكِ كمالِ الله. نصائحنا لك:

- تأمّل قوله تعالى: ﴿وَمَا قَدَرُوا اللَّهَ حَقَّ قَدْرِهِ﴾ (الأنعام:٩١).
- تقبّل دهشتَكَ بتواضع: فهي بابٌ لمعرفةِ عظمةِ الخالق.
- استخدم هذه اللحظاتِ لتعميقِ إيمانك: صلِّ بخشوعٍ، واقرأ القرآن بتدبُّر.

نص الشيخ الهروي

٦٨- باب الهيمان

قال الله عز وجل: (وخر موسى صعقا)(الأعراف:١٤٣).
الهيمان ذهاب عن التماسك تعجبا أو حيرة. وهو أثبت دواما وأملك بالنعت من الدهش.
وهو على ثلاث درجات
الدرجة الأولى: هيمان في شيم أوائل برق اللطف عند قصد الطريق؛ مع ملاحظة العبد خسة قدره، وسفال منزلته، وتفاهة قيمته.
والدرجة الثانية هيمان في تلاطم أمواج التحقيق؛ عند ظهور براهينه، وتواصل عجائبه، ولياح أنواره.
والدرجة الثالثة: هيمان عند الوقوع في عين القدم، ومعاينة سلطان الأزل، والغرق في بحر الكشف.

النصّ مكتوباً بلغة مبسّطة

٦٨- باب الهيمان

قال الله عز وجل: ﴿وَخَرَّ مُوسَىٰ صَعِقًا﴾ (الأعراف:١٤٣).

الهيمان هو ذَهابُ العقلِ من شدَّةِ الدهشةِ أمام عظمة الله، وهو أعمقُ من الدهشِ وأدوم.

وينقسم إلى ثلاث درجات:

الدرجة الأولى: هيمان البداية

يشعرُ العبدُ بالذهولِ عندما يلمحُ نورَ رحمةِ الله لأول مرةٍ، فيدركُ صِغَرَ نفسِه وضعفَ منزلتِه. كمن يقفُ لأول مرةٍ أمام محيطٍ هائلٍ فيَشعرُ بالضآلةِ.

الدرجة الثانية: هيمان الاكتشاف

يَغرقُ القلبُ في أمواجِ الأسرارِ الإلهيةِ التي تتكشفُ له، فيُصابُ بالحيرةِ من عجائبِ الخلقِ وأنوارِ الحقّ. كبحَّارٍ تُدهشُه الأمواجُ العاتيةُ وهو يحاولُ فهمَ أعماقِ البحرِ.

الدرجة الثالثة: هيمان الفناء

ذوبانٌ كاملٌ في شهودِ عظمةِ الله الأزليةِ، حيثُ يَختفي الشعورُ بالذاتِ، ويَغيبُ العقلُ في بحرِ الكشفِ الإلهيِّ. كشمعةٍ تذوبُ تمامًا في لهيبِ النورِ.

<u>الموجز والنصيحة العملية:</u>

الهيمانُ دليلُ عجزِ البشرِ عن إدراكِ كمالِ الله. نصائحنا لك:

- تأمّل قوله تعالى: ﴿سُبۡحَٰنَ رَبِّكَ رَبِّ ٱلۡعِزَّةِ عَمَّا يَصِفُونَ﴾ (الصافات:١٨٠).
- تقبّل عجزَكَ بتواضع: فالهيمانُ طريقٌ لتطهيرِ القلبِ من الكِبْرِ.
- استثمِر هذا الذهولَ: اجعله دافعًا لطلبِ المزيدِ من المعرفةِ والعبادةِ.

نص الشيخ الهروي

٦٩- باب البرق

قال الله عز وجل: (إِذْ رَءَا نَارًا)(طه:١٠).

البرق باكورة تلمع للعبد فتدعوه إلى الدخول في هذا الطريق. والفرق بينه وبين الوجد أن الوجد يقع بعد الدخول فيه، فالوجد زاد والبرق إذن.

وهو على ثلاث درجات

الدرجة الأولى: برق يلمع من جانب العدة في عين الرجاء؛ يستكثر فيه العبد القليل من العطاء، ويستقل فيه الكثير من الأعباء، ويستحلي فيه مرارة القضاء.

والدرجة الثانية: برق يلمع من جانب الوعيد في عين الحذر؛ فيستقصر فيه العبد الطويل من الأمل، ويزهد في الخَلق على القرب، ويرغب في تطهير السر.

والدرجة الثالثة: برق يلمع من جانب اللطف في عين الافتقار؛ فيُنشئ سحاب السرور، ويمطر قطر الطرب، ويُجري نهر الافتخار.

النصّ مكتوباً بلغة مبسّطة

٦٩- باب البرق

قال الله عز وجل: ﴿ إِذْ رَءَا نَارًا ﴾ (طه:١٠).

البرق هو ومضةٌ إلهيةٌ تُضيء طريقَ القلبِ نحو الله، تُنبِهُه لبدء الرحلة الروحية. وهو يختلف عن الوجد (الشعور العميق) الذي يأتي بعد السير في الطريق.

والبرق ثلاث درجات:

الدرجة الأولى: برق الرجاء

ومضةٌ تُظهر للمؤمنِ نِعَمَ الله الصغيرةَ كأنها عظيمة، وتُخفِّفُ عنه صعوبات الطريق، وتجعلُه يرضى بقضاء الله حتى لو كان مُرًّا. كمن يجدُ قطرة ماءٍ في الصحراء فيراها كنزًا.

الدرجة الثانية: برق الحذر

ومضةٌ تُذكِّرُه بعواقبِ الغفلة، فتُقلِّلُ تعلُّقه بالدنيا، وتدفعُه لتزكية سريرته. كمسافرٍ يُسرعُ خطاه عندما يسمعُ تحذيرًا من خطرٍ قريب.

الدرجة الثالثة: برق اللطف

ومضةٌ تُنشئُ في قلبه فرحًا لا ينتهي، وتُحيطُه برحمة الله، وتُشعرهُ بالفخرِ بانتسابه إليه. كمن يُفاجأ برَشَّةٍ من المطرِ تُنعِش أرضًا قاحلة.

<u>الموجز والنصيحة العملية:</u>

البرقُ دليلُ بدايةِ الرحلةِ إلى الله. نصائحنا لك:

- تأمّل قوله تعالى: ﴿أَلَا بِذِكْرِ اللَّهِ تَطْمَئِنُّ الْقُلُوبُ﴾ (الرعد:٢٨).
- استقبل هذه الومضاتِ بقلبٍ مفتوح: فهي دعوةٌ من الله لِتَقَرُّبٍ أعمق.
- لا تَغفل عن العبادة: البرقُ يُضيءُ الطريق، لكن السيرَ عليه بِجهدِك.

نص الشيخ الهروي

٧٠- باب الذوق

قال الله عز وجل: (هذا ذكر)(ص:٤٩).
الذوق أبقى من الوجد وأجلى من البرق.
وهو على ثلاث درجات:
الدرجة الأولى: ذوق التصديق طعم العدة؛ فلا يعقله ضن، ولا يقطعه أمل، ولا تعوقه أمنية.
والدرجة الثانية: ذوق الإرادة طعم الأنس؛ فلا يعلق به شاغل، ولا يفتنه عارض، ولا تكدره تفرقة.
والدرجة الثالثة: ذوق الانقطاع طعم الاتصال، وذوق الهمة طعم الجمع، وذوق المسامرة طعم العيان.

النصّ مكتوباً بلغة مبسّطة

٧٠- باب الذوق

قال الله عز وجل: ﴿هَٰذَا ذِكْرٌ﴾ (ص:٤٩).

الذوق هو شعورٌ عميقٌ بحلاوة الإيمان، أبقى من الوجد (المشاعر العابرة) وأوضح من البرق (الومضات الروحية).

وهو ثلاث درجات:

الدرجة الأولى: ذوق التصديق
يشعر المؤمنُ بطعم اليقين الذي لا يضعف أمام الشهوات، ولا ينقطع بالآمال الزائفة، ولا يعوقه تعلُّقٌ بالدنيا. كمن يتذوَّق عسلًا حقيقيًا فيميّزه عن المُحلَّى الصناعي.

الدرجة الثانية: ذوق الإرادة

هنا يجد القلبُ لذةَ الأنس بالله، فلا تشغله مشاغل الدنيا، ولا تُلهيه المُغريات، ولا تُكدِّره الخلافات. كمن يسمعُ لحنًا جميلًا فينصتُ له بكلِّ حواسِّه.

الدرجة الثالثة: ذوق الانقطاع

ذوقُ الوصول إلى حالةِ شعورٍ روحيٍّ مباشرٍ بالله، حيث تختفي الحواجز، ويُدرك العبدُ جمالَ الحضرة الإلهية. كمن يشربُ من نبعٍ صافٍ فيروي ظمأَه إلى الأبد.

الموجز والنصيحة العملية:

الذوقُ الروحيُّ ثمرةُ الإخلاصِ في الطريق. نصائحنا لك:

- تأمّل قوله تعالى: ﴿أَلَا بِذِكْرِ اللَّهِ تَطْمَئِنُّ الْقُلُوبُ﴾ (الرعد:٢٨).
- دَوِّن تجاربَكَ الروحية: فهي تُعمِّق إحساسَكَ بذوق الإيمان.
- لا تبحث عن الذوقِ لذاته: اجعل غايتك رضا الله، والذوقُ يأتي تلقائيًّا.

٨- قسم الولايات

وأما قسم الولايات فهو عشرة أبواب وهي:
اللحظ والوقت والصفاء والسرور والسر والنفس والغربة والغرق والغيبة والتمكن.

نص الشيخ الهروي

٧١- باب اللحظ

قال الله عز وجل: (ٱنظُرۡ إِلَى ٱلۡجَبَلِ فَإِنِ ٱسۡتَقَرَّ مَكَانَهُۥ فَسَوۡفَ تَرَىٰنِي)(الأعراف:١٤٣).
اللحظ لمح مسترق.
وهو في هذا الباب على ثلاث درجات:
الدرجة الأولى: ملاحظة الفضل سبقا؛ وهي تقطع طريق السؤال إلا ما استحقته الربوبية من إظهار التذلل لها، وتُنبت السرور إلا ما يشوبه من حذر المكر، وتبعث على الشكر إلا ما قام به الحق عز وجل من حق الصفة.
والدرجة الثانية: ملاحظة نور الكشف؛ وهي تُسبل لباس التولي، وتذيق طعم التجلي، وتعصم من عوار التسلي.
والدرجة الثالثة: ملاحظة عين الجمع؛ وهي توقظ لاستهانة المجاهدات، وتخلّص من رعونة المعارضات، وتفيد مطالعة البدايات.

النصّ مكتوباً بلغة مبسّطة

٧١- باب اللحظ

قال الله عز وجل: ﴿ ٱنظُرۡ إِلَى ٱلۡجَبَلِ فَإِنِ ٱسۡتَقَرَّ مَكَانَهُۥ فَسَوۡفَ تَرَىٰنِي﴾ (الأعراف:١٤٣).

اللحظ هو لمحةٌ روحيةٌ خاطفةٌ تُكشفُ للقلبِ أسرارًا إلهيةً.

وهو ثلاث درجات:

الدرجة الأولى: لحظ الفضل الإلهي

إدراكٌ مفاجئٌ لعظمةِ نعمِ الله، يَجعلُ العبدَ يتذلّلُ له شكرًا، لكنه يَخلطُ بين الفرحِ وخوفِ نقصانِ النعمة. مثل مَن يرى جمالَ الطبيعةِ فيتذكرُ خالقَها مع خوفٍ من زوالِها.

الدرجة الثانية: لحظ نور الكشف

ومضةٌ تُظهرُ للقلبِ حقائقَ خفيةً عن طريقِ الإلهام، فتُنقّيه من الشواغلِ وتُشعرهُ بلذةِ القربِ من الله. كمن يَسمعُ صوتَ مُرشدٍ في الظلامِ فيهديه إلى الطريقِ الآمن.

الدرجة الثالثة: لحظ الجمع مع الله

نظرةٌ روحيةٌ تُذيبُ اهتمامَ العبدِ بالدنيا، وتُريه أن كلَّ جهدٍ بشريٍّ صغيرٌ أمامَ عظمةِ الخالق. كعالمٍ يُدركُ فجأةً أن اكتشافاتِه ما هي إلا ذرةٌ في بحرِ علمِ الله.

<u>الموجز والنصيحة العملية:</u>

اللحظاتُ الروحيةُ هِباتٌ تُعزّزُ الإيمانَ وتُقرّبُ من الله. نصائحنا لك:

- تأمّل قوله تعالى: ﴿سَنُرِيهِمۡ ءَايَٰتِنَا فِي ٱلۡأٓفَاقِ وَفِيٓ أَنفُسِهِمۡ﴾ (فصلت:٥٣).
- دوّن اللحظاتِ الإلهيةَ: فكتابتُها تُعمّقُ فهمَكَ وتُذكّرُك بنعمِ الله.
- لا تنسَ التواضعَ: فكلُّ لحظةٍ روحيةٍ هي مِنّةٌ من الله، لا دَخلَ لكَ فيها.

نص الشيخ الهروي

٧٢- باب الوقت

قال الله عز وجل: (ثُمَّ جِئْتَ عَلَىٰ قَدَرٍ يَٰمُوسَىٰ)(طه:٤٠).
الوقت اسم لظرف الكون.
وهو اسم في هذا الباب لثلاثة معان على ثلاث درجات:
المعنى الأول: حينُ وجدٍ صادقٍ لإيناس ضياء فضلٍ جذبه صفاء رجاءٍ، أو لقصمة جذبها صدق خوف، أو لتلهيب شوق جذبه اشتعال محبة.
والمعنى الثاني: اسم لطريقِ سالكٍ يسير بين تمكن وتلون، لكنه إلى التمكن ما هو يسلك الحال ويلتفت إلى العلم، فالعلم يشغله في حين والحال يحمله في حين، فبلاؤه بينهما يذيقه شهودا طورا، ويكسوه غيرة طورا، ويريه غبرة تفرق طورا.
والمعنى الثالث: قالوا "الوقت الحق"؛ أرادوا به استغراق رسم الوقت في وجود الحق، وهذا المعنى يشق على هذا الاسم عندي.
لكنه هو اسم في هذا المعنى الثالث، لحين يتلاشى فيه الرسوم كشفا لا وجودا محضا، وهو فوق البرق والوجد، وهو يشارف مقام الجمع لو دام وبقي، ولا يبلغ وادي الوجود، لكنه يكفي مؤنة المعاملة، ويصفي عين المسامرة، ويشم روائح الوجود.

النصّ مكتوباً بلغة مبسّطة

٧٢- باب الوقت

قال الله عز وجل: ﴿ثُمَّ جِئْتَ عَلَىٰ قَدَرٍ يَٰمُوسَىٰ﴾ (طه:٤٠).

الوقت في طريق السائرين إلى الله له ثلاثة معاني رئيسية، كلُّ معنى ينقسم إلى ثلاث درجات:

المعنى الأول: وقت الشوق والرهبة. وهو على ثلاث درجات:

- الدرجة الأولى: لحظاتٌ يَشعر فيها القلبُ بجذبٍ نحو الله بسبب نقاء الأمل أو الخوف الصادق. مثل مَن ينتظر غائبًا عزيزًا فيُدرك قيمة الوقت.
- الدرجة الثانية: وقتٌ تُلهِبُه محبةُ الله، فيشتاق العبدُ لقُربه كاشتياق الظمآن للماء.
- الدرجة الثالثة: وقتٌ تختلط فيه المشاعر بين الفرح بالفضل الإلهي والخوف من زوال النعمة.

المعنى الثاني: وقت السير بين العلم والحال
وهو على ثلاث درجات:

- الدرجة الأولى: مرحلةٌ يتنقل فيها السالكُ بين التمسك بالعلم الشرعي والتجربة الروحية، كطالبٍ يدرس النظريات ثم يطبقها.
- الدرجة الثانية: وقتٌ يشهد فيه القلبُ تناقضات الطريق، فتارةً يغلب عليه اليقين، وتارةً يُصيبه القلق.
- الدرجة الثالثة: وقتٌ يَصِلُ فيه السالكُ إلى توازنٍ بين العلم والعمل، فيصبحُ الوقتُ جسرًا للقرب من الله.

المعنى الثالث: الوقت الحق (الوقت المطلق)
وهو على ثلاث درجات:

- الدرجة الأولى: لحظةٌ يذوب فيها إحساسُ العبدِ بالزمن، ويُدرك أن كلَّ شيءٍ بيد الله. كمن يغيب عن نفسه في الصلاة.
- الدرجة الثانية: وقتٌ يُدرك فيه العبدُ أن الدنيا ظلٌّ زائل، فيتعلق بالله وحده.
- الدرجة الثالثة: وقتٌ يُشرق فيه نورُ الحقِّ على القلب، فيرى العبدُ الكونَ بمنظورٍ جديدٍ، لكنه يبقى في حدود العبودية دون ادعاءِ الاتحاد.

الموجز والنصيحة العملية:

الوقتُ هو وعاءُ الأعمالِ وقيمةُ العمرِ. نصيحتنا لك:

- تأمّل قوله تعالى: ﴿وَهُوَ ٱلَّذِي جَعَلَ ٱلَّيۡلَ وَٱلنَّهَارَ خِلۡفَةٗ لِّمَنۡ أَرَادَ أَن يَذَّكَّرَ أَوۡ أَرَادَ شُكُورٗا﴾ (الفرقان:٦٢).
- استثمِرْ كلَّ لحظةٍ: في الذكر، والطاعة، والإحسان.
- ثِقْ بتدبير الله: فـ"الوقت الحق" هو حينُ تسليمِ القلبِ له.

نص الشيخ الهروي

٧٣- باب الصفاء

قال الله عز وجل: (وإنهم عندنا لمن المصطفين الأخيار)(ص:٤٧).
الصفاء اسم للبراءة من الكدر. وهو في هذا الباب سقوط التلون. وهو على ثلاث درجات:
الدرجة الأولى: صفاء علم؛ يهذب لسلوك الطريق، ويبصر غاية الجد، ويصحح همة القاصد.
والدرجة الثانية: صفاء حال؛ تشاهد به شواهد التحقيق، وتذاق به حلاوة المناجاة، وينسى به الكون.
والدرجة الثالثة: صفاء اتصال؛ يدرج حظ العبودية في حق الربوبية، ويغرق نهايات الخبر في بدايات العيان، ويطوى خسة التكاليف في عزل الأزل.

النصّ مكتوباً بلغة مبسّطة

٧٣- باب الصفاء

قال الله عز وجل: ﴿وَإِنَّهُمْ عِندَنَا لَمِنَ الْمُصْطَفَيْنَ الْأَخْيَارِ﴾ (ص:٤٧).

الصفاء هو التحرر من كلِّ شائبة، وثبات القلب على الحق دون تردد.

وهو ثلاث درجات:

الدرجة الأولى: صفاء العلم

- يصفّي الفهم لمعرفة طريق الله الصحيح.
- يُظهر الهدف الحقيقي من الجدِّ والاجتهاد.
- يُقوِّم نية السالك ويوجهها نحو الخير.

الدرجة الثانية: صفاء الحال

- يختبر القلب لذة المناجاة مع الله.
- يرى السالك آثار رحمة الله في كل شيء حوله.
- ينشغل بالحق حتى ينسى هموم الدنيا.

الدرجة الثالثة: صفاء الاتصال

- تذوب حدود الجهد البشري في إدراك عظمة الله.
- تتحول المعرفة النظرية إلى يقينٍ يشعُّ في القلب.
- تُرفع الأعباء النفسية بانسجام القلب مع حكمة الله.

الموجز والنصيحة العملية:

الصفاءُ مرآةُ القلب النقية. نصيحتنا لك:

- تأمّل قوله تعالى: ﴿قَدۡ أَفۡلَحَ مَن زَكَّىٰهَا﴾ (الشمس:٩).
- طهِّر قلبك: بالاستغفار، ومراقبة الله في الخلوات.
- اسعَ إلى اليقين: كلما زاد صفاؤك، اقتربتَ من فهم حكمة الله في حياتك.

نص الشيخ الهروي

٧٤- باب السرور

قال الله عز وجل: (قل بفظل الله وبرحمته فبذلك فليفرحوا)(يونس:٥٨).
السرور اسم لاستبشار جامع. وهو أصفى من الفرح لأن الأفراح ربما شابها الأحزان، ولذلك نزل القرآن باسمه في أفراح الدنيا في مواضع، وورد اسم السرور في الموضعين في القرآن في حال الآخرة.
وهو في هذا الباب على ثلاث درجات:
الدرجة الأولى: سرور ذوقٍ ذهب بثلاثة أحزان؛ حزن أورثه خوف الانقطاع، وحزن هاجته ظلمة الجهل، وحزن اغشته وحشة التفرق.
والدرجة الثانية: سرورُ شهودٍ كشف حجاب العلم، وفك رق التكلف، ونفي صغار الاختيار.
والدرجة الثالثة: سرور سماع الإجابة؛ وهو سرور يمحو آثار الوحشة، ويقرع باب المشاهدة، ويضحك الروح.

النصّ مكتوباً بلغة مبسّطة

٧٤- باب السرور

قال الله عز وجل: ﴿قُلْ بِفَضْلِ اللَّهِ وَبِرَحْمَتِهِ فَبِذَٰلِكَ فَلْيَفْرَحُوا﴾ (يونس:٥٨).

السرور هنا هو فرحٌ نقيٌّ لا تشوبه شوائب الدنيا؛ ولذلك خصّ الله كلمة السرور في القرآن الكريم في وصف أحوال اللآخرة.

وله ثلاث درجات:

الدرجة الأولى: سرور الذوق

- يُزيل ثلاثة أحزان:

- خوف الانقطاع عن الله.
- ظلام الجهل بحقائقه.
- وحشة التفرُّق عن محبته.

الدرجة الثانية: سرور الشهود

- يَكشِف حجابَ العقل المحدود.
- يُحرِّر القلبَ من التكلُّف والتصنُّع.
- يرفع الإنسان عن صغار الاختيارات الدنيوية.

الدرجة الثالثة: سرور سماع الإجابة

- يمحو آثار الوحشة بين العبد وربِّه.
- يُقرَع به باب المشاهدة القلبية لجمال الحق.
- يُنعِش الروحَ بلذة القرب الإلهي.

<u>الموجز والنصيحة العملية:</u>

السرورُ الحقيقيُّ ثمرةُ القرب من الله. نصيحتنا لك:

- تأمّل قوله تعالى: ﴿الَّذِينَ آمَنُوا وَتَطْمَئِنُّ قُلُوبُهُم بِذِكْرِ اللَّهِ﴾ (الرعد:٢٨).
- اشكر نِعَم الله: فكلُّ فضلٍ منه سببٌ للسرور.
- تَجاوَزْ همومَك: بالتوكل عليه، فهو كافيك.

نص الشيخ الهروي

٧٥- باب السر

قال الله عز وجل: (الله أعلم بما في أنفسهم)(هود:٣١).
أصحاب السر هم الأخفياء الذين ورد فيهم الخبر.
وهم ثلاث طبقات على ثلاث درجات:
الطبقة الأولى: طائفة علت هممهم، وصفت قصودهم، وصح سلوكهم، ولم يوقف لهم على رسم، ولم ينسبوا إلى اسم، ولم تشر إليهم الأصابع. أولئك ذخائر الله عز وجل حيث كانوا.
والطبقة الثانية: طائفة أشاروا عن منزل وهم في غيره، وورّوا بأمر وهم لغيره، ونادوا على شأن وهم على غيره؛ بين غيره عليهم تسترهم، وأدب فيهم يصونهم، وظرف يهذبهم.
والطبقة الثالثة: طائفة أسرهم الحق عنهم، فألاح لهم لائحا أذهلهم عن إدراك ما هم فيه، وهيمهم عن شهود ما هم له، وضن بحالهم على علمهم معرفة ما هم به؛ فاستسروا عنهم مع شواهد تشهد لهم بصحة مقامهم، من قصد صادق يهيجه غيب، وحب صادق يخفى عليهم علمه، ووجد غريب لا ينكشف لهم موقده. وهذا من أرق مقامات أهل الولاية.

النصّ مكتوباً بلغة مبسّطة

٧٥- باب السر

قال الله عز وجل: ﴿اللَّهُ أَعْلَمُ بِمَا فِي أَنفُسِهِمْ﴾ (هود:٣١).

أصحاب السر هم خُصوص عباد الله الذين تُخفي قلوبهم أسرار التقوى.

وهم ثلاث فئات:

الفئة الأولى: المخفيون المُختارون

- هممهم عالية لا تُحدها الدنيا.
- نواياهم صافية كالمرآة.
- لا يُعرفون بعلامات ظاهرة، فهم كنوز الله الخفية.

الفئة الثانية: المُتَّقون المُتخفون

- يُظهرون شيئًا ويُخفون أعظم منه.
- يُربّيهم أدبُ التواضع ويصونهم.
- تفوقهم الروحي يُنقّيهم من التكلُّف.

الفئة الثالثة: الغائبون عن أنفسهم

- استولى حبُّ الله على قلوبهم فنسوا ذواتهم.
- لديهم إخلاصٌ لا يشعرون به، وحبٌّ لا يدركونه.
- حالهم العجيب علامةٌ على قربهم من الله دون ادعاء.

الموجز والنصيحة العملية:

السرُّ جوهرُ الإخلاص. نصيحتنا لك:

-تأمّل قوله تعالى: ﴿أَلَا يَعْلَمُ مَنْ خَلَقَ وَهُوَ اللَّطِيفُ الْخَبِيرُ﴾ (الملك: ١٤).

-طهِّر سريرتك: فالله يعلم ما تُخفي الصدور.

-اعمل في صمت: فالأعمال الخفية أقرب إلى القبول.

نص الشيخ الهروي

٧٦- باب النفَس

قال الله عز وجل: (فَلَمَّآ أَفَاقَ قَالَ سُبۡحَٰنَكَ)(الأعراف:١٤٣).
يسمى النفس نفسا لتروح المتنفس به.
وهو على ثلاث درجات - وهي تشابه درجات الوقت.
والأنفاس ثلاثة:
النفس الأول: نفس في حين استتار؛ مملوء من الكظم، معلق بالعلم. إن تنفس تنفس نفس المتأسف. وإن نطق نطق بالحرب.
وعندي هو يتولد من وحشة الاستتار؛ وهي الظلمة التي قالوا إنها مقام.
والنفس الثاني: نفس في حين التجلي؛ وهو نفس شاخص عن مقام السرور إلى روح المعاينة، مملوء من نور الوجود، شاخص إلى منقطع الإشارة.
والنفس الثالث: نفس مطهر بماء القدس؛ قائم بإشارات الأزل، وهو النفس الذي يسمى صدف النور.
فالنفس الأول للغيور سراج، والنفس الثاني للقاصد معراج، والنفس الثالث للمحقق تاج.

النصّ مكتوباً بلغة مبسّطة

٧٦ -باب النَّفَس

قال الله عز وجل: ﴿ فَلَمَّآ أَفَاقَ قَالَ سُبۡحَٰنَكَ ﴾ (الأعراف:١٤٣).

النَّفَس في طريق السالكين علامةٌ على حال القلب مع الله.

وهو ثلاث درجات:

1. النَّفَس الأول: نَفَس الخفاء
   - ينشأ عندما يشعر القلب بالبُعد عن الله.
   - مليءٌ بالكظم (كتمان الألم)، ومتعلقٌ بالعلم النظري.
   - صاحبه يتنفَّس كمن يندم، وكلامه يعكس صراعه الداخلي.

2. النَّفَس الثاني: نَفَس التجلي
- يظهر عند إشراق نور المعرفة في القلب.
- ينتقل السالك من الفرح الروحي إلى شهود جمال الحق.
- يصعد به إلى مراحل تفوق الوصف بالكلمات.

3. النَّفَس الثالث: نَفَس القداسة
- مُطهَّرٌ بنور الله، مرتبطٌ بحكمته الأزلية.
- يُسمى "صَدَف النور" لشدة نقائه.
- هو ذروة القرب من الله دون زوال شخصية العبد.

دلالات رمزية:
- نَفَس الخفاء: مصباحٌ للغيورين على طاعة الله.
- نَفَس التجلي: سُلَّمٌ يصعد به السالك إلى المعرفة.
- نَفَس القداسة: تاجٌ للمحقِّقين في طريق الإخلاص.

<u>الموجز والنصيحة العملية:</u>

النَّفَسُ مرآةُ الروح. نصيحتنا لك:
- تأمّل قوله تعالى :﴿وَذَكَرَ اسْمَ رَبِّهِ فَصَلَّىٰ﴾ (الأعلى:١٥).
- تنفَّسْ بوعي :اجعل كلَّ نَفَسٍ ذكرًا لله.
- اسعَ إلى النقاء :طهِّر قلبك ليتحول نَفَسُك من كظمٍ إلى نور.

نص الشيخ الهروي

٧٧- باب الغربة

قال الله عز وجل: (فَلَوۡلَا كَانَ مِنَ ٱلۡقُرُونِ مِن قَبۡلِكُمۡ أُوْلُواْ بَقِيَّةٍ يَنۡهَوۡنَ عَنِ ٱلۡفَسَادِ فِي ٱلۡأَرۡضِ إِلَّا قَلِيلًا مِّمَّنۡ أَنجَيۡنَا مِنۡهُمۡ)(هود:١١٦).

الاغتراب اسم يشار به إلى الانفراد عن الأكفاء.

وهو على ثلاث درجات:

الدرجة الأولى: الغربة عن الأوطان. وهذا الغريب موته شهادة، ويقاس له في قبره من متوفاه إلى وطنه، ويجمع يوم القيامة إلى عيسى بن مريم عليه السلام.

والدرجة الثانية: غربة الحال. وهذا من الغرباء الذين طوبى لهم، وهو رجل صالح في زمان فاسد بين قوم فاسدين، أو عالم بين قوم جاهلين، أو صديق بين قوم منافقين.

والدرجة الثالثة: غربة الهمة. وهي غربة طلب الحق، وهي غربة العارف؛ لأن العارف في شاهده غريب، ومصحوبه في شاهده غريب، وموجوده فيما يحمله علم أو يظهره وجد، أو يقوم به رسم، أو تطيقه إشارة، أو يشمله اسم غريب. فغربة العارف غربة الغربة لأنه غريب الدنيا وغريب الآخرة.

النصّ مكتوباً بلغة مبسّطة

٧٧- باب الغربة

قال الله عز وجل: ﴿ فَلَوۡلَا كَانَ مِنَ ٱلۡقُرُونِ مِن قَبۡلِكُمۡ أُوْلُواْ بَقِيَّةٍ يَنۡهَوۡنَ عَنِ ٱلۡفَسَادِ فِي ٱلۡأَرۡضِ إِلَّا قَلِيلًا مِّمَّنۡ أَنجَيۡنَا مِنۡهُمۡ﴾ (هود:١١٦).

الغربة هنا هي انفراد السالك عن أقرانه في المجتمع بسبب تمسُّكه بصفات التقوى التي تُبعِده عن مسالكهم الدنيوية.

وهي ثلاث درجات:

الدرجة الأولى: الغربة الجسدية

- ترك الأوطان في سبيل الله (كالهجرة).
- يُعَدُّ صاحبها شهيدًا، ويُربط قبره بوطنه رمزًا لوفائه.
- يجتمع يوم القيامة مع الصالحين مثل عيسى عليه السلام.

الدرجة الثانية: الغربة الأخلاقية

- أن تكون صالحًا في مجتمع فاسد.
- عالمًا بين جهلة، أو مُخلصًا بين منافقين.
- هؤلاء هم "الغرباء" الممدوحون في الأحاديث.

الدرجة الثالثة: الغربة الروحية

- غربة العارف بالله؛ فهو يشعر باختلافٍ حتى في مشهوده الروحي.
- لا تَسَعُهُ العلامات الدنيوية ولا الأوصاف، فهو غريب عن الدنيا والآخرة معًا.
- همته العالية تجعله دائم السعي نحو الحق، كأنه في وطنٍ آخر.

<u>الموجز والنصيحة العملية:</u>

الغربةُ الحقيقيةُ هي ثمنُ السير إلى الله. نَصيحَتُنا لَكَ:

- تأمّل قوله تعالى: ﴿ إِنَّ ٱلَّذِينَ قَالُواْ رَبُّنَا ٱللَّهُ ثُمَّ ٱسۡتَقَٰمُواْ تَتَنَزَّلُ عَلَيۡهِمُ ٱلۡمَلَٰٓئِكَةُ﴾ (فصلت:٣٠).
- كن غريبًا بإرادتك: اختر ما يرضي الله حتى لو خالفت الجميع.
- لا تيأس: فكلما زادت غربتك، اقتربتَ من رحمة الله.

نص الشيخ الهروي

٧٨- باب الغرق

قال الله عز وجل: (فلما أسلما وتله للجبين)(الصافات:١٠٣).
هذا اسم يشار به في هذا الباب إلى من توسط المقام وجاوز حد التفرق.
وهو على ثلاث درجات:
الدرجة الأولى: استغراق العلم في عين الحال؛ وهذا رجل قد ظفر بالاستقامة، وتحقق في الإشارة، فاستحق صحة النسبة.
والدرجة الثانية: استغراق الإشارة في الكشف؛ وهذا رجل ينطق عن موجوده، ويسير مع مشهوده، ولا يحس برعونة رسمه.
والدرجة الثالثة: استغراق الشواهد في الجمع؛ وهذا رجل شملته أنوار الأولية، وفتح عينه في مطالعة الأزلية، فتخلص من الهمم الدنية.

النصّ مكتوباً بلغة مبسّطة

٧٨- باب الغرق

قال الله عز وجل: ﴿فَلَمَّا أَسْلَمَا وَتَلَّهُ لِلْجَبِينِ﴾ (الصافات:١٠٣).

الغرق هنا يعني الاندماج الكامل في طريق الله.

وهو ثلاث مراحل:

١ .المرحلة الأولى: غرق العلم في العمل

- يكون السالك مُستقيمًا في أفعاله، مُطابقًا علمه لعمله.
- يُدرك حقيقة الإخلاص، فيستحق أن يُنسب إلى الصالحين.

٢ .المرحلة الثانية: غرق الإشارة في الكشف

- يتحدث بلسان القلب لا بلسان العادة.
- يسير وفق ما يُشهد له روحانيًّا، دون التفاتٍ لرغبات النفس الدنيوية.

٣ .المرحلة الثالثة: غرق الشواهد في الجمع

- يُحيط به نور اليقين، فيرى كل شيءٍ بحكمة الله الأزلية.
- يتحرر من الأهواء الدنيوية، ويصبح همُّه الوحيد رضوان الله.

الموجز والنصيحة العملية:

الغرقُ الحقيقيُّ هو الاستسلامُ الكاملُ لله. نَصيحَتُنا لَكَ:

- تأمّل قوله تعالى :﴿وَمَنْ يُسْلِمْ وَجْهَهُ إِلَى اللَّهِ وَهُوَ مُحْسِنٌ فَقَدِ اسْتَمْسَكَ بِالْعُرْوَةِ الْوُثْقَى﴾ (لقمان:٢٢).
- وحِّدْ قولك وفعلك :ليكن عملك صدى لإيمانك.
- اطلب الفهم لا الشكل :فجوهر العبادة استسلام القلب.

نص الشيخ الهروي

٧٩- باب الغيبة

قال الله عز وجل: (وَتَوَلَّىٰ عَنْهُمْ وَقَالَ يَٰأَسَفَىٰ عَلَىٰ يُوسُفَ)(يوسف:٨٤).
الغيبة التي يشار بها في هذا الباب على ثلاث درجات:
الدرجة الأولى: غيبة المريد في مخلص القصد؛ عن أيدي العلائق ودرك العوائق، لالتماس الحقائق.
والدرجة الثانية: غيبة السالك؛ عن رسوم العلم، وعلل السعي، ورخص الفتور.
والدرجة الثالثة: غيبة العارف؛ عن عيون الأحوال والشواهد والدرجات، في حصن الجمع.

النصّ مكتوباً بلغة مبسّطة

٧٩- باب الغيبة

قال الله عز وجل: ﴿ وَتَوَلَّىٰ عَنْهُمْ وَقَالَ يَٰأَسَفَىٰ عَلَىٰ يُوسُفَ﴾ (يوسف:٨٤).

الغيبة هنا تعني انشغال القلب عن كل ما سوى الله.

وهي بثلاث مراحل:

١ .المرحلة الأولى: غيبة المريد (المبتدئ)

- ينفصل عن التعلقات الدنيوية والعقبات ليبحث عن الحقائق الإلهية.
- يُجاهد ليتحرر من شهوات النفس وهمومها.

٢ .المرحلة الثانية: غيبة السالك (المتقدم)

- يتجاوز التمسك الظاهري بالعلم والشكليات.
- يترك الكسل الروحي، ويسير بقلبٍ موقنٍ بلا تردد.

٣ .المرحلة الثالثة: غيبة العارف (الخواص)

- يغيب عن ملاحظة أحواله الروحية نفسها، فلا يشغله إلا الله.
- يستقر في "حصن الجمع" حيث لا مكان للانشغال بالذات أو المكاسب.

الموجز والنصيحة العملية:

الغيبةُ الحقيقيةُ انشغالُ القلبِ بالله. نَصيحَتُنا لَكَ:

- تأمّل قوله تعالى: ﴿أَلَا بِذِكْرِ اللَّهِ تَطْمَئِنُّ الْقُلُوبُ﴾ (الرعد:٢٨).
- طهِّر قلبك من الشواغل: بالذكر الدائم والصبر على الطاعة.
- لا تيأس من تكرار المحاولة: فكل خطوة تقرِّبك من الانعتاق الروحي.

نص الشيخ الهروي

٨٠- باب التمكن

قال الله عز وجل: (ولا يستخفنك الذين لا يوقنون)(الروم:٦٠).
التمكن فوق الطمأنينة، وهو إشارة إلى غاية الاستقرار.
وهو على ثلاث درجات:
الدرجة الأولى: تمكن المريد؛ وهو أن تجتمع له صحة قصد تسيره، ولمعُ شهودٍ يحمله، وسعة طريق تروحه.
والدرجة الثانية: تمكن السالك؛ وهو أن تجتمع له صحة انقطاع، وبرقُ كشفٍ، وصفاء حال،
والدرجة الثالثة: تمكن العارف؛ وهو أن يحصل في الحضرة، فوق حجب الطلب، لابسا نور الوجود.

النصّ مكتوباً بلغة مبسّطة

٨٠- باب التمكن

قال الله عز وجل: ﴿وَلَا يَسْتَخِفَّنَّكَ الَّذِينَ لَا يُوقِنُونَ﴾ (الروم:٦٠).

التمكن هو ثبات القلب في طريق الله بعد تجاوز مرحلة الطمأنينة.

وهو ثلاث درجات:

١ .الدرجة الأولى: تمكن المريد (المبتدئ)

- يجتمع لديه:
  - نية صادقة تُرشده في رحلته.
  - ومضات إلهامٍ تُعزز إيمانه.
  - طريق واضحٌ يمنحه راحةً في السير.

٢ .الدرجة الثانية: تمكن السالك (المتقدم)

- يجتمع لديه:

- انقطاع كامل عن الشواغل الدنيوية.
- لحظات كشفٍ تُظهر له الحقائق الروحية.
- صفاء داخليٌّ يجعله متوازنًا في جميع الأحوال.

٣ .الدرجة الثالثة: تمكن العارف (الخواص)

- يصل إلى:

- الحضور القلبي أمام الله دون حاجةٍ إلى طلب.
- النور الإلهي الذي يغلف وجوده باليقين.
- الاستقرار النهائي حيث لا تهزمه الشكوك.

<u>الموجز والنصيحة العملية:</u>

التمكنُ ثمرةُ الصبر والثقة بالله. نَصيحَتُنا لَكَ:

- تأمّل قوله تعالى: ﴿ وَٱسۡتَعِينُواْ بِٱلصَّبۡرِ وَٱلصَّلَوٰةِۚ﴾ (البقرة:٤٥).
- ثبِّت قدميك: بالعمل الدؤوب والذكر اليومي.
- لا تلتفت إلى المُشككين: فاليقينُ حصنك الأمين.

٩- قسم الحقائق

وأما قسم الحقائق فهو عشرة أبواب وهي:
المكاشفة والمشاهدة والمعاينة والحياة والقبض والبسط والسكر والصحو والاتصال والانفصال.

نص الشيخ الهروي

٨١- باب المكاشفة

قال الله عز وجل: (فأوحى إلى عبده ما أوحى)(النجم:١٠).
المكاشفة مهاداة السر بين متباطنين. وهي في هذا الباب بلوغ ما وراء الحجاب وجودا.
وهي على ثلاث درجات
الدرجة الأولى: مكاشفة تدل على التحقيق الصحيح، وهي أن تكون مستديمة. فإذا كانت حينا دون حين، لم يعارضه تفرق، غير ان الغين ربما شاب مقامه، على انه قد بلغ مبلغا لا يلفته قاطع، ولا يلويه سبب، ولا يقتطعه حظ. وهي درجة القاصد فإذا استدامت فهي الدرجة الثانية.
واما الدرجة الثالثة: فمكاشفة عين؛ لا مكاشفة علم، ولا مكاشفة حال. وهي مكاشفة لا تذر سمةً تشير الى التذاذ، أو تلجئ الى توقف، أو تنزل على ترسم.وغاية هذه المكاشفة المشاهدة.

النصّ مكتوباً بلغة مبسّطة

٨١- باب المكاشفة

قال الله عز وجل: ﴿فَأَوْحَىٰ إِلَىٰ عَبْدِهِ مَا أَوْحَىٰ﴾ (النجم:١٠).

المكاشفة هي إزالة الحواجز بين العبد وربه لرؤية الحقائق الإلهية.

وهي ثلاث مراحل:

١ .المرحلة الأولى: مكاشفة الاستدلال

- يستدلّ السالك بظواهر الكون على تجليات الخالق سبحانه وتعالى.
- كشفٌ متكررٌ يدل على صحة الطريق، لكنه قد يتخلله انقطاع.
- يصل السالك هنا إلى مرحلةٍ لا تُثنيه العقبات، لكنه قد يختبر فترات غفلة.

٢ .المرحلة الثانية: مكاشفة الثبات

- تصبح المكاشفة مستمرة دون انقطاع.
- يصل السالك إلى ثباتٍ لا يُضعفه شك، ولا يُبعده طمع، ولا يُشتته خوف.

٣ .المرحلة الثالثة: مكاشفة العيان

- رؤيةٌ مباشرةٌ للحقائق دون حاجة إلى أدلة أو تفسيرات.
- لا تترك هذه المكاشفة أثرًا للشهوة أو التوقف عند الظواهر، بل تنتهي بالمشاهدة القلبية الخالصة.

الموجز والنصيحة العملية:

المكاشفةُ هِبةٌ تُكتَسَبُ بالإخلاص. نَصيحَتُنا لَكَ:

- تأمّل قوله تعالى: ﴿ وَمَا كَانَ لِبَشَرٍ أَن يُكَلِّمَهُ ٱللَّهُ إِلَّا وَحْيًا أَوْ مِن وَرَآيِ حِجَابٍ﴾ (الشورى:٥١).
- طهّر نيتك: فالإخلاص مفتاح الكشف.
- لا تطلب الكشف لذاته: بل اسعَ إلى رضوان الله، فهو يهدي من يشاء.

نص الشيخ الهروي

٨٢- باب المشاهدة

قال الله عز وجل: (إن في ذلك لذكرى لمن كان له قلب أو ألقى السمع وهو شهيد)(ق:٣٧).
المشاهدة سقوط الحجاب بتّا، وهي فوق المكاشفة، لأن المكاشفة ولاية النعت، وفيه شيءٌ من بقاء الرسم، والمشاهدة ولاية العين والذات.
وهي على ثلاث درجات:
الدرجة الأولى: مشاهدة معرفةٍ؛ تجري فوق حدود العلم، في لوائح نور الوجود، منيخة بفناء الجمع.
والدرجة الثانية: مشاهدة معاينةٍ؛ تقطع حبال الشواهد، وتلبس نعوت القدس، وتخرس ألسنة الإشارات.
والدرجة الثالثة: مشاهدة جمع؛ تجذب إلى عين الجمع، مالكة لصحة الورود، راكبة بحر الوجود.

النصّ مكتوباً بلغة مبسّطة

٨٢- باب المشاهدة

قال الله عز وجل: ﴿إِنَّ فِي ذَٰلِكَ لَذِكْرَىٰ لِمَن كَانَ لَهُ قَلْبٌ أَوْ أَلْقَى السَّمْعَ وَهُوَ شَهِيدٌ﴾ (ق:٣٧).

المشاهدة هي رفع الحجاب تمامًا لرؤية الحقيقة مباشرةً دون وسيط،
وهي أعلى من المكاشفة لأنها تتجاوز العلامات الجزئية إلى اليقين الكامل.

وهي ثلاث مراحل:

١ .المرحلة الأولى: مشاهدة المعرفة

- تجاوزُ حدود العلم النظري إلى إدراكٍ ينيرُه نورُ الحق.
- يذوب السالك هنا في إشراقات الوجود ملتمساً القرب من إدراك معاني تجلّيات الحقّ.

٢ .المرحلة الثانية: مشاهدة العيان

- رؤيةٌ مباشرةٌ لحقائق الكون تُلغِي الحاجةَ إلى الشواهد الخارجية.
- يَلبَسُ القلبُ صفاتَ الطُّهر، وتصمتُ الألسنةُ عن الوصف لِعَجزها عن التعبير.

٣ .المرحلة الثالثة: مشاهدة الجمع

- اكتمالُ الوصال القلبي مع الحقيقة، حيث يُدرك السالكُ وحدةَ الوجود الإلهي دون التباس.
- يَسبحُ في بحر الحضرة الإلهية، مُتحررًا من قيود الزمان والمكان.

<u>الموجز والنصيحة العملية:</u>

المشاهدةُ ذروةُ السير إلى الله. نَصيحَتُنا لَكَ:

- تأمّل قوله تعالى: ﴿أَفَغَيْرَ اللَّهِ أَبْتَغِي حَكَمًا﴾ (الأنعام:١١٤).
- طهِّر قلبك: بالإخلاص والتوكل ليَهَبَكَ اللهُ البصيرة.
- اسعَ إلى العمق: لا تكتفِ بالظواهر؛ فالحقُّ يُرى بالقلب قبل العين.

نص الشيخ الهروي

٨٣- باب المعاينة

قال الله عز وجل: (ألم تر إلى ربك كيف مد الظل)(الفرقان:٤٥).
المعاينات ثلاث:
إحداها: معاينة الأبصار.
والثانية: معاينة عين القلب؛ وهي معرفة الشيء على نعته، علما يقطع الريبة ولا تشوبه حيرة. وهذه معاينة بشواهد العلم.
والمعاينة الثالثة: معاينة عين الروح؛ وهي التي تعاين الحق عيانا محضاً. والأرواح إنما طهرت وأكرمت بالبقاء لتناغي سناء الحضرة، وتشاهد بهاء العزّة، وتجذب القلوب إلى فِناء الحضرة.

النصّ مكتوباً بلغة مبسّطة

٨٣- باب المعاينة

قال الله عز وجل: ﴿أَلَمْ تَرَ إِلَىٰ رَبِّكَ كَيْفَ مَدَّ الظِّلَّ﴾ (الفرقان:٤٥).

المعاينة هي رؤية الحقائق بثلاث طرق:

١ .الرؤية الحسية (بالأبصار)

- إدراك المظاهر المادية كالظل والأشياء بالعين المجردة.

٢ .رؤية القلب

- معرفةٌ يقينيةٌ تنفي الشكَّ، تُدرَكُ بالإيمان العميق دون التباس.
- مثل: رؤية عظمة الله في الكون عبر آياته المُبْصَرة.

٣ .رؤية الروح

- إشراقٌ روحيٌّ تُدرَكُ به الحقائق الإلهية مباشرةً دون وسيط.
- الأرواح الطاهرة تُناغي جمال الحضرة الإلهية، وتجذب القلوب نحوها.

الموجز والنصيحة العملية:

المعاينةُ الحقيقيةُ رؤيةُ القلبِ والروح. نَصيحَتُنا لَكَ:

- تأمّل قوله تعالى: ﴿وَهُوَ مَعَكُمْ أَيْنَ مَا كُنتُمْ﴾ (الحديد:٤).
- نقِّ قلبك: بالتفكر في آيات الله لترى بعين البصيرة.
- لا تَقِفْ عند الظاهر: فكل شيءٍ يدل على عظمة الخالق.

نص الشيخ الهروي

٨٤- باب الحياة

قال الله عز وجل: (أَوَمَن كَانَ مَيْتًا فَأَحْيَيْنَٰهُ)(الأنعام:١٢٢).
اسم الحياة في هذا الباب يشار به إلى ثلاثة أشياء:
الحياة الأولى: حياة العلم من موت الجهل؛ لها ثلاثة أنفاس: نفس الخوف، ونفس الرجاء، ونفس المحبة.
والحياة الثانية: حياة الجمع من موت التفرقة؛ لها ثلاثة أنفاس: نفس الاضطرار، ونفس الافتقار، ونفس الافتخار.
والحياة الثالثة: حياة الوجود؛ وهي حياة بالحق، لها ثلاثة أنفاس: نفس الهيبة - وهو يميت الاعتلال، ونفس الوجود - وهو يمنع الانفصال، ونفس الانفراد - وهو يورث الاتصال. وليس وراء ذلك ملحظ للنظارة ولا طاقة للإشارة.

النصّ مكتوباً بلغة مبسّطة

٨٤- باب الحياة

قال الله عز وجل: ﴿ أَوَمَن كَانَ مَيْتًا فَأَحْيَيْنَٰهُ﴾ (الأنعام:١٢٢).

الحياة هنا ثلاث مراحل تُحيي القلب من موت الجهل والانفصال عن الله:

١ .الحياة الأولى: حياة العلم
- تنتشلُك من ظلام الجهل إلى نور المعرفة.
- تقوم على ثلاثة أسس:

  - خوفٌ من تقصيرك في حق الله.
  - رجاءٌ في رحمته ومغفرته.
  - محبةٌ تربطك به سبحانه.

٢ .الحياة الثانية: حياة الوحدة

- تتحررُ من انشغالات الدنيا وتتحدُ مع إرادة الله.
- تقوم على ثلاثة أسس:

- اضطرارٌ تدرك فيه أنك لا غنى لك عن الله.
- افتقارٌ تشعر فيه بضعفك أمام عظمته.
- افتخارٌ باختيارك طريق الحق رغم الصعاب.

٣ .الحياة الثالثة: حياة القرب الإلهي

- تذوبُ فيها الأنانية، ويصبح وجودك مرتبطًا بالحق.
- تقوم على ثلاثة أسس:

- هيبةٌ تُنسيك حاجاتك وتجلك عن السؤال.
- وجودٌ يملأ قلبك فلا تشعر بفراقٍ عنه.
- انفرادٌ تختلي فيه مع الله بلا شواغل.

الموجز والنصيحة العملية:

الحياةُ الحقيقيةُ قربٌ من الله. نَصيحَتُنا لَكَ:

- تأمّل قوله تعالى: ﴿ أَوَمَن كَانَ مَيۡتٗا فَأَحۡيَيۡنَٰهُ وَجَعَلۡنَا لَهُۥ نُورٗا يَمۡشِي بِهِۦ فِي ٱلنَّاسِ﴾ (الأنعام:١٢٢).
- اطلب العلم النافع: فهو يحيي القلب من موت الجهل.
- اخْلُ بنفسك: لترتقي من حياة الظاهر إلى حياة الروح.

نص الشيخ الهروي

٨٥- باب القبض

قال الله عز وجل: (ثُمَّ قَبَضۡنَٰهُ إِلَيۡنَا قَبۡضٗا يَسِيرٗا)(الفرقان:٤٦).
القبض في هذا الباب اسم يشار به إلى مقام الضنائن الذين ادخرهم الحق اصطناعا لنفسه.
وهم ثلاث فرق:
فرقة قبضهم إليه قبض التوفي، فضن بهم على أعين العالمين.
وفرقة قبضهم بسترهم في لباس التلبيس، وأسبل عليهم أكلة الرسوم، فأخفاهم عن عيون العالم.
وفرقة قبضهم منهم إليه، فصافاهم مصافاة سر، فضن بهم عليهم.

النصّ مكتوباً بلغة مبسّطة

٨٥- باب القبض

قال الله عز وجل: ﴿ثُمَّ قَبَضۡنَٰهُ إِلَيۡنَا قَبۡضٗا يَسِيرٗا﴾ (الفرقان:٤٦).

القبض هنا يعني أن الله يختار عباده المخلصين ويحفظهم في حالة خاصة قريبة منه.

وهم ثلاثة أنواع:

١ .الفئة الأولى: المقبوضون بالاعتزال

- يعتزلون عن العالم تمامًا، فلا يعرفهم أحدٌ من الناس.
- يَخفي اللهُ وجودَهم الروحيَّ، فيعيشون في خفاءٍ تامٍّ، كأنهم غائبون عن الأعين رغم حضورهم الجسدي.

٢ .الفئة الثانية: المقبوضون بالستر

- يُخفي اللهُ قدْرَهم الحقيقي تحت مظاهر عادية، فلا يُميّزهم الناس.
- قد يظهرون بسلوكٍ غامضٍ أو بسيطٍ لِيُحافظ الله على نقاء سرِّهم.

٣ .الفئة الثالثة: المقبوضون بالأسرار

- يربطهم الله به برباطٍ خاصٍّ غير مرئي، فيصبحون أقربَ إليه من أي شيءٍ آخر.
- هم مَحفوظون حتى من أنفسهم؛ فلا يدركون كامل حقيقتهم.

<u>الموجز والنصيحة العملية:</u>

القبضُ الإلهيُّ علامةُ حبٍّ ورحمة. نَصيحَتُنا لَكَ:

- تأمّل قوله تعالى: ﴿وَهُوَ مَعَكُمْ أَيْنَ مَا كُنتُمْ﴾ (الحديد:٤).
- لا تطلب الشهرة: فخيرُ العبادِ مَن اختبأَ عن الأعين.
- اخْلُصْ عملك لله: فالقربُ منه لا يُقاسُ بالظهورِ بل بالإخلاص.

نص الشيخ الهروي

٨٦- باب البسط

قال الله عز وجل: (يذرؤكم فيه)(الشورى:١١).
البسط أن ترسل شواهد العبد في مدارج العلم، ويسبل على باطنه رداء الاختصاص، وهم أهل التلبيس، وإنما بسطوا في ميدان البسط لأحد ثلاثة معان لكل معنى طائفة. فطائفة بسطت رحمة للخلق؛ يباسطونهم ويلابسونهم، فيستضئون بنورهم، والحقائق مجموعة، والسرائر مصونة.
وطائفة بسطت لقوة معانيهم وتصميم مناظرهم؛ لأنهم طائفة لا تخالج الشواهد مشهودهم، ولا تضرب رياح الرسوم موجودهم، فهم منبسطون في قبضة القبض.
وطائفة بسطت أعلاما على الطريق، وأئمة للهدى، ومصابيح للسالكين.

النصّ مكتوباً بلغة مبسّطة

٨٦- باب البسط

قال الله عز وجل: (يذرؤكم فيه)(الشورى:١١).

البسط هنا هو انفتاح القلب على الخير بثلاثة مظاهر:

١ .الفئة الأولى: البسط بالرحمة

- يعيشون بين الناس بقلوبٍ رحيمة، يُشرِقون عليهم بنور الإيمان، ويَحفظون أسرارهم دون تعالٍ.
- هدفهم: إرشاد الخَلق إلى الحق بلطفٍ وحكمة.

٢ .الفئة الثانية: البسط بالثبات

- أصحاب إيمانٍ راسخ لا تُزعزعه الشدائد، ولا تُشتته الماديات.
- قلوبهم مُطمئنَّة لأنهم يعلمون أن كل شيءٍ بقدر الله.

٣ .الفئة الثالثة: البسط بالهداية

- كالمصابيحِ في طريق السائرين إلى الله، يُبيِّنون المنهج القويم بالعلم والعمل.
- هم قدوةٌ عمليةٌ تُظهر جمال التمسك بالدين.

الموجز والنصيحة العملية:

البسطُ الحقيقيُّ انفتاحٌ على الخير دون تكلف. نَصيحَتُنا لَكَ:

- تأمّل قوله تعالى: ﴿وَاصْبِرْ نَفْسَكَ مَعَ الَّذِينَ يَدْعُونَ رَبَّهُم بِالْغَدَاةِ وَالْعَشِيِّ﴾ (الكهف:٢٨).
- كن رحيمًا: فالمؤمن مرآةُ رحمة الله في الأرض.
- ثبّت قلبك: بالذكر والتفكر في آيات الله.

نص الشيخ الهروي

٨٧- باب السكر

قال الله عز وجل: (قال رب أرني انظر إليك)(الأعراف:١٤٣).
السكر في هذا الباب اسم يشار به إلى سقوط التمالك في الطرب. وهذا من مقامات المحبين خاصة، فإن عيون الفناء لا تقبله، ومنازل العلم لا تبلغه.
وللسكر ثلاث علامات:
الضيق عن الاشتغال بالخبر والعظيم قائم، واقتحام لجة الشوق والتمكن دائم، والغرق في بحر السرور والصبر هائم.
وما سوى ذلك فحيرةٌ تنحل اسم السكر جهلا، أو هيمانٌ يسمى باسمه جورا.
وما سوى ذلك فكله نقائص البصائر؛ كسكر الحرص، وسكر الجهل، وسكر الشهوة.

النصّ مكتوباً بلغة مبسّطة

٨٧- باب السكر

قال الله عز وجل: ﴿قَالَ رَبِّ أَرِنِي أَنظُرْ إِلَيْكَ﴾ (الأعراف:١٤٣).

السكر هنا هو حالةٌ روحيةٌ يفقد فيها العبدُ الشعورَ بذاته من فرطِ فرحه بقربه من الله، وهي خاصّةٌ بالمُحبين الصادقين. له ثلاثة علامات:

١ .العلامة الأولى: انشغالٌ تامٌّ بالله
- يَنسى كلَّ شيءٍ سواه، حتى لو كان الأمرُ عظيمًا في عيون الناس.

٢ .العلامة الثانية: غوصٌ في بحر الشوق
- يَخوضُ في محبة الله بلا تردد، كمن يسبح في نورٍ لا ينتهي.

٣ .العلامة الثالثة: غمرةُ سرورٍ لا تُدرَك
- يَغرقُ في فرحٍ روحيٍّ يفوق الوصف، مع صبرٍ على ابتلاءات الطريق.

أما ما سوى ذلك من حالاتٍ تُسمَّى "سكرًا" – كسكر الجشع أو الشهوة – فهي ضلالٌ أو وَهْمٌ لا علاقةَ له بالسكر الروحي الحقيقي.

الموجز والنصيحة العملية:

السكرُ الحقيقيُّ هو ذوبانُ القلبِ في حبِّ الله. نَصيحَتُنا لَكَ:

- تأمّل قوله تعالى: ﴿ وَٱلَّذِينَ ءَامَنُوٓاْ أَشَدُّ حُبًّا لِّلَّهِ﴾ (البقرة:١٦٥).
- تَحلَّ بالتوازن: فلا يُلهيك الفرحُ الروحيُّ عن واجباتك الدنيوية.
- اطلب الإخلاص: فالسكرُ الحقيقيُّ ثمرةُ المحبةِ الخالصةِ لا الشهواتِ العابرة.

نص الشيخ الهروي

٨٨- باب الصحو

قال الله عز وجل: (حتى إذا فزع عن قلوبهم قالوا ماذا قال ربكم قالوا الحق)(سبأ:٢٣).
الصحو فوق السكر، وهو يناسب مقام البسط.
والصحو مقام صاعد عن الانتظار، مغن عن الطلب، طاهر من الحرج.
فإن السكر إنما هو في الحق، والصحو إنما هو بالحق. وكل ما كان في عين الحق لم يخل من حيرة، لا حيرة الشبهة، بل الحيرة في مشاهدة نور العزة. وما كان بالحق لم يخل من صحة، ولم يخف عليه من نقيصه، ولم تتعاوره علة.
والصحو من منازل الحياة، وأودية الجمع، ولوائح الوجود.

النصّ مكتوباً بلغة مبسّطة

٨٨- باب الصحو

قال الله عز وجل: ﴿حَتَّىٰ إِذَا فُزِّعَ عَن قُلُوبِهِمْ قَالُوا مَاذَا قَالَ رَبُّكُمْ ۖ قَالُوا الْحَقَّ﴾ (سبأ:٢٣).

الصحو هو حالةٌ روحيةٌ راقيةٌ تلي مرحلةَ السكر (النشوة)، تتميز بالوضوح والاستقرار. وهو أعلى من النشوة لأنه يرتبط بالاتزان الروحي وليس الغياب عن الوعي.

خصائصه الرئيسية:

١ .الوضوح الكامل:

- يرى السالكُ الحقائقَ بقلبٍ مُستنيرٍ دون تشويشٍ أو التباس.
- لا يحتاج إلى طلبٍ أو انتظارٍ؛ لأنه وصل إلى مرحلةِ اليقين المُطمئن.

٢ .التحرر من القيود:

- مَن تسير حياتُه وفقًا لمشيئة الله، لا يُخشى عليه الوقوعَ في الأخطاء؛ لأن استقامتَه في طريق الحقِ تحميه.
- يعيش في سلامٍ مع حكمة الله، واثقًا أن كلَّ شيءٍ يجري بتقديره، فلا قلقَ ولا تردد.

٣ .الصحة الروحية:

- حالةٌ نقيةٌ لا تشوبها شائبةٌ أو نقص، كالمرآةِ الصافية التي تعكس نورَ الحق.
- لا تؤثر فيه تقلبات الدنيا، فهو مُستقرٌّ في إيمانه.

الموجز والنصيحة العملية:

الصحوُ هو ذروةُ الاتزانِ الروحي. نَصيحَتُنا لَكَ:

- تأمّل قوله تعالى: ﴿قُلْ هُوَ رَبِّي لَا إِلَٰهَ إِلَّا هُوَ عَلَيْهِ تَوَكَّلْتُ وَإِلَيْهِ مَتَابِ﴾ (الرعد: ٣٠).
- اطلب الوضوح: بالتفكر في آيات الله والاستغفار.
- ثبِّت قدميك: فاليقينُ الحقيقيُّ لا يَزولُ بتغيير الظروف.

نص الشيخ الهروي

٨٩- باب الاتصال

قال الله عز وجل: (ثم دنا فتدلى . فكان قاب قوسين أو أدنى)(النجم:٨-٩).
أيْأس العقول فقطع البحث بقوله (أو أدنى),
وللاتصال ثلاث درجات:
الدرجة الأولى: اتصال الاعتصام، ثم اتصال الشهود، ثم اتصال الوجود. فاتصال الاعتصام تصحيح القصد، ثم تصفية الإرادة، ثم تحقيق الحال.
والدرجة الثانية: اتصال الشهود؛ وهو الخلاص من الاعتلال، والغنى عن الاستدلال، وسقوط شتات الأسرار.
والدرجة الثالثة: اتصال الوجود؛ وهذا الاتصال لا يدرك منه نعت ولا مقدار، إلا اسم معار، ولمح إليه مشار.

النصّ مكتوباً بلغة مبسّطة

٨٩- باب الاتصال

قال الله عز وجل: ﴿ثُمَّ دَنَا فَتَدَلَّىٰ . فَكَانَ قَابَ قَوْسَيْنِ أَوْ أَدْنَىٰ﴾ (النجم:٨-٩).

الاتصال هنا يعني القُرب الشديد من الله بثلاث مراحل، دون أيِّ وَهمٍ بالاتحاد أو الحلول:

١ .المرحلة الأولى: اتصال الاعتصام (التعلُّق بالله)

- تصحيح القصد :توجيه النية خالصةً لوجه الله.
- تنقية الإرادة :التحرر من الأهواء الشخصية.
- تحقيق الحال :الثبات الروحي في الطاعة.

٢ .المرحلة الثانية: اتصال الشهود (المشاهدة القلبية)

- التحرر من الحاجة إلى البراهين العقلية.
- رؤية الحقائق الإلهية بقلبٍ مُوقنٍ دون شك.
- زوال تشتت الأسرار؛ لانكشاف الحق بوضوح.

٣ .المرحلة الثالثة: اتصال الوجود (القُرب المطلق)

- قُربٌ لا يُوصفُ بالكلمات، يُدركُه السالكُ كإشراقة روحية.
- لا يُعبر عنه إلا بالإشارة، كالنور الذي يُبصرُه القلب دون أن يحويه.

<u>الموجز والنصيحة العملية:</u>

الاتصالُ الحقيقيُّ هو قُربُ القلبِ من الله. نَصيحَتُنا لَكَ:

- تأمّل قوله تعالى :﴿وَإِذَا سَأَلَكَ عِبَادِي عَنِّي فَإِنِّي قَرِيبٌ﴾ (البقرة:١٨٦).
- طهّر نيتك :فالقُربُ يبدأ بالإخلاص.
- لا تيأس :فالله يُقرّبُ من يشاءُ بِرَحمته

نص الشيخ الهروي

٩٠- باب الانفصال

قال الله عز وجل: (ويحذركم الله نفسه)(آل عمران:٢٨).
ليس في المقامات شيء فيه من التفاوت ما في الانفصال.
ووجوهه ثلاثة:
أحدها: انفصال هو شرط الاتصال؛ وهو الانفصال عن الكونين، بانفصال نظرك إليهما، وانفصال توقفك عليهما، وانفصال مبالاتك بهما.
والثاني: انفصال عن رؤية الانفصال الذي ذكرناه؛ وهو أن لا يتزنا عندك في شهود التحقيق شيئا يوصل بالانفصال منهما إلى شيء.
والثالث: انفصال عن الاتصال؛ وهو انفصال من شهود مزاحمة الاتصال عين السبق، فإن الانفصال والاتصال على عظم تفاوتهما في الاسم والرسم في العلة سيان.

النصّ مكتوباً بلغة مبسّطة

٩٠- باب الانفصال

قال الله عز وجل: ﴿وَيُحَذِّرُكُمُ اللَّهُ نَفْسَهُ﴾ (آل عمران:٢٨).

الانفصال هنا هو قطع التعلُّق بكل ما يُبعد عن الله.

وهو ثلاث أنواع:

١ .الانفصال الأول: الانفصال عن العالمين (المادي والروحي)

- ترك النظر إليهما: عدم الاهتمام المفرط بملذات الدنيا أو المكاسب الروحية الزائفة.
- التوقف عن الاعتماد عليهما: الاستغناء عن كل شيء سوى الله في الحاجات والطموحات.
- عدم الاكتراث بهما: تحرير القلب من الخوف أو الطمع في ما لدى الخلق.

٢ .الانفصال الثاني: الانفصال عن إدراك الانفصال نفسه

- الوصول إلى مرحلةٍ لا يشغُلك حتى التفكير في أنك "منفصل"، لأن قلبك مُنشغل بالله تمامًا.
- كمن يسبح في البحر فلا يفكر في الماء؛ لأنه جزءٌ من وجوده.

٣ .الانفصال الثالث: الانفصال عن الاتصال (المفارقة الروحية)

- فهم أن القرب من الله لا يحتاج إلى ادعاءات اتصالٍ أو انفصال، فالحقيقة فوق الأوصاف.
- مثل نور الشمس: تراه ولا تستطيع امتلاكه، فتسلم بوجوده دون محاولةِ التقيد به.

<u>الموجز والنصيحة العملية:</u>

الانفصالُ الحقيقيُّ هو تحريرُ القلبِ ليكون لله وحده. نَصيحَتُنا لَكَ:

- تأمّل قوله تعالى: ﴿قُلِ اللَّهُ ثُمَّ ذَرْهُمْ فِي خَوْضِهِمْ يَلْعَبُونَ﴾ (الأنعام:٩١).
- طهِّر قلبك من التعلقات: بالاستغفار والتوكل على الله في كل أمر.
- لا تَخَفِ الفقدَ: فمن يفقد ما سوى الله يَجدُ كلَّ شيءٍ فيه.

١٠- قسم النهايات

وأما قسم النهايات فهو عشرة أبواب وهي:
المعرفة والفناء والبقاء والتحقيق والتلبيس والوجود والتجريد والتفريد والجمع والتوحيد.

نص الشيخ الهروي

٩١- باب المعرفة

قال الله عز وجل: (وإذا سمعوا ما أنزل إلى الرسول ترى أعينهم تفيض من الدمع مما عرفوا من الحق)(المائدة:٨٣).
المعرفة إحاطة بعين الشيء كما هو.
وهي على ثلاث درجات، والخلق فيها ثلاث فرق:
الدرجة الأولى: معرفة الصفات والنعوت. وقد وردت أساميها بالرسالة، وظهرت شواهدها في الصنعة، بتبصير النور القائم في السر، وطيب حياة العقل لزرع الفكر، وحياة القلب بحسن النظر بين التعظيم وحسن الاعتبار. وهي معرفة العامة التي لا تنعقد شرائط اليقين إلا بها. وهي على ثلاثة أركان؛ أحدها إثبات الصفة باسمها من غير تشبيه، ونفى التشبيه عنها من غير تعطيل، والإياس من إدراك كنهها وابتغاء تأويلها.
والدرجة الثانية: معرفة الذات مع إسقاط التفريق بين الصفات والذات. وهي تنبت بعلم الجمع، وتصفو في ميدان الفناء، وتستكمل بعلم البقاء، وتشارف عين الجمع.
وهي على ثلاثة أركان؛ إرسال الصفات على الشواهد، وإرسال الوسائط على المدارج، وإرسال العبارات على المعالم. وهي معرفة الخاصة التي تؤنس من أفق الحقيقة.
والدرجة الثالثة: معرفة مستغرقة في محض التعريف، لا يوصل إليها الاستدلال، ولا يدل عليها شاهد، ولا تستحقها وسيلة. وهي على ثلاثة اركان؛ مشاهدة القرب، والصعود عن العلم، ومطالعة الجمع. وهي معرفة خاصة الخاصة.

النصّ مكتوباً بلغة مبسّطة

٩١- باب المعرفة

قال الله عز وجل: ﴿وَإِذَا سَمِعُوا مَا أُنزِلَ إِلَى الرَّسُولِ تَرَىٰ أَعْيُنَهُمْ تَفِيضُ مِنَ الدَّمْعِ مِمَّا عَرَفُوا مِنَ الْحَقِّ﴾ (المائدة:٨٣).

المعرفة هي الفهم العميق للحقائق الإلهية.

وهي ثلاث درجات:

١ .الدرجة الأولى: معرفة الصفات (للعوام)

- تُدرك صفات الله (كالرحمة، العدل) دون تشبيهها بصفات البشر.

- تقوم على ثلاثة أسس:

- الإيمان بالصفات كما وردت في القرآن دون تحريف.
- نفي التشبيه بين الله وخَلقه.
- التسليم بأن كُنْهَ ذات الله فوق إدراك العقل.

٢ .الدرجة الثانية: معرفة الذات (للخاصة)

- دمج صفات الله في فهمٍ واحدٍ لذاته، دون فصلٍ بينها.

- تقوم على:

- التحرر من الوسائط في الفهم.
- التخلص من التعلق بالشكليّات.
- الوصول إلى حالةِ اطمئنانٍ قلبيٍّ بوحدانية الله.

٣ .الدرجة الثالثة: المعرفة المُطلقة (لخاصة الخاصة)

- تجربةٌ روحيةٌ مباشرةٌ مع الله، لا تحتاج إلى أدلةٍ أو كلمات.

- تقوم على:
- رؤية قُرب الله بالقلب.
- تجاوز العلم النظري إلى المعايشة.
- الاتحاد الروحي مع الحق دون اختلاطٍ أو حلول.

<u>الموجز والنصيحة العملية:</u>

المعرفةُ الحقيقيةُ تُذيبُ القلبَ في محبة الله. نَصيحَتُنا لَكَ:

- تأمّل قوله تعالى: ﴿إِنَّمَا يَخۡشَى ٱللَّهَ مِنۡ عِبَادِهِ ٱلۡعُلَمَٰٓؤُاْۗ﴾ (فاطر:٢٨).
- اطلب العلم النافع: بقلبٍ خاشعٍ لا بغرضِ الظهور.
- لا تَقِفْ عند الظاهر: فكلما تعمَّقتَ في المعرفة، ازدادَ يقينُك.

نص الشيخ الهروي

٩٢- باب الفناء

قال الله عز وجل: (كل من عليها فان . ويبقى وجه ربك)(الرحمن:٢٦-٢٧).
الفناء في هذا الباب اضمحلال ما دون الحق؛ علما، ثم جحدا، ثم حقاً.
وهو على ثلاث درجات:
الدرجة الأولى: فناء المعرفة في المعروف، وهو الفناء علما؛ وفناء العيان في المعاين، وهو الفناء جحدا؛ وفناء الطلب في الوجود، وهو الفناء حقا.
والدرجة الثانية: فناء شهود الطلب لإسقاطه، وفناء شهود المعرفة لإسقاطها، وفناء شهود العيان لإسقاطه.
والدرجة الثالثة: الفناء عن شهود الفناء، وهو الفناء حقا، شائما برق العين، راكبا بحر الجمع، سالكا سبيل البقاء.

النصّ مكتوباً بلغة مبسّطة

٩٢- باب الفناء

قال الله عز وجل: ﴿كُلُّ مَنْ عَلَيْهَا فَانٍ . وَيَبْقَىٰ وَجْهُ رَبِّكَ﴾ (الرحمن:٢٦-٢٧).

الفناء هنا هو تلاشي كل ما سوى الله في القلب والوجود.

وهو ثلاث مراحل:

١ .المرحلة الأولى: فناء المعرفة والرؤية

- فناء العلم: إدراك أن كل شيء زائل إلا الله.
- فناء الجحود: ترك الاعتماد على المخلوقات.
- فناء الحق: تحوُّل الوجود كله إلى شعورٍ بوحدانية الله.

٢ .المرحلة الثانية: فناء الشهود (المشاهدة)

- التحرر من حاجة طلب الدنيا أو الآخرة.
- زوال التعلق حتى بالمعرفة الروحية نفسها.
- الوصول إلى حالةٍ لا يرى فيها السالك إلا الله في كل شيء.

٣ .المرحلة الثالثة: الفناء عن الفناء نفسه

- اختفاء شعور "الفناء" ذاته، لأن القلب أصبح مُنعكسًا بأنوار الله.

<u>الموجز والنصيحة العملية:</u>

الفناءُ الحقيقيُّ هو ذوبانُ الأنانيةِ في محبة الله. نَصيحَتُنا لَكَ:

- تأمّل قوله تعالى: ﴿هُوَ ٱلۡأَوَّلُ وَٱلۡأٓخِرُ وَٱلظَّٰهِرُ وَٱلۡبَاطِنُۖ﴾ (الحديد:٣).
- طهِّر قلبك: بالاستغفار وترك التعلق بغير الله.
- اسعَ إلى الخلود: بالعمل للآخرة، فما عند الله باقٍ.

نص الشيخ الهروي

٩٣- باب البقاء

قال الله عز وجل: (والله خير وأبقى)(طه:٧٣).
البقاء اسم لما بقي قائما بعد فناء الشواهد وسقوطها.
وهو على ثلاث درجات:
الدرجة الأولى: بقاء المعلوم بعد سقوط العلم، عينا لا علما؛ وبقاء المشهود بعد سقوط الشهود، وجودا لا نعتا؛ وبقاء ما لم يزل حقا، بإسقاط ما لم يكن محوا.

النصّ مكتوباً بلغة مبسّطة

٩٣- باب البقاء

قال الله عز وجل: ﴿وَاللَّهُ خَيْرٌ وَأَبْقَىٰ﴾ (طه:٧٣).

البقاء هنا هو استمرارُ حضورِ الله في القلب بعد زوال كلِّ ما سواه.

وهو ثلاث درجات:

١ .الدرجة الأولى: بقاء المعلوم (الحقائق الإلهية)

- يَبقى إدراكُ وجود الله كحقيقةٍ ملموسةٍ حتى بعد زوال المعرفة العقلية المجردة.

٢ .الدرجة الثانية: بقاء المشهود (التجربة الروحية)

- يقينٌ بأن الله – الخالق الدائم – يبقى بعد فناء الحياة الدنيا وزوال مظاهرها.
- يشعر السالكُ في هذه الحالة وكأنه يعيش في عالمٍ روحيٍّ خالدٍ، لا يزول بزوال الأجساد.

٣ .الدرجة الثالثة: بقاء الحق الأزلي

- يَبقى الله وحده كحقيقةٍ سرمديةٍ بعد زوال كلِّ ما هو زائلٌ ووهميٌّ.
- هذه المرحلة لا تُوصف بالكلمات؛ فمن أدركها لا يحتاج إلى عبارة، ومن لم يدركها لا تنفعه العبارات.

الموجز والنصيحة العملية:

البقاءُ الحقيقيُّ هو تمسُّكُ القلبِ بالله وحده. نَصيحَتُنا لَكَ:

- تأمّل قوله تعالى: ﴿كُلُّ شَيْءٍ هَالِكٌ إِلَّا وَجْهَهُ﴾ (القصص:٨٨).
- رَكِّزْ على الأبديّ: لا تُفرِغْ وقتَك إلّا فيما يُقرِّبُك إلى الله.
- اعملْ لِلْباقي: فالدُّنيا فانيةٌ، وما عند الله خيرٌ وأبقى.

نص الشيخ الهروي

٩٤- باب التحقيق

قال الله عز وجل: (أو لم تؤمن قال بلى ولكن ليطمئن قلبي)(البقرة:٢٦٠).
التحقيق تلخيص مصحوبك؛ من الحق، ثم بالحق، ثم في الحق، وهذه أسماء درجاته الثلاث.
أما درجة تلخيص مصحوبك من الحق: فأن لا يخالج علمك علمه.
وأما الدرجة الثانية: فأن لا ينازع شهودك شهوده.
وأما الدرجة الثالثة: فإن لا يناسم رسمك سبقة.
فتسقط الشهادات، وتبطل العبارات، وتفنى الإشارات.

النصّ مكتوباً بلغة مبسّطة

٩٤- باب التحقيق

قال الله عز وجل: ﴿أَوَلَمْ تُؤْمِنْ قَالَ بَلَى وَلَٰكِنْ لِيَطْمَئِنَّ قَلْبِي﴾ (البقرة:٢٦٠).

التحقيق هو الوصول إلى اليقين الكامل بالله عبر ثلاث مراحل:

١ .المرحلة الأولى: التحقيق مِنَ الحق

- تطهير العلم من الشكوك، بحيث لا يختلط إيمانك بجهلٍ أو تردد.
- مثل: يقين أم موسى حين ألقت بابنها في اليم، واثقةً بحفظ الله.

٢ .المرحلة الثانية: التحقيق بالحق

- انسجام المشاهدات الروحية مع الحق الإلهي، دون تعارضٍ أو تناقض.
- مثل: رؤية آيات الله في الكون دون تشويشٍ بالشهوات.

٣ .المرحلة الثالثة: التحقيق في الحق

- ذوبان كلِّ ما سوى الله في القلب، حتى تختفي الحاجة إلى العبارات أو الإشارات.
- هنا يسقط كلُّ وصفٍ، لأن القلب أصبح مرآةً تعكس حضور الله دون حجاب.

<u>الموجز والنصيحة العملية:</u>

التحقيقُ هو ذروةُ اليقينِ بالله. نَصيحَتُنا لَكَ:

- تأمّل قوله تعالى: ﴿الَّذِينَ آمَنُوا وَتَطْمَئِنُّ قُلُوبُهُمْ بِذِكْرِ اللَّهِ﴾ (الرعد:٢٨).
- اطلب الطمأنينة: بالتأمل في آيات الله وترك الشكوك.
- لا تكتفِ بالظاهر: فاليقين الحقيقيُّ يتجاوز العقل إلى القلب.

نص الشيخ الهروي

٩٥- باب التلبيس

قال الله عز وجل: (وللبسنا عليهم ما يلبسون)(الأنعام:٩).
التلبيس تورية بشاهد معار عن موجود قائم.
وهو اسم لثلاثة معان
أولها: تلبيس الحق بالكون على أهل التفرقة، وهو تعليقه الكوائن بالأسباب والأماكن والأحايين، وتعليقه المعارف بالوسائط والقضايا بالحجج والأحكام بالعلل، والانتقام بالجنايات والمثوبة بالطاعات. فأخفى الرضى والسخط اللذين يوجبان الوصل والفصل، ويظهران السعادة والشقاوة.
والتلبيس الثاني: تلبيس أهل الغيرة؛ على الأوقات بإخفائها، وعلى الكرامات بكتمانها، والتلبيس بالمكاسب والأسباب، وتعليق الظاهر بالشواهد والمكاسب، تلبيسا على العيون الكليلة، والعقول العليلة، مع تصحيح التحقيق، عقدا وسلوكا ومعاينة. وهذه الطائفة رحمة من الله عز وجل على أهل التفرقة والأسباب في ملابستهم.
والتلبيس الثالث: تلبيس أهل التمكن على العالم؛ ترحّماً عليهم بملابسة الأسباب، توسيعا على العالم لا لأنفسهم. وهذه درجة الأنبياء، ثم هي للأئمة الربانيين الصادرين عن وادي الجمع المشيرين عن عينه.

النصّ مكتوباً بلغة مبسّطة

٩٥- باب التلبيس

قال الله عز وجل: ﴿وَلَبَسْنَا عَلَيْهِم مَّا يَلْبِسُونَ﴾ (الأنعام:٩).

التلبيس هو حكمة إلهية تُخفي الحقائقَ عن بعض الناس وفقًا لحكمته.

وهو ثلاثة أنواع:

١ .التلبيس الأول: تلبيس الحق بالعالم المادي

- يُظهِر اللهُ الأحداثَ وكأنها مرتبطةٌ بأسبابٍ ظاهرية (مثل الزمان أو المكان أو الأسباب المادية)، ليختبر إيمان الناس.
- مثال: ربط النجاح بالجهد البشري دون إدراك أن التوفيق من الله.

٢ .التلبيس الثاني: تلبيس أهل الإخلاص

- يُخفي اللهُ عن الصالحين كراماتهم أو يقينهم حتى لا يَفتخروا، أو يُلهَمون بسلوكٍ بسيطٍ يُوهم الآخرين أنهم عاديون.
- مثال: مُصلٍّ يُداوم على الصلاة بخشوعٍ لكنه يُخفي عن الناس دموعَه أثناء الدعاء.

٣ .التلبيس الثالث: تلبيس الأنبياء والأولياء

- يتعامل الأنبياءُ مع الناس بأسلوبٍ يتناسب مع عقولهم، فيُظهرون الأسبابَ رغم علمهم أن الله هو الفاعل الحقيقي.
- مثال: نبيٌّ يدعو قومه للجهاد مع توكله الكامل على نصر الله.

<u>الموجز والنصيحة العملية:</u>

التلبيسُ حكمةٌ إلهيةٌ لا تُدرَكُ إلا باليقين. نَصيحَتُنا لَكَ:

- تأمّل قوله تعالى: ﴿وَمَا تَشَاءُونَ إِلَّا أَن يَشَاءَ اللَّهُ﴾ (الإنسان:٣٠).
- اسأل اللهَ الفهمَ: فالحقائقُ قد تُخفى لِحكمةٍ.
- لا تَحكُمْ بالظاهر: فاللهُ يُدبِّرُ الأمورَ بما لا تَعلمون.

نص الشيخ الهروي

٩٦- باب الوجود

أطلق الله عز وجل في القرآن اسم الوجود صريحا في مواضع، فقال:
(يجد الله غفورا رحيما)(النساء:١١٠).
(لوجدوا الله توابا رحيما)(النساء:٦٤).
(ووجد الله عنده)(النور:٣٩).
الوجود اسم للظفر بحقيقة الشيء.
وهو اسم لثلاثة معان:
أولها: وجود علم لدني، يقطع علوم الشواهد في صحة مكاشفة الحق إياك.
والثاني: وجود الحق وجود عين، مقتطعا عن مساغ الإشارة.
والثالث: وجود مقام اضمحلال رسم الوجود فيه، بالاستغراق في الأولية.

النصّ مكتوباً بلغة مبسّطة

٩٦- باب الوجود

قال الله عز وجل:

- ﴿يَجِدِ اللَّهَ غَفُورًا رَحِيمًا﴾ (النساء:١١٠).
- ﴿لَوَجَدُوا اللَّهَ تَوَّابًا رَحِيمًا﴾ (النساء:٦٤).
- ﴿وَوَجَدَ اللَّهَ عِنْدَهُ﴾ (النور:٣٩).

الوجود هنا هو إدراكُ حقيقةِ الله في القلب والكون.

وهو ثلاث درجات:

١ .الوجود الأول: وجود العلم

- معرفةُ صفات الله (كالمغفرة والرحمة) من خلال آياته في الكون والحياة.
- مثل: إدراك المؤمن أن الله غفورٌ رحيمٌ حين يتوب إليه، فيشعر بالطمأنينة.

٢ .الوجود الثاني: وجود الذات الإلهية

- إيمانٌ بأن الله موجودٌ بذاته المقدسة، لا يشبه شيئًا ولا يُوصف بحدود الخيال.
- مثل: الشعور بقرب الله في لحظات الدعاء دون تصوُّر شكلٍ أو مكان.

٣ .الوجود الثالث: وجود الفناء في الأزلية

- ذوبان الشعور بالوجود الشخصي في نور الألوهية، مع بقاء القلب مرتبطًا بالله.
- مثل: انشغال العابد بالصلاة حتى ينسى نفسه، لكنه يبقى مُدركًا لعظمة خالقه.

<u>الموجز والنصيحة العملية:</u>

الوجودُ الحقيقيُّ هو حضورُ القلبِ مع الله. نَصيحَتُنا لَكَ:

- تأمّل قوله تعالى: ﴿وَهُوَ مَعَكُمْ أَيْنَ مَا كُنْتُمْ﴾ (الحديد: ٤).
- اشكر نِعَمَ الله: ففي كل ذرةٍ دليلٌ على وجوده.
- طهِّر قلبك: بالإخلاص؛ حتى ترى الحقائقَ بنور اليقين.

نص الشيخ الهروي

٩٧- باب التجريد

قال الله عز وجل: (فاخلع نعليك)(طه:١٣).
التجريد انخلاع عن شهود الشواهد.
وهو على ثلاث درجات:
الدرجة الأولى: تجريد عين الكشف عن كسب اليقين.
والدرجة الثانية: تجريد عين الجمع عن درك العلم.
والدرجة الثالثة: تجريد الخلاص من شهود التجريد.

النصّ مكتوباً بلغة مبسّطة

٩٧- باب التجريد

قال الله عز وجل: ﴿فَاخْلَعْ نَعْلَيْكَ﴾ (طه:١٢).

التجريد هو التحرر من التعلق بالظواهر المادية للتركيز على الحق الإلهي.

وهو ثلاث مراحل:

١ .المرحلة الأولى: تجريد اليقين

- التخلص من الحاجة إلى الأدلة الخارجية، بعد وصول القلب إلى يقينٍ داخليٍّ راسخ.
- مثال: الإيمان بالله دون الحاجة إلى براهين معقدة، كشعور الأم بوجود طفلها دون رؤيته.

٢ .المرحلة الثانية: تجريد المعرفة

- تجاوز الفهم العقلي إلى الاختبار الروحي المباشر، حيث تصبح المعرفة حضورًا قلبيًّا.
- مثال: تذوق حلاوة الإيمان في الصلاة، بعيدًا عن النقاشات الفلسفية.

٣ .المرحلة الثالثة: تجريد الذات

- نسيان حتى الشعور بالتجريد نفسه، والانشغال الكامل بالله دون وعيٍ بالذات.
- مثال: انغماس العالم في بحثه العلمي حتى ينسى الوقت، لكن هنا يكون الانشغال بالله.

<u>الموجز والنصيحة العملية:</u>

التجريدُ الحقيقيُّ هو تحريرُ القلبِ ليكون خالصًا لله. نَصيحَتُنا لَكَ:

- تأمّل قوله تعالى: ﴿وَمَا خَلَقْتُ الْجِنَّ وَالْإِنسَ إِلَّا لِيَعْبُدُونِ﴾ (الذاريات:٥٦).
- اختَرِ البساطة: في العبادة والتفكير، بعيدًا عن التعقيدات.
- جاهد نفسك: لتنقية قلبك من الشوائب يوميًّا.

نص الشيخ الهروي

٩٨- باب التفريد

قال الله عز وجل: (ويعلمون أن الله هو الحق المبين)(النور:٢٥).
التفريد اسم لتخليص الإشارة؛ إلى الحق، ثم بالحق، ثم عن الحق.
فأما تفريد الإشارة إلى الحق فعلى ثلاث درجات: تفريد القصد عطشا، ثم تفريد المحبة تلفا، ثم تفريد الشهود اتصالا.
وأما تفريد الإشارة بالحق فعلى ثلاث درجات: تفريد الإشارة بالافتخار بوحا، وتفريد الإشارة بالسلوك مطالعة، وتفريد الإشارة بالقبض غيرة.
وأما تفريد الإشارة عن الحق: فانبساط ببسط ظاهر، يتضمن قبضا خالصا، للهداية إلى الحق والدعوة إليه.

النصّ مكتوباً بلغة مبسّطة

٩٨- باب التفريد

قال الله عز وجل: ﴿وَيَعْلَمُونَ أَنَّ اللَّهَ هُوَ الْحَقُّ الْمُبِينُ﴾ (النور:٢٥).

التفريد هو توجيهُ القلبِ والعملِ خالصًا لله وحده. وهو ثلاث مراحل:

١ .المرحلة الأولى: توجيه النية والقصد إلى الله

- اشتياقٌ شديدٌ لرضا الله دون سواه.
- حبٌّ عميقٌ يُذهِلُ عن كل ما سوى الله.
- رؤيةٌ قلبيةٌ تُثبت وحدانية الله في كل شيء.

٢ .المرحلة الثانية: توجيه السلوك بالحق

- افتخارٌ بالانتماء إلى طريق الله دون مظاهر زائفة.
- سيرٌ روحيٌّ يُظهر جمال العبادة الخالصة.
- غيرةٌ على حفظ القلب من الانشغال بغير الله.

٣ .المرحلة الثالثة: توجيه الدعوة إلى الله

- نشر الخير ببساطةٍ ووضوح، دون تكلفٍ أو تعقيد.
- دعوةٌ تُظهر محاسن الإسلام بأفعالٍ قبل أقوال.
- توازنٌ بين الصدع بالحق ورحمة الخلق.

الموجز والنصيحة العملية:

التفريدُ هو إخلاصُ القلبِ والعملِ لله. نَصيحَتُنا لَكَ:

- تأمّل قوله تعالى: ﴿قُلْ هُوَ اللَّهُ أَحَدٌ﴾ (الإخلاص:١).
- طهِّر نيتك: اجعل كل أعمالك لوجه الله.
- كن قدوةً: دع أفعالك تُعلّم غيرك دون حاجةٍ إلى خطبٍ طويلة.

نص الشيخ الهروي

٩٩- باب الجمع

قال الله عز وجل: (وما رميت إذ رميت ولكن الله رمى)(الأنفال:١٧).
الجمع ما اسقط التفرقة، وقطع الإشارة، وشخص عن الماء والطين، بعد صحة التمكين، والبراءة من التلوين، والخلاص من شهود الثنوية، والتنافي من إحساس الاعتلال، والتنافي من شهود شهودها.
وهو على ثلاث درجات:
جمع علم، ثم جمع وجود، ثم جمع عين.
فأما جمع العلم: فهو تلاشي علوم الشواهد في العلم اللدني صرفا.
فأما جمع الوجود: فهو تلاشي نهاية الاتصال في عين الوجود مَحْقاً.
فأما جمع العين: فهو تلاشي كل ما تقله الإشارة في ذات الحق حقا.
والجمع غاية مقامات السالكين، وهو طرف بحر التوحيد.

النصّ مكتوباً بلغة مبسّطة

٩٩- باب الجمع

قال الله تعالى: ﴿وَمَا رَمَيْتَ إِذْ رَمَيْتَ وَلَٰكِنَّ اللَّهَ رَمَىٰ﴾ (الأنفال: ١٧).

الجمع هو حالةٌ يتلاشى فيها الابتعاد بين العبد وربه،
ويختفي الشعور بالحاجة إلى الإشارات أو الرموز،
ويَبرُز القلبُ من ظلمات المادّة (الماء والطين) بعد رسوخ الإيمان،
وتطهير النفس من التلوثات النفسية،
والتحرر من رؤية الأسباب وكأنها شريكة لله،
والانعتاق من الشعور بالضعف أو الاعتماد على غير الله.

للجمع ثلاث مراحل:

- جمع العلم: حيث تذوب العلوم الظاهرية في نور العلم الإلهي الذي يمنحه الله لقلوب عباده المخلصين.
- جمع الوجود: حيث تختفي فكرة الانفصال بين العبد والله، فيدرك أن وجوده الحقيقي هو بوجود الله، لا بذاته.
- جمع العين: حيث يزول كل ما يُشار إليه في الكون، فلا يرى السالك إلا الحق سبحانه مصدرَ كل شيء.

الجمع هو غاية طريق السائرين إلى الله، وهو بداية دخول بحر التوحيد الخالص.

<u>الموجز والنصيحة العملية:</u>

الجمع هو ليس الحلول أو الاتحاد.

الجمع يعني أن ترى يد الله في كل شيء، فتتخلص من التعلق بالأسباب، وتستيقن أن القلوب بيده وحده.

- ابدأ بتدبر الآية الكريمة: ﴿ وَٱلَّذِينَ جَٰهَدُواْ فِينَا لَنَهۡدِيَنَّهُمۡ سُبُلَنَا ﴾ (العنكبوت: ٦٩).
- اجعل قلبك مرآةً تنعكس عليها أنوار المعرفة، وداوم على ذكر الله ("ألا بذكر الله تطمئن القلوب")، واطلب العون منه في كل خطوة.
- طريق التزكية طويل، لكن خطواته الأولى تكون بإخلاص النية والصبر على الطاعة.

نص الشيخ الهروي

١٠٠- باب التوحيد

قال الله عز وجل: (شهد الله أنه لا إله إلا هو)(آل عمران:١٨).
التوحيد تنزيه الله تعالى عن الحدث. وإنما نطق العلماء بما نطقوا به وأشار المحققون بما أشاروا إليه في هذا الطريق لقصد تصحيح التوحيد.وما سواه من حال أو مقام فكله مصحوب العلل.
والتوحيد على ثلاثة وجوه:
الوجه الأول: توحيد العامة، الذي يصح بالشواهد.
والوجه الثاني: توحيد الخاصة، وهو الذي يثبت بالحقائق.
والوجه الثالث: توحيد قائم بالقدم، وهو توحيد خاصة الخاصة.

فأما التوحيد الأول، فهو شهادة أن لا إله إلا الله وحده لا شريك له الأحد الصمد الذي (لم يلد ولم يولد . ولم يكن له كفوا أحد)(الإخلاص:٣-٤).هذا هو التوحيد الظاهر الجلي الذي نفى الشرك الأعظم وعليه نصبت القبلة، وبه وجبت الذمة، وبه حقنت الدماء والأموال، وانفصلت دار الإسلام من دار الكفر، وصحت به الملة للعامة، وإن لم يقوموا بحق الاستدلال، بعد أن سلموا من الشبهة والحيرة والريبة بصدق شهادة صححها قبول القلب.هذا توحيد العامة الذي يصح بالشواهد؛ والشواهد هي الرسالة والصنائع، يجب بالسمع، ويوجد بتبصير الحق، وينمو على مشاهدة الشواهد.
وأما التوحيد الثاني، الذي يثبت بالحقائق، فهو توحيد الخاصة. وهو إسقاط الأسباب الظاهرة والصعود عن منازعات العقول، وعن التعلق بالشواهد. وهو أن لا تشهد في التوحيد دليلا، ولا في التوكل سببا، ولا للنجاة وسيلة؛ فتكون مشاهدا سبق الحق بحكمه وعلمه، ووضعه الأشياء مواضعها، وتعليقه إياها بأحايينها، وإخفائة إياها في رسومها، وتحقق معرفة العلل، وتسلك سبيل إسقاط الحدث. هذا توحيد الخاصة، الذي يصح بعلم الفناء، ويصفو في علم الجمع، ويجذب إلى توحيد أرباب الجمع.
وأما التوحيد الثالث، فهو توحيد اختصه الحق لنفسه، واستحقه بقدره، وألاح منه لائحا إلى أسرار طائفة من صفوته، وأخرسهم عن نعته، وأعجزهم عن بثه.

والذي يشار به إليه على ألسن المشيرين أنه إسقاط الحدث وإثبات القِدَم، على أن هذا الرمز في ذلك التوحيد علة لا يصح ذلك التوحيد إلا باسقاطها. هذا قطب الإشارة إليه على ألسن علماء هذا الطريق وإن زخرفوا له نعوتا وفصلوه فصولا فإن ذلك التوحيد تزيده العبارة خفاء، والصفة نفورا، والبسط صعوبة.وإلى هذا التوحيد شخص أهل الرياضة وأرباب الأحوال، وله قصد أهل التعظيم، وإياه عَنَى المتكلمون في عين الجمع. وعليه تصطلم الإشارات، ثم لم ينطق عنه لسان، ولم تشر إليه عبارة، فإن التوحيد وراء ما يشير إليه مكوَّن، أو يتعاطاه حين، أو يقلُّه سبب.
وقد أجبت في سالف الزمان سائلا سألني عن توحيد الصوفية بهذه القوافي الثلاث:

ما وحد الواحد من واحد   إذ كل من وحده جاحد
توحيد من ينطق عن نعته   عارية أبطلها الواحد
توحيده إياه توحيده   ونعت من ينعته لاحد

النصّ مكتوباً بلغة مبسّطة

١٠٠- باب التوحيد

قال الله تعالى: ﴿شَهِدَ اللَّهُ أَنَّهُ لَا إِلَٰهَ إِلَّا هُوَ﴾ (آل عمران: ١٨).

التوحيد هو تنزيه الله عن كل ما لا يليق بجلاله، مثل الحدوث (التغير أو الزوال). ما ذكره العلماء وأشار إليه الصوفيّة عن التوحيد هدفه تأكيد إخلاص الإيمان بالله وحده. أما الحالات الروحية أو المنازل الأخرى فكلها قد تشوبها الشوائب إن لم تُبنَ على أساس التوحيد الصحيح.

للتوحيد ثلاثة مستويات:

توحيد العامة:
وهو الإقرار باللسان والقلب أن "لا إله إلا الله"، كما في سورة الإخلاص: ﴿لَمْ يَلِدْ وَلَمْ يُولَدْ . وَلَمْ يَكُن لَّهُ كُفُوًا أَحَدٌ﴾. هذا التوحيد يحمي من الشرك الظاهر، ويُعتبر أساس قبول الأعمال، وبه تُفرّق دار الإسلام عن دار الكفر. وهو كافٍ لعامة الناس، حتى لو لم يدركوا كل البراهين العقلية، ما دام القلب سليمًا من الشك.

توحيد الخاصة:
وهو إدراك أن الأسباب المادية لا تأثير لها إلا بمشيئة الله، فلا تعلق القلب بها، ولا اعتماد على الحواس أو العقل وحده. هنا يرى السالك أن الله هو الفاعل الحقيقي وراء كل شيء، فيتخلى عن المناقشات العقيمة، ويعرف أن علم الله وقدرته سبقت كل سبب.

توحيد خاصة الخاصة:

وهو مرتبة لا يُعبّر عنها بالكلمات، اختص الله بها من يشاء من عباده. هنا يزول كل وصف أو تصور بشري عن الله، فلا يُرى إلا قِدَمُه (أزليته) دون حَدَثِ الخلق. هذا التوحيد يتجاوز كل رمز أو عبارة، وحتى محاولة وصفه تُعتبر تقصيرً ونقصًا!

الموجز والنصيحة العملية:

التوحيد هو جوهر الإيمان: من "لا إله إلا الله" البسيطة إلى إدراك عظمة الله التي لا تُحد.

- ابدأ بتدبر قوله تعالى: ﴿هُوَ ٱلْأَوَّلُ وَٱلْآخِرُ وَٱلظَّاهِرُ وَٱلْبَاطِنُ﴾ (الحديد: ٣).
- لا تكتفِ بالإقرار باللسان، بل حسّن يقينك بأن الله هو المدبر الوحيد.
- راقب قلبك: هل تعلق بغير الله؟ هل تخشى الفقر أو المرض أكثر من خوفك منه؟
- اجعل التوحيد منهج حياة، واطلب من الله الثبات، فـ﴿وَمَن يُؤْمِن بِاللَّهِ يَهْدِ قَلْبَهُ﴾ (التغابن: ١١).

تمّ الكتاب و لله الحمد